THE ARABS

BOOKS BY
BERTRAM THOMAS

THE ARABS

ARABIA FELIX

ALARMS AND EXCURSIONS IN ARABIA

BERTRAM THOMAS.

(By courtesy of the artist, Sir Walter Russell, R.A.)

THE ARABS

The life-story of a people who have left their deep impress on the world.

Bertram Thomas

Simon Publications

2001

Originally published by T. Butterworth Ltd, London and Doubleday, Doran & Co. Garden City NY.

Library of Congress Control Number: 37016320

ISBN: 1-931541-20-5

Printed by Lightning Source Inc. La Vergne, TN

Published by Simon Publications, P. O. Box 321, Safety Harbor, FL 34695

FOREWORD

FIRST I would acknowledge my indebtedness to ex-President A. Lawrence Lowell of Harvard University, at whose invitation I was privileged, last year, to deliver the Lowell Lectures on 'The Arabs' at the Lowell Institute, Boston. The researches necessary for those lectures, following fourteen years residence in many Arab countries, prompted this setting forth, in a single volume, of a life story of the Arab people, a story of wide scope and varied interest for so small a compass, attempting as it does an outline of their history, religion, medieval civilization and later-day politics. In these pages my address is to the general reader.

Orientalist authorities in many fields of learning have been freely drawn upon, and this brings me to another acknowledgment of deep obligation. A list of such authors and their works forms a brief selected bibliography at the end of the book.

The index I owe to my wife's devotion and many of the illustrations to the kindness of friends whose names are acknowledged in appropriate places. Finally, the help of those who have been so good as to read through my manuscript and make valuable suggestions—Professor Margoliouth, Professor Gibb, Mr Mahmood Zada, Mrs D. L. R. Lorimer and Sir Percy Cox—is gratefully remembered. The viewpoints are not always theirs, of course, but my own.

BERTRAM THOMAS

Christmas 1936
THE WHITE FRIARS
SANDWICH
KENT

is summed up for us in the person of Ishmael. 'He will be a wild man; his hand will be against every man, and every man's hand against him.' This of course is the traditional view throughout the ages and down to this day, the view of the neighbouring settled man, the agriculturalist and the trader, the man who has accumulated possessions and cherishes security.

The inhabitants of Arabia have always comprised these two types, the militant nomad and the peaceful settler. A mutual antagonism has divided them. In a land where famine and ignorance combined to prevent a rational way of life the settled man regarded the nomad as a natural enemy, the nomad regarded the settled man as a legitimate prey. Arabia Deserta was an unsubjugated and savage, if thinly populated world, whose denizens, in the intervals of their pastoral pursuits, issued forth on plundering raids into the lands of the settled dwellers towards the coasts. Shedding innocent blood had no terror for them. They had their own code of tribal honour and tribal sanctions. Nor was it entirely without mercy. The right of asylum, for instance, was sacrosanct, the custom whereby a refugee from another's wrath once given protection by a desert tribe could feel as safe as they; they would never surrender him whatever his offence, however influential the pursuer or tempting the inducement—an honourable tradition to which the desert dwellers of our time are true.

There was not much godly religion in Arabia before Muhammad's day. Those nomads who worshipped anything at all (for by nature they were not spiritually minded men) seem to have had a predilection for trees and stones, believing these to be the abodes of spirits. The single stone or monolith was probably a widely spread Semitic cult and possibly the prototype of the altar. The settled man doubtless tended to evolve religious observances, but here again there was no uniformity. Every settlement had its own favourite local spirit. Mana, the spirit of doom, was preferred here; Gadd, the spirit of good luck, there; others were Yaghuth, the helper; Wadd, the spirit of friendship. Many of these spirits appear to have been propitiated or exorcised rather than worshipped, their influence dreaded rather than invoked, and to this day a cult of propitiating and exorcising spirits is practised throughout the coasts of eastern and southern Arabia, covertly where the authorities are religious and active, elsewhere quite openly.[1] In immediate pre-Islamic times idol worship, a late innovation from Syria, was practised in the settlements along the old trade routes, and some of the spirits came, too, to be represented by images.

Marriage with the Arabs of antiquity was probably at first a very casual link bordering on promiscuity. It is likely to have differed little from the practice attributed to most primitive cultures, whereby the woman remained in her own tribe and the children she bore came to be members of her totem. Indeed, at the beginning of the Christian Era it would appear that Arab children customarily took their names from their mothers rather than their fathers, after the model of Simon son of Miriam rather than Simon son of Jonas, and this practice survives to this day among the nomadic tribes of the deserts, though rarely found among settled Arabs. As time went on men came to take wives unto themselves on the more enduring basis familiar to us, and children were born into the father's tribe. Endogamous marriages between cousins were doubt-

[1]For description of the rites see my *Alarms and Excursions in Arabia.*

TAPPING A FRANKINCENSE BUSH.

A DESERT SCENE.

desert, would ensure no lack of recruits for the most dangerous adventure. Their camels—in later times their horses, too—carrying scarcely any weight, could swoop down and disappear as swiftly as they came, easily eluding the less mobile troops of a civilized enemy, who would be unable to pursue the raiders very far from ignorance of pastures and water holes and fear of the forbidding heat of the burning deserts. Depredations must have grown serious indeed when, in the middle of the sixth century B.C., the last Babylonian king led an army across the desert to ancient Taima, which he invested and where he built a palace, only to yield it erelong to a Persian conqueror.

The maritime Arabs of the eastern seaboard, through these early times, were doubtless engaged in carrying on the sea trade between Babylonia and India. Their country, too, may well have been the Land of Magan, whence Sumer drew her copper and the wood used by the Priest-King Gudea in the making of his temple at Lagash. But eastern Arabia remained unknown to the west until the approach of the Christian Era, when the veil was lifted by one of Alexander the Great's campaigns.

Fresh from his conquests across western Asia, Alexander arrived at the mouth of the Indus near where Karachi now stands. With Babylon for his objective he planned his long march westwards, skirting the coasts of Baluchistan and Persia, and to make the journey possible built a fleet of ships to sail along these desolate coasts in attendance on him, landing food and supplies at frequent intervals. That march, bristling with difficulties, would tax even a modern army's resources, but the forces led by Alexander achieved it in 327 B.C. On the historic voyage Nearchus, the admiral of the Greek fleet, secured the services of a Persian Gulf pilot and learned from him that Arabia was a peninsula and that it was all but possible to circumnavigate it. Later on some of the Greek ships set out to make the attempt, but perhaps, fortunately for themselves, turned back, possibly intimidated by the maelstrom that normally lashes Cape Musandam.

Arabia was by this time becoming known not merely as the land of spices, but as the highway of trade between India and the Hellenistic world, for Egypt and Babylonia were now in decline. Indian and Arab ships came, braving the winter northeast monsoon, loaded with such luxuries as pearls, beryls, ginger and pepper. The early Ptolemies had particularly encouraged the Red Sea trade and had by diplomatic means established small mercantile communities on the African and Socotra coasts to serve its needs, but such was the fear of piracy in those waters that it was customary to send armed guards in the ships. Within living memory a British ship was driven ashore on the south Arabian coast; she was plundered and every member of her crew ruthlessly murdered: an echo, as it were, of Arabian exploits in the time of the later Ptolemies when the Red Sea was ravaged by pirates and freebooters, trade suffered, ships were taken and all on board sold into slavery.

To the Romans, who became masters of Egypt in 30 B.C., this condition of things was intolerable, and they soon found an excellent reason for dealing effectively with it, though their main objective was the unlocking of the fabulous riches of supposed Eldorado in south Arabia. A fleet of one hundred and thirty Roman ships set out from Aqaba in 26 B.C. with ten thousand Roman infantry, one thousand Nabatæan Irregulars, and fifty Jews. Ælius Gallus, the eparch of Egypt, was himself in command and had for his guide and adviser on tribal matters and terrain—what we should term today 'political officer to the force', a role the writer has filled in the stormy days of the Arab rebellion in Mesopotamia—a Nabatæan, named Syllæus. The force was disembarked at Leuke Kome, a point some way down the Red Sea coast, and thence the march was begun into the interior. It is impossible to follow with certainty the actual route taken, because the place names of those days are no longer identifiable, but for the first fifty days Syllæus led the army through waterless and trackless wastes, and the men suffered terribly from scurvy of the gums and legs. It is suspected that Syllæus had a personal motive for not wishing the Romans to succeed too well, and that in accompanying them at all his object was to gain knowledge of settlements he hoped one day to make his own.

Whether or not, six months passed by. The Romans had won battles but no treasure, and, disillusioned, they began their retreat. Since a retreating force may expect to have to fight a rearguard action in Arabia, where superior arms excite covetous eyes, and an enemy, particularly at night, is swift and elusive, it is remarkable that Ælius Gallus seems only to have been involved in one action on his way back to the coast, which he was able to reach in sixty days. From Strabo, who accompanied the expedition as war correspondent, we learn that Syllæus, the discredited guide, was sent a prisoner to Rome, where he was beheaded in the streets as a traitor, while the Romans consoled themselves with the boast that despite all their losses from disease, toil and hunger only seven Roman soldiers were actually killed in action. But the truth seems to be that their plans had been ill-conceived and the army was not properly equipped for a tropical campaign; they were disappointed, too, in finding wilderness and barbarous villages where they expected a prosperous countryside and thriving towns. They never invaded Arabia again, and this expedition is the isolated example of a European invasion of Arabia Proper throughout the centuries.

Clearly the southern principalities had already declined, and Minæans, Sabæans, Qatabanis and Attramatei disappear in the mists of antiquity. When the classical writers again speak of the southwest they no longer mention these peoples individually nor tell us of their fate; henceforward they speak of one people, the Homeritæ or Himyarites. But the days of the Himyarites were as grass, for by the year A.D. 350 the Abyssinian king numbered Himyar and Yemen among his dominions.

The next two centuries witnessed a fitful Abyssinian occupation of southwest Arabia. It was probably little more than a shadowy hold on the Yemen coast, except intermittently at times of actual military invasion. Abyssinia had meanwhile become the client of a new power that had arisen in Egypt, the Byzantine, and had adopted the religion of her patrons; and hence Christianity came to be introduced into south Arabia by the Abyssinians.

Jewish colonies already existed there, and these also had their rival imperial connection. The Sassanids, the great Persian dynasty of Zoroastrian creed (a nonproselytizing and nationalistic religion to which, indeed, none but Persians were admitted), had arisen out of the ashes of Babylon. For the next four hundred years Persians and Byzantines struggled one with another for supremacy in world politics, a conflict that was not without its influence on Arabia.

That Christianity was the religion of foreign invaders —the Abyssinians—must have militated against its acceptance by the local Himyarites. Judaism, on the other hand, though not a proselytizing system, made considerable headway in southwest Arabia, where whole tribes are believed to have embraced it. Whether this was from spiritual conviction or political convenience is not clear, but traditions concerning the events that followed suggest that the two religions stood for opposing political factions, in which case Judaism came to connote a particular political allegiance. This faction must have grown powerful in the early sixth century, when it rose successfully to throw off the Abyssinian yoke. Tradition speaks of a trench filled with fire, of Christian captives offered the choice between apostasy and burning, of a bishop's martyrdom and wholesale Christian massacre. The Abyssinian invasion that immediately followed was undertaken ostensibly to avenge these wrongs, though another tradition represents the Abyssinians and Himyarites as struggling at this time for the control of the Red Sea trade. Abyssinian victory at length brought to an end the last Himyaritic kingdom under its Jew-convert insurgent leader. The new viceroy from Aksum, with the new bishop, set immediately to work to restore the great dam of Mar'ib which had been destroyed by a flood more than half a century before, as a commemorative tablet bearing an inscription with a Christian invocation to the Holy Trinity testifies to this day.

Medievally recorded Arab tradition attaches enormous importance to this famous waterwork. The ancient prosperity of the south is bound up with it; the south's decay with its destruction. But the tradition must embody a series of disasters stretching back over four or five centuries, probably more, for, as we saw, the Roman invaders even before the Christian Era found not continuous fertility and walled cities as they had expected, but comparative desolation. It is unlikely that Arab memory went back so far as the ancient southern kingdoms: the civilization of the south, in any case, had rested on frankincense and spices, not on irrigated crops.

The last Abyssinian occupation of the Yemen endured for a brief half century. Whether from the decline of the colonists, as is probable, or from their despotic temper, as one tradition has it, the local opposing faction that leaned towards Persia soon got the upper hand again. Southeastern Arabia had already been conquered by the Persians in the fourth century, Oman already ruled by Persian viceroys for two hundred years[8] so that the extension of Persian influence westwards into the Yemen presented few difficulties, and that influence had not entirely disappeared when the Prophet arose.

The vast interior spaces of Arabia remained inviolate. The mass of the Arabs lived their lives remote from, and uninfluenced by, these foreign imperialistic activities along the fringes of the peninsula. In the north Persians and Byzantines secured themselves against unwelcome attentions of desert marauders by encouraging the growth of two small Arab buffer states along their desert frontiers. Hira and Ghassan were states which may well have owed as much to their strategic location as to inherent virtues, however these abounded. We have seen that the nomadic Beduin, goaded by hunger, were an immemorial nuisance to the neighbouring civilizations. At best, when impelled by some powerful impulse such as that which governed later historic migrations that revolutionized the world, they showed themselves capable of developing an impressive civilization; at worst, they were ever ready, in return

[8]My grammar and vocabulary of the surviving Iranian dialect found in southeastern Arabia was published in the *JRAS.* of October 1930.

for proper remuneration, to give up their raiding and, indeed, to act as escorts to caravans and keep off others like themselves who would attack their patrons; for the nomads, in spite of tribal associations, are incorrigible individualists. So all down the centuries it has been the policy of Powers to enlist the support, by the lure of financial and political advantage, of the Arabs nearest their frontiers, and these, given the right inducements, have co-operated and afforded an effective rampart against the hosts of their less favoured kinsmen in the deserts beyond.

To start with there was probably small difference between them. The men of Hira like those under Ghassan, not improbably, came originally as marauders to batten on the industry of the settled cultivators. Their political value as a potential buffer against the desert was appreciated, the right was conceded them to exact a landlord's tribute, and they were encouraged to give themselves up to a life of hunting and war and lavish hospitality while their bards produced poetry—an aristocratic mode of life exactly suited to the desert temper.

The Ghassanid principality, successor to the vanished Palmyrene state, adopted, as the client of the Byzantines, the Christian faith of its patrons, and Justinian made its kings patricians of his empire. These kings, claiming aristocratic Yemeni origin, lived a seminomadic life inherited from recent ancestors, eschewing a capital city and spending the seasons now in one, now in another of their favourite resorts, where beyond the Jordan the ruins of their palaces and churches of Byzantine architecture still occasionally serve to shelter modern Beduin. The Lakhmids of Hira, who also claimed Yemeni origin, were even more renowned, for they had a capital city and professed a pagan creed that was not the creed of their Persian patrons: indeed, they later flirted with Christianity, the religion of the Byzantine enemy, so that the princes of Hira were compelled publicly to abjure that faith, though the common folk came in time to embrace it, as indeed did their last prince. To the desert Arabs the luxurious life of these prosperous borderland kinsmen seemed idyllic indeed, and the earliest Arab poetry sings mostly of their ancient glories. But in the latter part of the sixth century both Byzantines and Persians had begun to reduce their commitments in these northern buffer states, and the borderland Arabs were fain to revert to their primitive ways.

Ancient Arabia had many tongues, all of them belonging to one Semitic family, though spoken by peoples who appear to have been of different racial origin.[4] In the northern borderlands were many settled peoples, all of them possessing written languages.[5] In the south were the four distinct lettered peoples, already mentioned as known to the Greeks, who made the Arabia of antiquity famous. Their languages belonged, as their inscriptions show, to the south Semitic group. The mass of the Arabs occupying the great heart of the peninsula were, on the other hand, unlettered. They spoke a dialect of Semitic which was not a literary language before the sixth century of our era, when the Prophet arose. The curious thing about this north and central Arabian speech is that its most correct form was spoken not in the settlements such as Mecca and Yathrib, but among the nomads. Modern Arabic is its offspring.

These various Arabian languages were no mere local

[4]The reader interested is referred to an Appendix, pp. 337 et seq.

[5]Aramaic, Syriac, Lihyani and Hebrew.

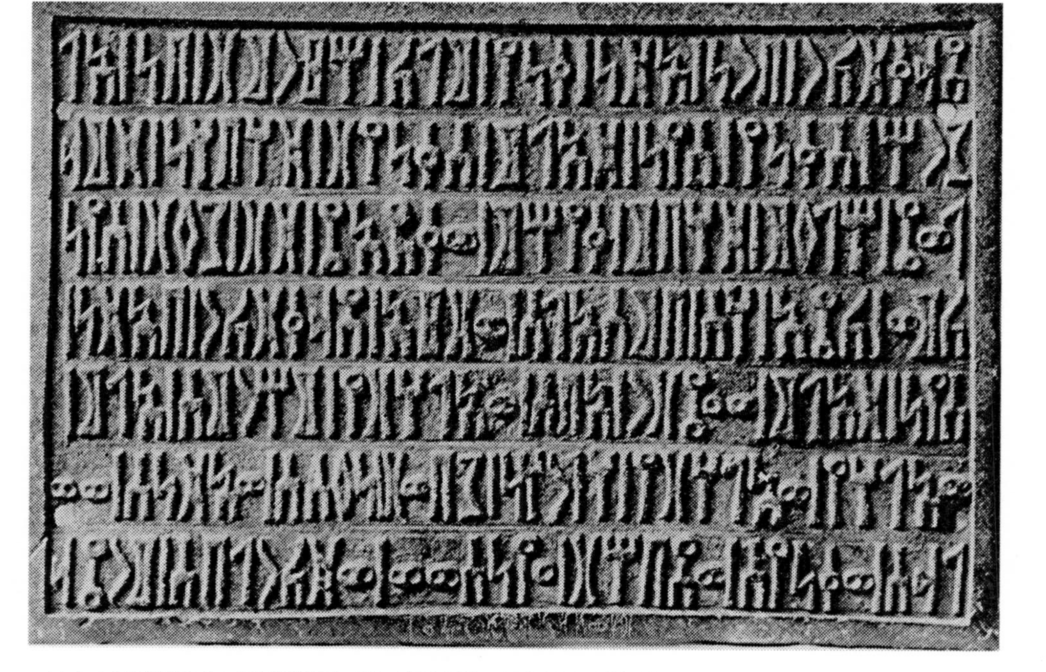

AN ANCIENT SOUTH ARABIAN INSCRIPTION (IN RAISED CHARACTERS ON BRONZE PLATE FROM SHABWA).

(By courtesy of the British Museum 'Dedication by Sadig Dhakir Barran, vassal of the King of Hadhramaut, son of Ilsharah, to Sin Dhu-ilum, his sanctuary, and the gods and goddess of Shabwat, his own soul and feeling, children and property, his eyesight and the thoughts of his heart, which he prays may be agreeable [to them]')

dialects. There existed between them differences comparable to those that divide the Romance languages. There must, of course, have been an ancient Semitic parent tongue, corresponding to the Latin ancestor of the Romance languages, and, says Dr Margoliouth, 'the classical language of the peninsula should naturally have been not the patois of the Beduin, but the idiom which had for so long served for inscriptions commemorating laws, contracts, treaties, dedications, vows, epitaphs and the like.'[2]*

In early times the languages of the south would almost certainly have enjoyed a superior prestige[6] because they were the languages of a civilization, but the position came naturally to be reversed in the seventh and succeeding centuries, by which time they were in decay, because the Prophet arose where the northern dialect was spoken. As the tongue of Muhammad and the tongue of the divine revelations recorded in the Holy Qur'an, thence as the language of Arab armies that swept the world, it became the lingua franca of an empire, and its pre-eminence today is the natural consequence. But this Arabic of the Islamic period—it was then about to enjoy what in English corresponds to an Elizabethan age—needs no superior antiquity among Semitic tongues to establish its greatness; it is inherently great. The pride of the Arabs in their language could rest alone on its own marvellous structural design, its comprehensiveness, its flexibility. 'From its own inner resources it could evolve the *mot juste,*' and it provided, centuries before our Renaissance, a ready in-

[6]The Hebraisms which have been traced in the inscriptions of the ancient south that are found lacking in northern Arabic, the established descent of Ethiopic of Abyssinia from south Semitic and the marked philological affinities of the ancient Akkadian language of Babylonia with south Semitic, alike suggest a superior antiquity for the southern forms.

strument for the translation of the lore of ancient Greece. Even today, incredible as it may seem, the Arabs have seldom to go outside this ancient language of the deserts to express the terminology of modern sciences.

It is odd that the Arabs, whose tongue this was, should have shown so scant a memory of the Sabæan and cognate cultures, yet the old Greek classical authorities tell of the sending of gold and silver plate to south Arabia, and the archaeological spade of recent times has unearthed Greek statuary there, from which we may judge of Hellenistic influences penetrating Arabia before Muhammad's day. According to the Arabs, however, the times which preceded the Prophet, i.e., sixth–seventh century A.D., are par excellence the Days of Ignorance, the Dark Ages, the *Jahiliya*. Arabia—such is the conventional view—was wholly deficient of enlightenment. Savagery and ignorance stalked the land. The Arabs were pagan, remote in their deserts, sequestered from outside influences.

The great mass of the Arabs, it is true, were pagans. Yet Arabia, as we have seen, had its leaven of Judaism and Christianity in settled areas, north, south, east and west. Jewish communities particularly had been established for centuries in the principal settlements along the ancient trade route, notably at Taima, Yathrib and Najran.

Jewish penetration of Arabia is known to have been going on in the early Christian centuries by way of the north. Some colonists were possibly those Jews who had been turned out of Judea by Hadrian and Trajan and who, we are told, built synagogues in the wilderness; others are supposed to have been Edomites from Nabatæa, and Hebrew inscriptions have been found in the far southwest. Settled Arab tribes of the settlements, as we saw, also embraced Judaism; indeed the Jewish colonies found surviving in Najran today Arab tradition prefers to regard as of the religion, rather than of the blood, of Israel.

The Jews from Palestine seem to have come as agriculturalists; hence their chief colony was founded among the agricultural community of Yathrib, but they soon took to arts and crafts, in which they easily excelled the Arabs, and also to commerce, so that they tended to be town dwellers. In spite of their origin among lettered societies they are supposed, after a few centuries of Arabian domicile, to have given up their old native tongue and to have called their tribes and their sons by Arab names, though at the time of the Prophet Muhammad they are represented at Yathrib as still possessing tables of the law, attaching great importance to their rabbis and observing the Sabbath by certain food taboos. Their monotheistic religion, as we shall see later, had an early attraction for the Arab Prophet and a considerable influence on his teachings. It does not appear, however, to have been the only monotheistic cult at the time, for there were Arab communities with one god, Rahman, and some suppose that many so-called Judaistic communities of ancient Arabia may have been Arab ones professing Rahmanism. The law of the market place of Yathrib, the Jewish stronghold, is said to have been Jewish law even as late as the time that Muhammad made his home there in the seventh century, though Jewish influence was already in decline.

Christianity, too, in forms however diverse and crude, was practised in the two northern Arab buffer states of renown, Ghassan and Hira; it was practised in Najran in the south, a settlement rivalling Mecca itself, and in the half-settled townships of the Persian Gulf littoral, the Bahrain. Not improbably it penetrated even to Nejd, for the legendary Kinda whose seat was at Yamama numbered among his following Imru al Kais, the famous Christian warrior-poet of the Arabs. Scattered Christian communities like these would doubtless, however, have been small minorities, and where Beduin professed such a religion it is unlikely that the allegiance had anything spiritual about it; more probably it had some political connotation.

Yet it would appear that the more enlightened merchants of the settlements having trade intercourse with Jews and Christians both inside and outside the peninsula and caravaners and travellers who annually went up to Syria and to Mesopotamia were, during the centuries that led up to the Prophet's birth, not unfamiliar with religious cults that taught the existence of one supreme God, creator of all things, whose instruments were angels and prophets, who sent down oracles to earth and declared himself by miracles: cults that taught a Judgment Day when the dead should rise, the believers enter into everlasting life, the unbelievers into everlasting damnation. The very emphasis which conventional Arab tradition places on the ignorance and barbarism of the Arabs before the time of the Prophet has led some Western authorities to stress, perhaps unduly, their contrary opinion. 'Arabia,' says Dr O'Leary, 'was not so self-centred nor so self-contained; indeed to a great extent its later segregation seems largely due to the influence of Islam, . . . and consequently the religion of Islam was not evolved among remote tribes with only very slight contact with the outside world, but in the midst of the general tide of West Asiatic Civilization.'[1]*

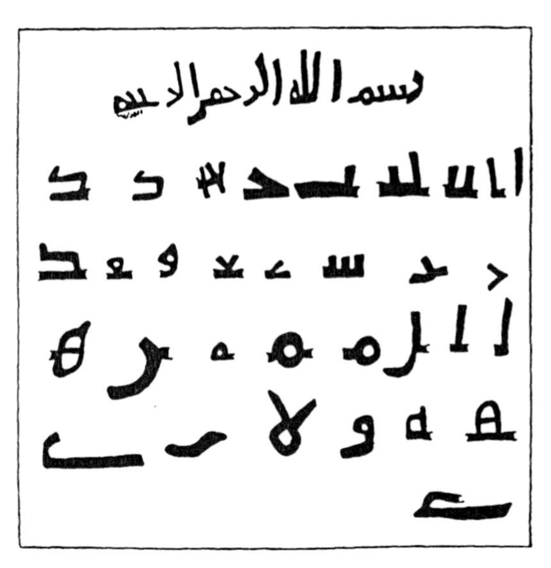

THE EARLY ARABIC ALPHABET FROM THE TOMBSTONE BELOW.

(By courtesy of the Royal Asiatic Society)

THE MOST ANCIENT ISLAMIC MONUMENT KNOWN, THE TOMBSTONE OF ABD AL RAHMAN IBN KHAIR AL HAJRI (A.D. 652).

(In the Cairo Museum of Arab Art)

CHAPTER II

The Prophet Muhammad

His humanity extended itself to the lower creation. He forbade the employment of living birds as targets for marksmen and remonstrated with those who ill-treated their camels. When some of his followers had set fire to an ant-hill he compelled them to extinguish it. Foolish acts of cruelty which were connected with old superstitions were swept away by him. . . . No more was a dead man's camel to be tied to his tomb to perish of thirst and hunger. No more was the evil eye to be propitiated by the bleeding of a certain proportion of the herd. No more was the rain to be conjured by tying burning-torches to the tails of oxen. . . . The manes and tails of horses were not to be cut, the former being meant by nature for their warmth and the latter as a protection against flies: nor were asses to be branded.[3]* MARGOLIOUTH

IN THE YEAR A.D. 570 or thereabouts was born in Mecca a son of the Arabs whose fame today places him among the greatest men of all time: one who was destined to found a world religion, to inspire a revolution which raised his fellow countrymen from obscurity to eminence and to change the whole course of history.

Muhammad, son of Abdullah son of Abd al Muttalib, came into the world amid lowly surroundings, of good tribal ancestry, which his followers came later to ennoble, and which his detractors have uncharitably sought to debase. His father had died before his birth; his mother was to die soon after it, leaving the orphan boy to be reared by relations, first a grandfather and then an uncle. Both were kind to him, but both were poor, and the boy grew up in homes that knew hardship.

The Arabia of his day was the primitive land we have described. The greater part of its people consisted of pagan nomadic tribesmen, who combined the roles of herdsmen and warriors; they were also proud and brave men who were accustomed to much freedom and who had never bent the neck under the yoke of foreign conqueror. Each tribe had its hereditary chief, but he was regarded as little more than a senior among equals, to whom allegiance of a light and precarious kind was due in times of crisis. Life in the great spaces of the desert encouraged equality. No man approached another there with those varying degrees of regard to which men in closely regimented societies today are accustomed. Other nations might boast of national freedom. The freedom of the desert was a personal freedom, a freedom to kill neighbour or brother, maybe, without fear of any constituted authority, a freedom to forgive the murderer of a kinsman for the consideration of blood money, again without recourse to authority. The Arabs were men of inflammable temper, quick to anger and swift to shed blood, capable of being roused to battle by an appeal to the emotions, by an impassioned recital of some poem enshrining a valiant exploit. The frugal pastoral life of the deserts bred the soldier or the bandit. Periodical drought demanded self-discipline or drove to rapine and plunder; inherited blood feuds perpetuated a lust for vengeance; insecurity necessitated unremitting vigilance as well as skill in the art of riding and the use of weapons. With a sense of self-esteem went a suspicion of others and intolerance of strangers. The Beduin were the products of a cruel environment, volatile men whose friendship and enmity were alike capricious. Such were the men to whom Muhammad's teachings came early to be addressed.

But it was not from among such men that his religion drew its inspiration. Islam was to take shape not in the deserts, but among the settled Arabs of entirely different temper. Its early life was cradled by the cultural influences of the city of Muhammad's birth. Mecca at that time was probably as well known and progressive a settlement as existed within the peninsula, though perhaps no Arab city had at this time acquired outside fame. It had grown up around the well of Zem Zem, where, according to local tradition, Hagar had found refreshment for her son Ishmael when they were cast adrift by Abraham in the wilderness. Whether or not this was at the root of a belief in the sanctity of its environs, Mecca was already a holy city and had been so for some centuries before the Prophet's coming. It was indeed to the trade brought by an annual pilgrimage rather than to any local industry that the settlement owed its rise, and its importance increased as it came to dominate the trade route after the decline of the south and the decay of Byzantine shipping in the Red Sea.

The inhabitants of Mecca belonged chiefly to a tribe called the Quraish. They formed a settled population such as is usual in Arabian townships to this day; tribal, that is, in name, origin and organization, but essentially different in function, being composed of merchants, shopkeepers, caravaners and the like. As a settlement its interests were served by peace and security and its outlook doubtless marked by anti-Beduin sentiment. It had its own miniature government, for now that the old northern confederations of Hira and Ghassan had decayed there were few, if any, political organizations in the peninsula more comprehensive than the city-state. Its religious cult was principally the worship of an idol named Hubal, recently introduced from Syria; it had other idols, too, representing the much older Arabian deities, Al Uzza, Al-lat and Mana; a monotheistic creed was held by a tiny sect of Arabs known as Hanifs; and Christianity and Judaism were both professed, probably among a small foreign community and by occasional visitors.

We know as little of the authentic childhood of Muhammad as of Jesus of Nazareth. While yet a boy he found employment minding camels. At the age of twelve he is believed to have accompanied his uncle on a long caravan journey, not improbably on one of those two Meccan caravans that went up yearly to the fairs of Syria.

We may picture young Muhammad with other boys at the time of Mecca's own annual fair, held in the month of Dhul Hijja. A vast concourse of pilgrims crowded the streets and alleyways. Townsmen from Yathrib and Najran jostled Beduin from the near-by deserts, a motley stream into which boys, naturally curious, would be drawn by the appeal of a variety of accent, of dress and of weapons. In the hostelries Muhammad would hear the news of the desert told with intent voice and excited gesture; he would listen breathlessly to caravaners fresh from Syria or Mesopotamia bringing tidings of the wars between Greeks and Persians, of strange beliefs and foreign practices, and doubtless the youthful imagination would be fired to share such wonderful experiences and see great armies marching.

The gala days of the fair were those when the pilgrims

brought gifts to the heathen temple in the middle of the city square where the idols were housed. There, at a distance from the *Ka'ba,* as it came to be called, they disrobed and circled round in procession at a quick pace, clapping their hands and singing. He would see them reverently kissing the black stone in the wall of the sanctuary and then follow them as they withdrew to make seven visits to the neighbouring hills and seven times throw stones into the Valley of Mina, and so to the scene of a wholesale sacrifice of camels and sheep that brought the rites to an end. This ritual must have burnt deep into the young impressionable mind, for the grown man was to incorporate much of it into his own religion. Trading in Mecca went briskly on for these thirty days, and then an end came to the Pilgrimage Fair with public contests in oratory and poetry, arts to which the illiterate Arabs were fondly addicted.

When these Beduin came again they would do so by stealth, probably to raid the grazing grounds of Meccan merchants and carry off camels, killing as by immemorial custom anyone who stood in their way. The youth Muhammad, as a Meccan herdsman, doubtless experienced many scares of raiders, if not the reality, and tradition gives him his first military adventure at eighteen when he accompanied his uncle, probably in pursuit of desert braves who had been paying some such unwelcome visit.

At twenty-four Muhammad, now in the service of Khadija, a rich widow merchant of Mecca, found himself leader of a caravan going to Syria. This journey, affording contacts with the outside world to a man who was of mature age and commanding position, may well have had a profound influence on his religious outlook, but whether or not, it was to be the turning point in his domestic life.

For so well did Muhammad conduct his patron's affairs that on his return he won her admiration, and they were married. Khadija was already the widow of two husbands. She was many years older than Muhammad, but the marriage with her brought him independence and an enhanced status in the life of Mecca.

Muhammad was greatly devoted to Khadija. His life with her seems to have been entirely happy, and so long as she lived he did not marry again, an unusual fidelity perhaps in the polygamous society of Mecca at that time. During those fifteen years of early married life, as early manhood passed into middle age, he lived unobtrusively as a fond husband and father and like any other well-to-do private citizen.

Tradition speaks of him as a man of striking appearance with a fine sagacious face, black piercing eyes and a flowing beard; a sincere man, rather taciturn in speech, but gifted with penetrating insight and a natural rugged eloquence—a man whose rectitude won him the title of 'the trustworthy'; a kindly man and a lover of children. He was illiterate; indeed, few of the Meccan merchants of his day are thought to have acquired literacy and then only as much as served the purpose of their business accounts, for books were as yet a rarity in Arabia. But illiteracy was no greater handicap to him than it was to our own medieval English kings or to many illustrious oriental potentates of our day who can just read and write their own language. Book learning carries less prestige in backward societies than the moral and intellectual qualities of natural leadership, and with these Muhammad was abundantly endowed. He had an unusual grasp of realities, a deep intuitive understanding of man and nature; he was a man that other men could believe in. Although religion seems to have been a late development, there being scarcely any mention of it until the commencement of his ministry in his middle age, he must have been a man of serious mind and pious disposition, one who in his travels abroad and intercourse at home had been curious to learn what other men believed and practised. There were no religious books in his native Arabic, and Muhammad could not have understood the foreign scriptures of the Jews and Christians even if they had been read aloud to him. His knowledge of these and other systems could only have been such as he heard on 'the lips of men.'

Suddenly Muhammad came to have remarkable religious experiences. He had reached his fortieth year when in his retreat on Mount Hira he had a vision which he believed to be supernatural, a vision to call men to repentance and the better life, to give up idol worship and to confess the one and only true God, an inspiration that man's strength and peace of mind were to be found in resignation to the divine will.

From now on he began to speak of visions, of a faithful spirit, later identified as the angel Gabriel, who came and put God's words into his mouth; they were communications, he claimed, of supernatural origin, and he himself was but the medium. He made no personal claims to divinity or even that he had the gift of prophecy or of performing miracles. On the contrary, he was to assert with lifelong consistency that he was a mortal man. This disclaimer of divine origin brings him in one way into line with the Old Testament prophets. It is a reason, too, why our English word for his religion is really a misnomer. It is not Muhammadanism or Muhammadan to the Arab. They do not worship Muhammad, so there is really no analogy with our words 'Christianity' and 'Christian' from the word 'Christ', though Buddhism and Confucianism offer closer parallels. The name of the religion, according to its devotees, is not Muhammadanism but Islam: the Arab believer calls himself not Muhammadan but Muslim. These words, 'Islam' for the religion and 'Muslim' (='Moslem') for the believer, derive from an Arabic root word which means 'surrender', or, as we should say, 'resignation': its full connotation being 'a sublime resignation to God's will.'

Muhammad spent much time in prayer and fasting, and while in this condition the revelations of Allah came to him. As he sat, silent and musing, he would suddenly be overcome by great trembling, his face would change colour, and he would pass into a trance. By his followers these seizures were accepted as signs of divine revelation. Non-Moslem authorities, on the other hand, have observed that they are the symptoms of epilepsy, and some hold that Muhammad was an epileptic, an opinion which Gibbon branded as an absurd calumny of the Greeks.

While in the trance or perhaps on regaining consciousness, Muhammad 'recited' what he had seen and heard to the intimate friends about him, who, according to Arab tradition, wrote down the revelations on leaves of grass or shoulder bones of mutton or whatever other material availed. These recitations were couched in language of great authority purporting to be the voice of God, in a literary style of ecstatic beauty recalling the prophetic manner of the Old Testament.

Muhammad, in the first flush of these religious experiences, declared that 'There is but one God, and Muhammad is a messenger of God'[1]; that this God is the God of

[1]The word used in Arabic means 'sent-one'; the term 'prophet', however, has the authority of established usage.

the Jews and the God of the Christians; and that it is folly and wickedness to worship idols such as men rub with wax.

The proclamation of such beliefs would doubtless have given offence to his idol-worshipping fellow Meccans, and at first Muhammad did not go out and preach publicly. At the outset the revelations were disclosed within the family circle. Some members believed and some did not. Khadija, his wife, was an early convert, and so was his cousin, Ali, but his uncle, Abu Talib, who brought him up, remained an unbeliever to the end of his life, which came a few years later. Of Muhammad's own conviction and sincerity there would appear to be no doubt. He became aflame with zeal to destroy the idolatrous cults of his native Mecca and convert his fellow Arabs to monotheism; in other words to bring their attitude into conformity with the underlying conception of Judaism and Christianity.

Muhammad's first principle was the oneness of God and the universality of God. Although God of the Jews, He was no narrow, exclusive tribal God; although God of the Christians, He was not composed of Father, Son and Holy Ghost. His fundamental attribute was oneness. It is the slogan of the Arabs of the ages, and to this day they are fanatical on this issue. The very word 'Trinity' is a blasphemy to their ears.

Simplicity was the dominant note. The abstruse, and to Muhammad incomprehensible, doctrines of the Incarnation and the Trinity were utterly inacceptable. To Muhammad Jesus was just another prophet. The orthodox Christianity of his day was thus less attractive to him than Judaism; indeed, the revelations not only required the concept of a pure monotheism, but even the ritual of the Jews, the prayer ablutions, turning towards Jerusalem in prayer, the banning of pig's flesh as unclean. Christians were rebuked for giving up these laws which had been observed by Jesus and His apostles.

Muhammad clearly did not claim to be the founder of a new religion but the restorer of an old one—which he called the religion of Abraham. We may indeed suppose theological differences to have been a subordinate part of his teachings, for the masses he addressed were pagans. Intellectual differences of opinion were doubtless of less moment to Muhammad than the sins of the world. It was to save humanity from their sins, to make men and women realize their duty to the one true God and their duty to one another, that filled his heart and mind.

When Muhammad first went out into the highways and byways to preach, his converts were at first very few. Many were of lowly or even slave origin; others, notably Abu Bakr, Othman and Ali, were men of position and influence. It required courage to damn the city gods and to rebuke practically the whole of his fellow Meccans. At first people thought him mad. His claims to be a prophet in the old patriarchal tradition excited their derision. How could they accept his teachings? They much preferred their own ancestral cults to the established foreign religions of Jews and Christians, even as they knew them locally, and Muhammad's teachings must have looked to them like a hotchpotch. In any case they rejected outright his pretensions to be a prophet. They challenged him to perform miracles if he was really a prophet of God. For reply Muhammad disclaimed the power of working miracles. To him the whole creation was a miracle: the earth, the sky, man himself. To him the truth of his message was a miracle, and, said Muhammad, God 'refused to give signs and wonders that would lessen the merit of faith and increase the guilt of unbelief.'

Later votaries of Muhammad have, in spite of this, ascribed to him supernatural attributes. His nocturnal visit to Jerusalem, for instance, and thence to heaven for an interview with the Almighty (neither place, incidentally, is mentioned in the Qur'an, where a vision may be intended, or, if some Moslem scholars are right, a dream) has been believed literally by some of his followers who claim Palestine as having a special significance for them on that account. By old traditional belief Muhammad was carried from Mecca through the air on a mysterious animal called Boraq and set down at the temple in Jerusalem. There he dismounted, tethered Boraq and thence, escorted by the angel Gabriel, ascended through the seven heavens, visiting the various patriarchs, prophets and angels in their apartments. Beyond the seventh heaven Gabriel was left behind and Muhammad permitted to pass on alone, towards the throne. While he was still two bowshots off he felt a cold shiver pass through his heart and the hand of God on his shoulder. The deity imposed upon Muhammad the duty of believers to pray fifty times a day, but this was reduced to five on the advice of Moses. Descending to Jerusalem, he remounted his aerial Boraq[2] and so passed through the skies back to Mecca, 'thus performing in the tenth part of a night the journey of many thousand years.'[11]*

We may dismiss literal interpretation as being inconsistent with Muhammad's claims and teachings. His precepts were a simple and rational piety, observances such as prayer and fasting, the sinfulness of idolatry, the worship of one true and only God and claim to men's acknowledgment of the divine authority behind his message.

Still the Meccans scoffed. They believed, doubtless,

[2]The word *Barq* in Arabic means lightning.

that his teachings were subversive of the social order. As men of business they were naturally averse from changes which they thought might be to their loss, and clearly any change in the traditional cult which brought thousands of pilgrims to Mecca each year was to be looked on askance. Was not Muhammad preaching that the city idols were ineffectual and abhorrent? Some members of Muhammad's own family were, doubtless for political reasons, among his bitterest opponents, though some, like Uncle Abu Talib, who was now his protector, were well disposed but too good conservatives to abandon lightly the gods of their fathers. Muhammad was doubtless counselled by the doubters to walk warily and avoid trouble. Could he not keep his revelations to himself instead of bringing embarrassment or worse upon his family?

The early converts were obliged to meet secretly. They listened to Muhammad's sermons, prayed according to a formula and postures he had devised for them, their faces turned towards Jerusalem, and pledged themselves to abstain from the particular sins he most inveighed against—idolatry, fornication, falsehood, theft, infanticide.

Muhammad's converts grew, and the revelations increased. The passages of the Qur'an assigned to this early period are few and short and deal mainly with three subjects: the unity and attributes of God, morality and the coming Judgment Day. His teachings about the first two were the teachings of the Jews; the third was the Christian doctrine of the Resurrection, Judgment Day and the life to come.

The sensual picture of paradise is presented as 'a garden of delight existing for eternity; below it flow cooling streams, perpetual, and in it also are streams of water uncorrupted, and streams of milk whose flavour changes not, and streams of wine which are a delight to the drinkers, and streams of purified honey. Those who dwell there will enjoy fruits of every kind and have the forgiveness of their Lord. Each of the blessed will recline upon a richly decked bed, on either side a garden in which the fruits grow within reach of his hands. Therein are maidens of modest glances whom neither men nor *jinn* have touched before. . . . As though they were rubies or pearls.'

'Hell will be brought within sight of every beholder, on Judgment Day, as a burning fire. Those who are damned, whether man or *jinn,* remain in it for a long time, tormented by flames, all escape from which is prevented by long fetters. Above the hearts of the damned the fires of Hell shall be raised on columns outstretched, behind which there is no shadow or any protection against the flames, for they throw off sparks like castles or like yellow camels. The denizens of Hell shall taste no coolness, nor any drink save boiling water and ichor, nor any food but what chokes the eaters. All must pass through Hell, but Allah delivers from it those whom He wishes. They are those who have followed the way of Allah, but only for them is intercession permitted.'[9]*

An allegorical interpretation of heaven and hell is held by enlightened Moslems as by enlightened Christians. The rude Arabs of Muhammad's day, however, could probably only have grasped a sensual presentation as was accepted by Christians up to quite recent times. But the sensual presentation is only one side of the picture. Muhammad taught a spiritual heaven, too, where there shall be no sin, where the presence of the Highest shall infinitely transcend all other joys, where all grudges shall be taken out of men's hearts, and peace and concord shall reign.

With this vision of the life to come went an insistence

on a life here below to be lived by a far stricter ethical code than that to which the people were then accustomed.

But if all these teachings were already familiar enough to tiny Jewish and Christian communities they were revolutionary indeed to a great mass of the nomadic inhabitants of Arabia who lived segregated lives, many indeed seldom if ever visiting Mecca or Yathrib or any other big settlement, and the bulk of them not caring for religion at all, certainly not for the gods of the settled Arabs.

Muhammad's consuming desire to save the Meccans from their sins was in vain. One revelation referred to the Ka'ba, where the idols were enshrined, as 'the House of God', but if the Meccans mistook the toleration of their sanctuary for a gesture or a sop, it was in any case insufficient for them. They scoffed at this fellow townsman of theirs setting up as a prophet—Muhammad, one of themselves, Muhammad, whom they remembered as a boy, whose father and mother they knew and everybody connected with him. It was this individual that now dared to be contemptuous of the deities sacred to them all and dared suggest abolishing the source of the city's prosperity. They must threaten him. They bullied and mocked his converts, ill-treating those who had no family or tribal connections to afford them protection. The plight of these followers of Muhammad—estimated in the fifth year of his ministry at eighty-three families, perhaps six hundred souls—grew more serious. Taking counsel with the Prophet, they decided upon flight to Abyssinia. There they went, were sympathetically received by its Christian king and given asylum.

Muhammad and a tiny band of faithful followers remained in Mecca. But he was, figuratively speaking, driven underground for the time. The Meccans were alarmed by the growth of the movement and were resolved to crush it. The Quraish were intent on silencing Muhammad or expelling him or worse. They issued an ultimatum to his section of the tribe, the Bani Hashim, demanding that he should be outlawed. The Bani Hashim were unbelievers, but to withdraw their protection from one of their own number at the dictation of others would have been a shameful thing to do; the issue for them was a different one. They proudly refused to outlaw Muhammad; in other words declined to abrogate their right to revenge one of their members. The Quraish thereupon renounced intercourse with them, commercial and social.

Persecution was hence the lot of any who dared follow the Prophet. The loss of his beloved wife, Khadija, and his uncle and protector, Abu Talib, his strong shield and a counsellor of the Bani Hashim, made his position parlous indeed. Mecca was no longer safe for him. He turned for a refuge to the neighbouring city of Taif, but Taif, too, proved hostile, and he returned once more to Mecca under the protection of an influential heathen merchant. Ten years had passed since the commencement of his ministry. He was now fifty: he had few friends and few followers. Two years longer he remained in Mecca, but he had to exercise great care, though he was free to address himself to pilgrim visitors, and if these generally treated him with indifference or ridicule and the Meccans still reviled and persecuted him, his converts increased.

One day a party of pilgrims arrived who listened to the preacher with more than ordinary interest. They had come an eleven days journey from neighbouring Yathrib, a city to the north, that had had its Jewish sect for hundreds of years and a city whose citizens are thought to have had no love for the Meccans. To these pilgrims the Islamic message made an appeal. They felt drawn to the saintly man who delivered it and was the object of Meccan persecution. During their sojourn they came more and more under Muhammad's influence. Their conversion, indeed, was to be the turning point in the fortunes of the whole movement.

These Yathrib converts went back to their city carrying with them the tidings of a new-found salvation and of a religious wonder. They yearned for the fellowship of the great teacher and began to consider how they could persuade the elders of the city to allow him to come and settle in their midst.

Muhammad, as we have seen, had of late been living on sufferance in Mecca. Mecca was solid against this, the greatest of her sons. The adage that no man is a prophet in his own country might well have been said of Muhammad up to this time. Hostility had never abated to this renegade citizen, guilty of deserting the city's deities, this man who dared imply that the Arabs of past ages were ignoramuses and fools; how could Meccans feel anything but loathing for such imputations and repugnance for their author!

Two years thus passed. The Yathrib converts had come to the Mecca Fair again, this time bringing with them an invitation to Muhammad to return with them for good. A secret meeting was called and a solemn promise of protection and succour given. He was ready, nay, eager but felt he could not abandon his Meccan followers. These in any case had small reason for wishing to remain behind. They therefore decided to fly too. They left as gradually and as unobtrusively as possible. The Prophet himself remained to the end, then he, too, crept away in disguise, eluding those more extreme Meccan elements who sought to slay him. For two days he hid in a cave outside Mecca, then continued his perilous flight (*hijra*[3]) northwards along the coast. Sixteen days later he entered Yathrib, perhaps quietly and unnoticed, though one tradition gives him a public entry riding a she-camel, his turban flying ominously in the breeze like a standard, and being hailed with acclamation by five hundred citizens who had come out to welcome him. Yathrib in any case had done well. She had gained for herself the title to be known as 'The City of the Prophet'; in Arabic *Medinat al Nabi,* soon to be shortened to Medina, as we know it today.

The people of Medina who sympathized with the refugees gave them of hospitality; those who did not suffered them with an ill grace. Some there were who opposed them and intrigued against them, and among this number were the Jews. At the outset a plot of ground was provided, and on this was built the Prophet's house and the first mosque, the two possibly under one roof, the mosque being a simple room in which a palm tree served the purpose of chair or pulpit as befitted the essential puritanism of the Prophet's teachings. Revelations came, converts multiplied.

For ten years Medina was the home of the Prophet and the refuge of his followers. He continued throughout this

[3]The hijra is the starting point of the Islamic Era. Such manner of dating differs conspicuously from that of our Christian calendar. We date our era from the birth of Christ, of course, but the Moslems do not date theirs from the birth of Muhammad or even from the year in which he commenced his ministry. They date it from the year of his flight to Medina (from the hijra, hence A.H.) when he had reached the age of fifty-two. This reckoning is not without significance, for the year of flight marks the year when Muhammad first enjoyed 'temporal protection to preach openly.' Islam was to become a theocracy, temporal power to have a valid and intimate connection with instituted religion, and the orthodox Islamic tradition, right down to the War, has been that the strongest temporal Islamic power, latterly Turkey, was the appropriate seat of the Prophet's successor—the caliph.

time with unabated vigour to teach the message which was being revealed to him. He taught men to pray[4] and inspired them to lead better lives. He taught the wayward Arabs respect for authority. These ten years were also to witness the development of the movement from a religion to a theocratic state. The faithful, hitherto a persecuted minority, became involved in a series of military operations that resulted in their becoming a majority: the Prophet, hitherto missionary, became soldier and statesman, too, which, at the end of his life, led to a temporal mastery not only of Mecca and Medina, but of the Yemen southwards and Najran.

The early revelations which had counselled liberty of conscience and religious toleration had been utterly inacceptable to the unbelieving Meccans. They had hounded the Prophet forth, they had sent an embassy off to Abyssinia demanding the expulsion of his followers, and now they stretched forth their arm to strike at the movement that, to their alarm, was growing in Medina.

The enmity of the Meccans was a perpetual menace. Muhammad as a God-fearing man would have preferred peace, but as a good Arab was not for peace at any price. The Moslems believed that the Meccans were set upon their extermination. Islam must now draw the sword in defence of itself.

Persecution made Islam militant. To the Arabs of all time battle had been an honourable arbiter. The Arabs were a warlike people. They possessed the manly virtues. 'The sword is the key of heaven and of hell; a drop of blood shed in the cause of God, a night spent in arms, is of more avail than two months of fasting and prayer:

[4]In the second year at Medina a revelation changed the direction of prayer from facing Jerusalem to facing Mecca.

whosoever falls in battle, his sins are forgiven: at the Day of Judgment his wounds shall be respendent as vermilion and odoriferous as musk and the loss of his limbs shall be supplied by the wings of angels and cherubim.' To ascribe this to the Prophet himself, as Gibbon does, is inconsistent with the revelations in which peace is exalted, yet the Arab writers who came to compose in this vein with the zeal of patriotism or devotion give us an insight into the psychology of the desert man who was soon to sweep across the world and make himself master of it.

The intrigues of the Meccans with the faction in Medina opposed to Muhammad grew from provocation to threat. A revelation came, justifying recourse to the sword under the compulsion of tyranny, but it was a qualified use of the sword, justifying defence but not attack. This led the Prophet to despatch reconnoitring parties from time to time to keep a watch on the enemy's movements, such parties being given instructions to avoid collisions. One party, however, responding to its old-time impulses, raided a caravan of the Quraish, killed a Meccan and took two other prisoners. Now the raid in Arabia is the equivalent of war. By desert canons, then as now, one is as honourable with them as the other is with us: for the spoils are taken in combat, a feature differentiating it from petty theft, which to the Arabs of all ages is wholly despicable. In a hungry land raiding is a natural condition, and, as with aggression in Western war, the motive is material self-interest.

Muhammad no sooner heard of this aggression than he condemned it; it had indeed taken place in defiance of his orders. But even now, had the Quraish been as peacefully disposed as the Prophet the matter could have been composed amicably by the normal payment of blood money and restitution of the spoils.[5] This course the Quraish spurned. The incident gave them the pretext for war.

Thus in the second year of Muhammad's exile a thousand Meccans marched north to encounter the Prophet and three hundred men at a well, not far from Medina, called Badr. Not only numerically were the odds overwhelmingly against the Moslems, but the Meccans were far better equipped. The Prophet retired into a small hut and offered up special prayers, then emerged, reciting the Qur'anic verse, revealed long since: 'Soon shall the hosts be routed, and they shall turn their backs.'[4]*

It was a custom in Arab warfare of old, as a prelude to battle, for a champion from each side to enter the lists in individual combat. Of Badr Arab tradition records three such combats, and in each case the Moslem was the victor. The Meccans, goaded to fury, fell upon their adversaries, but in vain, and at last were obliged to fall back for lack of water and, being better mounted, were able to retire from the field, leaving, however, seventy killed and as many wounded. Although this was the first battle of its kind between those who had been exiled from Mecca and those who had exiled them, believers and unbelievers, Muhammad commanded the kindly treatment of prisoners, and some of these remained and embraced Islam. Others, who were rich, were ransomed; those who were poor were freed. The success of Badr naturally had an influence on Medina opinion. Success against such odds connoted divine

[5]The division of the spoils in the wars to follow the Prophet's death, whether of gold or silver, captives, cattle or merchandise, was determined by the division that followed this incident at Nakhla. One fifth was the Prophet's share and set aside for pious and charitable purposes; the remainder was equally divided between the raiders; later practice gave a double share to a horseman as an inducement to increase the mounted arm, and the share of the slain went to the widows and children.

blessing; those Moslems who fought at Badr were honoured throughout life and those who were slain counted martyrs.

Mecca, smarting under the defeat, raised a force of a thousand horse and two thousand foot to move against the city that dared give Muhammad protection. Now Medina was not a commercial city like Mecca, but a group of village settlements that lived by agriculture, so that its outlying fields were exposed to the ravages of an attacker, and Muhammad, doubtless with this consideration uppermost in his mind, marched out with his smaller force of only a thousand men to outlying Uhud. The Meccans advanced, accompanied by their women. (I have myself witnessed the women of the Bani Bu Ali tribe in southeast Arabia running at the heels of their advancing men, carrying full water skins. Another custom of the Arabs of antiquity was for men to go into battle shouting the names of their sisters that they might do nothing ignoble in the face of an enemy.)

Before the battle was joined three hundred of Muhammad's force defected under the leadership of a hypocritical ally, yet so valiantly did the Moslems fight that the enemy at last withdrew, having gained no advantage. Rumour had reached them that Muhammad had been slain—he had indeed fallen to a javelin wound, but a faithful few had rallied to his help and saved him—so that the Meccans left the field of Uhud with Badr unavenged.

Medina now lived under the continual peril of invasion. The hostility of Mecca was implacable, and soon came news of a great army assembling there with a large Beduin contingent whose object was to crush Muhammad once for all. All the resources of Medina were clearly necessary to parry the coming blow. On this occasion there was no marching out as at Uhud. Not only were Muhammad's forces concentrated within Medina's defences, but these defences were of a novel kind. A trench was dug across the side of the city that was most exposed to attack—a practice of the Persians—whence the battle that ensued came to be known as the Battle of the Trench.

A tradition of prophetic vision recorded by Muhammad Ali runs thus: 'In the course of the excavation they came to a hard stone. All exerted themselves to their utmost but they could not break it. It was therefore suggested to the Prophet, who had chalked out the limits with his own hands, to allow a slight deviation from the original plan. Taking up a pickaxe he addressed himself to the task which others had failed to accomplish. Getting down into the ditch, he struck hard at the stone which gave way, emitting at the same time sparks of fire, on which the Prophet, followed by his companions, raised a cry of "God is Great" and said that he saw in the spark that he had been awarded the keys of the Palace of the Syrian King. A second stroke and the stone was split, the same spark of light coming out. Once more "God is Great" was shouted aloud, the Prophet observing that he had been given the keys of the Persian kingdom. The third attempt broke the stone to pieces, and the Prophet announced to have seen the keys of Yemen coming into his possession. Then he explained that he had been informed that his followers would gain possession of all those countries.'[6] [4]*

The Meccans were now to advance. Although they made no sustained attack, preferring the methods of siege, troops of their horsemen made occasional sorties

[6]Many Arabs hold that the military enterprises which subsequently brought about the spread of Islam across the world were ordained by God and known to the Prophet: to them the true world religion, Islam, was in full vigour from the moment of its revelation.

only to withdraw from the trench under a shower of arrows and stones. A deciding handicap was a shortage of supplies, for the Medina gardens failed to yield that which was expected of them. This also affected the defenders, and both forces would have welcomed an honourable compromise, but the supply factor was favourable to the besieged, and a tempest of wind, hail and rain arose to scatter the tents of the Meccans. They had already suffered from desertions and were compelled ignominiously to withdraw.

The course of events, not of Muhammad's seeking, had elevated him to the leadership of Medina. His followers had steadily been increasing, though a hostile faction still existed and became active, particularly in times of crisis. Belonging to this faction were the Medina Jews, and Muhammad had to turn aside from time to time to punish them for their treachery. Following Badr he had banished the prime offenders to Syria; from the Battle of Uhud he had occasion to expel another Jewish tribe, who had sought to encompass his murder, to neighbouring Khaibar; and after the Battle of the Trench he laid siege to the fastnesses of the intriguing Quraiza. After their surrender Arab tradition makes them prefer that their fate should be settled not by the Prophet, but by a Jewish convert to Islam. His judgment was duly carried out. It accorded with the Jewish way prescribed in the Scriptures of Deuteronomy XX, 13, 14—the males (three hundred) were put to death, females and children were enslaved, their property was confiscated.[4]*

Within a year of the Battle of the Trench Muhammad set forth from Medina to visit Mecca for the purpose of making the pilgrimage. Although the few hundred faithful followers who accompanied him went unarmed the Meccans were suspicious. They marched out with Beduin allies to block the Prophet's approach. He was forbidden entry. A ten years truce was entered into between the two cities, and an agreement made by which Muhammad should withdraw on this occasion but would be allowed to make the pilgrimage the following year, provided his followers again came unarmed and remained for no more than three days.

Pilgrimage time came round again. The Prophet set forth for Mecca with two thousand devoted followers. This time there was no hindrance, and he performed the traditional ceremonies. But his outward homage at the holy shrine that contained the idols concealed an inward resolution to sweep them away when the favourable hour should strike. The strength and devotion of his following and his own bearing impressed the Meccans, and two eminent converts were made, Khalid ibn al Walid and Amr ibn al As, destined to be great military leaders in wars of world conquest.

The Prophet returned to Medina, of which place he was now the master, and according to Arab historians forthwith despatched embassies to the great rulers of the earth, the Byzantine emperor, the Chosroes of Persia, the Aziz of Egypt, and the Negus of Abyssinia, summoning them to accept God and His apostle. The fire-worshipping Persian emperor is supposed to have treated the demand with contempt, whereas the Christian Byzantine emperor received the embassy favourably, but he must fain conceal his hand because he feared his ecclesiastical hierarchy.

A tragedy, to which momentous consequences are attached by Arab authorities, attended the return of this mission. Muhammad's messengers were killed on the Syrian border. It was a contravention of the laws of tribal morality, an act of war. A force of three thousand men was hastily got together in Medina and marched north. It encountered an unexpectedly large opposing force of the lieges of Byzantium at Muta, just south of the Dead Sea and after suffering the loss of three commanders was driven to retire on Medina.

During this time the Meccans had broken their truce with Medina by killing an ally of the Prophet's and, although offered alternative terms, preferred to accept the consequences of their action. Losing no time, the Prophet gathered ten thousand men, placed himself at their head and marched southwards towards Mecca.

In spite of the way the Meccans had treated him through life Muhammad, now an old man of sixty, bore them no grudge. He forbore to declare war though his object was investment. The city capitulated without a blow, and the Prophet marched in. A general amnesty was proclaimed for all but ten offenders. The Ka'ba was purified by the destruction of Hubal and the other idols; the black stone of special sanctity which pilgrims had been accustomed to stroke and kiss and which was said to have been placed there by the prophet Abraham was spared, the old ceremonies being incorporated into the rites of the Islamic pilgrimage.

The conquest of Mecca had its inevitable moral effect. Even the Quraish soon became converts, and if their idols were destroyed before their eyes their material interests were not only to be safeguarded under the new dispensation, but to be enhanced. The surrounding tribesmen were stampeded by the conquest. Godless by inclination, they would doubtless have sought their own advantage. At first this led them into opposition, to support the intransigeance of Taif, but within a year Taif had capitulated, and thus Muhammad lived to see even the surrounding Beduin submit. Thus did the Prophet also become a temporal ruler, the master of a state, the middle-western province of Arabia, familiar to us today as the Hijaz.

The dissensions and the enmity which had divided the settled man and the nomad, had divided Mecca and Medina, were thus brought to an end. Unity took their place. Rumour of an impending Byzantine invasion is held to have led the Prophet to collect a force and march north towards the Syrian border. The rumour proved insubstantial, and the Arabs swept through Jewish and Christian villages, subjugating them. The religious toleration which Muhammad showed was an example which his followers were faithfully to follow in the subsequent wars. The inhabitants were not asked to forswear their religion, and they were left in possession of their property; they were compelled only to pay tribute.

The pilgrims to Mecca now contained an ever-increasing majority of those professing the faith. It was as profitable to be a Moslem now as it had been unprofitable in those days of persecution before the hijra. Muhammad issued a proclamation that only Moslems were in future to be permitted to make the pilgrimage, and to this day no non-Moslem has gone to Mecca for this purpose without affirming his belief in Allah and His prophet.

It was one of Muhammad's last acts. On returning to Medina from his final pilgrimage, his health declined and he was overtaken by a mortal fever. For twelve days he presided at public prayers, and three days later the end came calmly. He died in the arms of his favourite wife, A'isha, at the age of sixty-two in the year A.D. 632.

Our knowledge of Muhammad's life and works is derived from Arab sources. There are no contemporary non-

Moslem authorities. Western authorities today suppose that much of this knowledge derives from oral tradition, cherished by companions, mostly illiterate and recorded later by believers in much the same way as our Gospels. This is not the view of pious Arabs. They believe that his utterances were faithfully recorded verbatim at the time, that the texts of the Qur'an were committed to writing at the moment of revelation; it was only the collection into book form that came about after the Prophet's death. Significant, they hold, is the fact that Muhammad ended his life in triumph, a national hero, a ruler as well as a prophet, so that his every saying, every action, every manner, every incident of his life would naturally have been the object of interest and investigation; indeed, they believe schools sprang up immediately after his death dedicated to his service in which A'isha, his wife, and Ali, his son-in-law, were foremost among the lecturers. According to the Arabs 'more is known of the life and character of Muhammad than of any other figure in history.'

He was a man without pride, without ostentation, without cant, not a mealymouthed man, but a strong, just man and a generous man. Such indeed was the munificence of his good works that he died in debt, some of his belongings in pawn with a Jew—among them his only shield, for which he obtained three measures of meal.

By the standards of his people and times Muhammad lived a normally moral life. He was a bachelor till twenty-six, the husband of one wife till fifty. After Khadija's death he married a second wife, Sauda, in Mecca, and from the time he came to Medina, at the age of fifty-two, he acquired many wives. Eleven of them occupied chambers around his house at one time, a revelation having absolved him from the limit of four wives which the revelations imposed upon his followers. All appear to have been elderly widows except A'isha, the daughter of Abu Bakr, who was nine when she was betrothed to Muhammad and fourteen at the time of marriage (a normal age in Arabia, where twenty is considered passée—the oriental girl of fourteen is indeed the equal of the European one of eighteen). The elderly wives were widows of companions who had fallen in the wars, and Muhammad married them to shelter them and provide them with homes. None bore children; indeed, after Khadija, A'isha is thought to have been Muhammad's only real wife, except the Copt slave girl, Mary, who was one of the presents sent by Makawkis of Egypt in reply to the embassy summoning him to accept the Prophet's divine mission. Mary Muhammad freed before marrying and she won favour in his sight by bearing him a son, but the child died in infancy. Khadija, the wife of the Prophet's middle age, bore him four sons and four daughters. The sons all died in infancy, and the daughters all predeceased Muhammad except the youngest one, Fatima, who as the wife of Ali became the mother of a considerable posterity.

Muhammad despised pomp and lived an utterly simple life. Wine he forbade. Barley bread, dates and water, milk and honey formed his simple diet, but mortification of the flesh was no part of his religion. Except for the Fast of Ramadhan it is thought to have been odious to him, and Moslem fakirs and dervishes made their appearance only some centuries after his death, and then not generally among the Arabs. He lived in great humility, performing the most menial tasks with his own hands; he kindled the fire, swept the floor, milked the ewes, patched his own garments and cobbled his own shoes. There was an essential puritanism in his system. Divine revelation forbade the believer to wear either gold or silk—a curb on covetous passions.

His moral teachings sprang from a pure and exalted mind aflame with religious enthusiasm. From being a persecuted preacher, exiled to Medina, he rose, by a militant statecraft—the Arabs believe a civil war not of his choosing—to political power.

This he enjoyed only in the last few years of his life, and this he used for the spiritual and material welfare of Moslems. He must clearly have acted in accordance with the best traditions of the Arabs, for without real sincerity and sustained goodness on his part those first ardent converts would not have stood by him through all the vicissitudes of a crowded and critical twenty-three years. His authority clearly sprang from moral as well as intellectual qualities.

Muhammad, as we saw, made no claims to miracles, yet the sociological reforms he was instrumental in setting in motion among his fellow countrymen were little short of the miraculous. Before his coming the Arabs, animated by the fiercest passions, were immemorially at feud one with another. The incident following the Battle of Uhud when Hind tore the liver out of Hamza and chewed it, strung his internal organs and garlanded herself, shows the manner of man to whom Muhammad brought the message of brotherhood.

Another barbarous practice of the Arabs of those times was that of putting girl children to death at birth—a practice found today only in China, engendered there as in Arabia of the seventh century by hunger and poverty. To this day you do not congratulate the wild man of the deserts on the birth of a daughter: it is a matter that may with propriety be passed over in silence. One revelation deplores this attitude: 'And when a daughter is announced to one of them his face becomes dark and full of anger. He hides himself from the people because of the evil of that which is announced to him. Shall he keep it with disgrace or bury it in the dust.'

The tradition remains of a companion who used to weep in repentance at having buried so many of his female children alive. This horrible practice the Prophet denounced and swept away. 'Whoever has a female child,' says a tradition ascribed to him, 'and does not bury her alive, nor hold her in contempt, nor prefer his male child to her, shall enter Paradise.'

His humanity was all embracing. He never ceased to champion the cause of woman against the ill-treatment of his contemporaries. He condemned the practice of inheriting the widow with the rest of an estate as though she were a chattel. She must not be a despised creature to be ashamed of and to be ill-treated any more, but a person to love and cherish and respect: at her feet lay the gates of paradise.

And so with slavery: he laboured for the amelioration of the slaves' lot, liberating any that were presented to him. He taught that the slave mother should never be separated from her children—a precept not always observed in later-day Arabian slavery—extolled the freeing of slaves as a penance, lauded the feeding of the orphan in times of famine and 'the poor man who lies in the dust.'

Muhammad was clearly a man of sound judgment. He was a realist. He was a gradualist. To have attempted to achieve his reforms in a single stroke would doubtless have imperilled them. He first forbade his followers' using wine before coming to prayers lest they should not understand what they were saying; at a later stage came total prohibition. Similarly polygamy without limit was radically restricted. 'You may marry as many wives as two or three or four; but if you fear you cannot be equitable between them, then marry only one. And you will never be able to be just between women no matter how much you may strive to do so.' Modern Moslem thought is persuaded that Muhammad was working towards the abolition of slavery and the institution of monogamy, but whether or not, the Arabs of his day were not ripe for these things. What he achieved, however, was a great and wonderful advance.

The obstacles that stood in the way of his aims Muhammad overcame as a practical man. A visionary idealism would have left untouched the savage tribal culture of seventh-century Arabia. Muhammad had recourse to the sword, but his supposed zest for war is scouted by Arabs as a Western prejudice. And in spite of fond boasts of their own prowess in battle—the theme of so much of their verse—they are unanimous in the assertion that Muhammad never killed a man with his own hands. To him war was utterly distasteful, and he only took up arms and justified the taking up of arms in self-defence. 'Fight in the way of God against those who attack you but begin not hostilities,' he said. 'Verily God loveth not the aggressors. . . . And if they incline towards peace thou shalt also incline towards it.'

The revelations which are ascribed to the early period before the Prophet's flight from Mecca had, as we have seen, chiefly to do with faith and morals, but as a community professing Islam grew in Medina, so the divine revelations came to take on a political character. Positive secular as well as religious enactments are found in the part of the Qur'an assigned to the post-hijra period. Each revelation is said to have arisen out of some particular political situation.[6]*

The great bulk of the Moslem scriptures is, however, devoted to the inculcation of high moral precepts. The essential teachings are a belief in an all-embracing universal God, one and indivisible, merciful and compassionate; a belief that God has revealed Himself through the prophets (in other words, a revealed religion); a belief in a future life to which death is the portal and which is a continuation of the present life. In a fundamental sense, therefore, Islam has a large common basis with our own religion, both, of course, having their roots in Judaism. The Moslem differs from the Christian in that he denies that God sent His Son into the world for its redemption by His suffering, for the Divine Essence was neither begotten nor can beget. The Moslem conception of God is therefore less personal than ours: His decrees are absolute and predestined and not to be swayed by intercession or sacrifice. There are, therefore, no priests in Islam, no confession, no intercession, no absolution, no sacrificial redemption.

The Qur'an denies that Jesus Christ or any other person can be the Son of God; asserts, however, that Jesus was a true prophet, born of a virgin, and could work miracles. It denies His crucifixion; instead His enemies were permitted by God to crucify a criminal or a phantom, believing it to be Jesus. Jesus was a mortal man and on the Day of Judgment will reproach both the Jews and the Christians, the one for denying Him, the other for deifying Him. Yet Jesus, according to Muhammad, was a true prophet every bit as much as himself, and references to

Him, both in the Qur'an and by Islamic usage, take the form of 'Our Lord', while His Mother is never referred to except as 'Our Lady.' When the name of either is mentioned, moreover, it is followed by the phrase 'on whom be peace.' It seems quite clear that Muhammad treated Christians with tolerance and respected their religion and their places of worship. It was the misunderstanding and misrepresentation that grew out of subsequent wars that led to the bitterness and the hatred, now happily dying.

A fundamental difference between Moslem and Christian is in the respective attitude towards their scriptures. To the former the Qur'an is the very word of God, so that the contradictions between it and the Bible are, in a Moslem's eyes, God's rectification of the mistakes that have crept into the scriptures of Christians and Jews. This conception does not invalidate the earlier prophets' message, for their message and Muhammad's message are held to have been the same: the earlier scriptures became corrupted and hence Muhammad's mission to restore them. Muhammad was not teaching a new religion: it was but an extension or a modification of the earlier religions, which he pronounced equally God-revealed in their pristine purity.

On Muhammad's lips our familiar Bible stories seem to us to be garbled versions, and Western authorities suppose that they were forms current in the largely unlettered Arabian society of Muhammad's day, for by tradition the Jews of Arabia had in many places forgotten the Hebrew tongue and had become illiterate. Moslems answer that the change will be found to be in the interests of reason, morality or decency; that according to the Qur'an the prophets did not commit the sins attributed to them in the Bible.

More difficult of acceptance in the West is the form of creation 'jinn', which the revelations showed God to have created out of fire before He created man out of clay, among whom are believers and unbelievers and to whom God sent apostles. As with Christian scholars faced in the Gospel with first-century beliefs in evil spirits, such as figure in the Gadarene miracle, so also modern Moslem scholars look for a more rational interpretation of 'jinn' than the traditionally accepted one.

But orthodoxy demands of the Moslem the acceptance of the Qur'anic revelations in their entirety. To the faithful the Qur'an is not a man-made book, not the work of Muhammad, who was just its passive medium, nor of later compilers. It is not merely divinely inspired as our Christian Scriptures are held to be. It is in itself divine. 'Its substance is uncreated and eternal subsisting in the Essence of the Deity. Its text is incorruptible.' Its ordinances, its precepts and its sanctions are held to have been not revealed for the exclusive regeneration of seventh-century Arabia, they are applicable to all countries and all times—the revealed word of God in man's midst.

The form and institutions of Islam came to take a final shape during those last ten years of the Prophet's life. Five cardinal tenets emerged:

(1) Acceptance of the unity of God and the message of Muhammad.

(2) The due performance of daily prayers.

(3) The poor rate.

(4) Fasting throughout the month of Ramadhan.

(5) Making if possible the pilgrimage to Mecca.

The Moslem rule of life is no easy one. Alcohol is forbidden. The poor rate is an obligation rather than a merit, for religious law has decided that one fortieth of the believer's income is the property of the poor: to give less is a sin, to give more is alms—a meritorious act and a pious duty. The Fast of Ramadhan, when no morsel of food, no drop of drink may pass a believer's lips between dawn and sunset, is more rigorous, particularly in hot climates, than our Lenten Fast. Prayer five times a day is de rigueur wherever the believer finds himself at the appointed hour between dawn and early evening[7]—in the street, at his house, his place of business or elsewhere; he must suspend his activities, free his mind from worldly thoughts and perform the set devotions. The spirit of Islam in its pure religious conception, like that of Christianity, is to elevate and ennoble the believer.

As has been noticed, Islam is not a sacerdotal religion. It condemns mediation between man and his Maker, 'who knew him before he was born, and is closer to him than his jugular vein.' Any Moslem of good character can lead the prayers in the mosque, though in practice an *imam*, a leader recognized for his piety and scholarship and devoted to the service of the mosque, does so.[8] It is a simple, dignified form of worship following a set formula of postures and devotions[9] (petitions and responses faintly suggesting an unintoned litany in the English church service). The worshippers do not bare their heads; they remove their shoes or sandals, perform certain ritualistic ablutions and then assemble to form a long line facing Mecca (the Ka'ba), the leader taking up a position a little to the front of them in the centre.

[7](1) Dawn or sunrise. (2) Midday. (3) Midafternoon. (4) Sunset. (5) Evening (bedtime).

[8]Friday is the Moslem day for congregational worship in the mosque, corresponding to the Saturday of the Jews, the Sunday of Christians.

[9]For those here given I am indebted to my friend Mr Mahmood Zada, of the Royal Legation of Sa'udi Arabia in London.

Posture 1.—They stand in a reverent way, with the palms of their hands raised to the ears.

Affirmations and prayers in a low reverent voice.

'God is greater than all else.'

Posture 2.—Still standing, the arms are lowered and the right hand placed over the left one.

'Glory and praise to Thee, O God! Blessed is Thy name and exalted is Thy Majesty. There is no one worthy of worship and service but Thee. In the Name of God, the Merciful, the Compassionate. Praise be to God the Lord of the Worlds, the Merciful, the Compassionate. The Master of the day of Judgment. Thee, O God, Thee only do we worship, and Thee only do we beseech for help. Guide us unto the right path, the path of those Thou hast blest, not of those with whom Thou art displeased, nor of those who have gone astray.'

The worshipper then recites a portion of the Qur'an he has committed to memory, e.g.—

Say 'Verily my prayers and my worship, my life and my death are unto God; the Lord of the Worlds. No associate has He. Thus have I been commanded and I am the first to surrender myself unto Him.'
'God is greater than all else.'

Posture 3.—Bodies are bent forward at right angles, the hands are lowered and placed on the knees.

'Glory to my Lord, the Exalted.'

A bow that is repeated twice more, each time with the same words.

Posture 4.—The standing position is resumed.

'God accepts him who is grateful to Him.
O our Lord! All praise be to Thee.
God is greater than all else.'

Posture 5.—The worshippers next kneel down, their bodies bowed over, supported with the hands on the ground, palms downwards, their heads bowed reverently, so that their brows touch the ground.

'Glory to my Lord, the Most High.'

A bow that is repeated twice more, each time with the same words and ending—

'God is greater than all else.'

Posture 6.—A sitting-kneeling position follows with the hands resting on the knees.

'Glory to my Lord, the Most Exalted.'
(repeated thrice)
'God is greater than all else.'

Posture 7.—The words and obeisances as in Posture 5.

Posture 8.—Is like Posture 6 and concludes the first phase of the devotions and is called a *Rakat*. Prayers are some of two, some of three, some of four Rakats. To end with, a prayer is said for the Prophets, the faithful and for the worshippers in some such form as the following—

'Homage be to God and all sincere worship is unto Him.

'Peace and the mercy of God and His blessings be upon thee, O Prophet! Peace be upon us and all righteous servants of God.

'I bear witness that there is but one God and that Muhammad is His servant and His messenger.

'May it please Thee, O God, to be gracious to Muhammad and the followers of Muhammad as Thou wast gracious to Abraham and the followers of Abraham and to bless Muhammad and the followers of Muhammad as Thou didst bless Abraham and the followers of Abraham, for surely Thou art Praised and Magnified.'

This is usually followed by—

'O Lord! Grant that I may always observe my prayers and that my offspring may do so also and accept, O our Lord, this supplication of mine. Our Lord! Forgive me and forgive my parents and all believers on the day of reckoning.'

And finally the worshippers turn their heads to right and left with the greeting—

'Peace be with you, and the mercy of Allah.'

10 POSTURES OF PRAYER 11

[10]From D. S. Margoliouth's *Mohammed.*
[11]By courtesy of G. P. Putnam's Sons.

CHAPTER III

Arab World Conquest—Eastwards

THE PROPHET was dead. And now the rude Arabs were to surge out of Arabia under the banner of Islam and vanquish the great nations of the earth and set going a movement that went on for upwards of a century to follow, which history remembers as the wars of the Saracenic expansion. (See map at end of book.)

The traditional view that the Arabs, following the birth of Islam, were fired by religious zeal to march forth on a mission of proselytizing the world is no longer acceptable. Although Arabs themselves believe that the widespread propagation of the faith, of which they were the militant instruments, came about as God willed, it is extremely unlikely that the Beduin hosts at the time of the Prophet's death had any strong spiritual convictions; and Arab authorities, moreover, tell us that the wars were precipitated by acts of aggression on the part of their enemies, that the early expedition against Syria was to check the depredations of the Christian Roman Empire against peaceful Moslems over the border, that the raids against the Persians were the outcome of Persian provocation in eastern Arabia. The militant policy of the Medina caliphate they thus hold to have been imposed by outside political events, which necessitated massing the Arabs to meet the invasion of two formidable powers.

Here we must part company with the Arab interpretation of history to follow those Western authorities who believe that the Arab wars were in their inception neither purely religious nor purely political, but chiefly economic.[7]*

It was hunger and want that drove the Arabs forth to their wars of world conquest. Arabia was immemorially hungry, as is reflected in her earlier population movements: the Canaanite migration was one; possibly the Hyksos and Akkadian movements were others. A historic role of hers seems to have been that of a human reservoir that periodically overflowed, and in the centuries before the Prophet there were signs of another welling up. South to north waves of peoples from the decaying Yemen are associated with the tradition of the bursting dam of Mar'ib, and doubtless a steady spilling over of borderline Arabs into the fertile plains of Syria and the Euphrates Valley was always going on. Now in the new powerful state that was emerging within Arabia the two old safety valves that had relieved population-pressure—infanticide and internecine warfare—were forbidden.

To return to that day in Medina when the Prophet died. He left no son to succeed him. Tradition represents his death as a surprise and a shock to the faithful, who had come to regard him, in spite of his protestations, as more than mortal man. He does not seem to have foreseen a near end or to have named a successor, but among his companions must have been those who thought on these things. So long as he lived, however, personal rivalries lay dormant. His decease was now to raise the thorny issue of succession.

The Prophet's nearest kinsman was Ali, his cousin and 'the legatee', the husband of his daughter Fatima, the father of the Prophet's grandchildren, whom he was known to love, the son of Abu Talib, who had shielded the Prophet in his dark early days. Ali was one of the first converts, too, and his zeal for the cause, both in peace and war, had never wavered. His claims looked incontestable. But Ali's enemies were many. The aged Abu Bakr, father of A'isha, the Prophet's favourite wife, was an older and more venerable companion. He, too, was one of the earliest converts, and one on whose advice the Prophet was known to have placed the greatest reliance. The issue was decided by Omar, a companion of the greatest influence, and Omar sided with Abu Bakr. Their more powerful and active following lost no time in forestalling a feud and rallying the faithful to one leader. They met and acclaimed Abu Bakr *khalifa* (=caliph). This term, originally denoting no more than 'successor', came to be a title rivalling 'emperor' in majesty. Ali, greatly mortified that another was preferred before him, retired for a time. The indecent haste, as it seemed to him, of the selection has been suggested as the reason for his precipitate burial of the Prophet in the room where he died, though tradition has it that Muhammad had expressed a wish that public ceremonial attaching to a formal funeral should be avoided.

Arabia, according to an Arab view, had achieved something like unity under the Prophet's genius. Its tribes are supposed already to have been in adherence; but now some of them, supposing Islam to be dead with its founder, seceded. Military expeditions had therefore to be sent out from Medina to compel, at the point of the sword, the return of the renegades to the allegiance. This view that Arabia, vast and uncontrollable land that it was, should at the very outset have formed a political and religious entity is thought by Western authorities to be historically improbable, for even Mecca itself and its surrounding tribes were in opposition to the movement up till a year or two before the Prophet's death. It is more probable that at the time of Abu Bakr's succession only the middle-western province about Mecca and Medina with the neighbouring Yemeni and Nejdi tribes formed a Moslem polity. Here indeed the Prophet had founded a theocratic state, but only very suddenly and at the end of his life. Except for the nominal adherence of Beduin tribes on its borders, therefore, the greater part of the peninsula would appear to have lain outside the pale of his political dominion, and certainly not to have been deeply affected as yet by the spiritual teachings of Islam.

Abu Bakr now found himself the temporal and religious head of this first Islamic state. The moment was one when it would have been opportune to distract attention from the disintegrating effects of the Prophet's sudden and unexpected end, prudent to find active employment for those Beduin who had been lured by its prizes to take up a profession of arms in the service of the state.

For the tribes close at hand, who had become Moslems from political expediency, promptly seceded on the death of the Prophet to rally round other leaders—pronounced 'false prophets' by the orthodox. Khalid ibn al Walid, who had earned military distinction when serving with the Prophet, was sent against those who deserted to one named Tulaiha and later won renown as the 'Sword of God', the greatest soldier in the Islamic cause. Khalid passed on to deal equally successfully with still more formidable opposition under another false prophet named Musailima. These and other expeditions sent against the seceders achieved their appointed end and extended the dominion of Medina throughout the peninsula. Their effect was to transform the wild Beduin into something like military organizations and to spread the belief that soldiers in the Islamic cause were licensed to plunder or exact tribute from unbelievers with whom the Moslems were at war, while to the pious, to die in the cause insured the believer the delights of paradise. During the brief caliphate of Abu Bakr the peninsula was brought under one political hegemony; there were no tribes left within whom it was lawful for others to attack. The Arabs were a unity. The spoils of the raid could only legitimately be looked for in the outside world. If in Medina and Mecca a pure religious ardour found for the wars a religious or a political mandate, the Beduin who waged them were doubtless actuated by worldly considerations. Products of a cruel environment and of ages of war, their resultant psychology was such that it did not change in a flash with the change of political or even religious allegiance.

Arabia's powerful neighbours, Byzantines and Persians, had in the days of their strength been able to keep the peninsular peoples pent up, but at the time of the Prophet these powers themselves were declining. Their ancient rivalry had grown into a death struggle of continuous warfare. The year of the Prophet's birth coincided with a Persian invasion of Syria, and Aleppo was in Persian possession. While he was not yet thirty, maybe while still away on that caravan visit to Syria undertaken at the behest of his future wife, a Greek army was marching into Persia to place its own protégé on the throne. At the time he was telling the unbelieving Meccans of those early visions caravans from Syria must have been bringing news that the Persians were back again, overrunning Syria and Palestine, invading Egypt and Asia Minor; these followed shortly by news of a Byzantine army advancing through Armenia to attack Persia in the rear and enter the royal city of Dastagird. (See map B at end of book.) At one period six sovereigns had ascended the throne of Persia in the course of six months, so riven was she by internal dissension. Both these great powers on Arabia's borders were exhausted, their outlying dependencies in chronic unrest from neglect and discontent. For them there was a writing on the wall. The way was opening for the hungry, virile and warlike Arab hosts. The old ramparts to the north had crumbled.

It was a mistake then to suppose that when these hosts did first appear they came like Cromwell's Roundheads, inspired with a fanatically religious mission. It was not primarily a beneficent eagerness to share with others the blessings of Islam that brought them. Nor indeed did they come to impose Islam, for Islam in a political sense had only recently been imposed on many of themselves.

We cannot suppose the Beduin to have been pious, God-fearing zealots like the companions of the Prophet; they were principally raiding bands of desert warriors whose allegiance to the new state was based primarily on self-interest. And whatever the higher motives of the caliphs of Medina and the enlightened Moslems of the settlements, there can be little doubt that the desert man himself was principally inspired by the hope of plunder.

Those earlier expeditions of bona fide religious converts, one under the leadership of the Prophet himself, were clearly not proselytizing missions: for the Jews and Christians subjugated were allowed to keep their own religion if they cared to. What they must do, however (for the Arabs conceived of themselves as being at war with Byzantines) was to pay tribute. Higher motives can scarcely be ascribed to later activities carried out by desert warriors of less religious zeal and to whom, doubtless, Islam was primarily a political allegiance.

But however cause and purpose of the raiders themselves may for the most part have been economic, the immediate and stupendous success met with gave the movement a new impetus and a new goal. The possibility of permanent conquest was forced upon the Arab imagination by the very feebleness of the resistance, so easily overcome. The Arabs marched from victory to victory, from ambition to ambition; the modest pillaging raids grew to be wars of territorial conquest; Arab sovereignty came to be the inspiration of the desert hosts.

Before his death the Prophet had planned another expedition against the Byzantine borderlands. This was now allowed to go forward by Abu Bakr, while Khalid, less eminent for religious zeal than for military prowess, next seized an opportunity of going off with five hundred braves to raid Iraq, his appetite whetted for fresh fame and riches. Khalid, on this latest adventure, had the luck that proverbially attends the successful general. His arrival at Hira, at this time the seat of a Christian bishop, coincided with an upheaval in Persia. The garrison was depleted and, though able to maintain itself within the fortification, was powerless to issue forth for open warfare, so that the country round was at the raiders' mercy. Hira was therefore well content to buy off the raiders and promise to pay henceforward annual tribute as the price of peace. The raiders thereupon withdrew, some to return to their local tribes, while Khalid and the nucleus of his force turned north up the Euphrates, plundering as they went, to join forces with other Medina elements operating in Syria. For it was Syria rather than Iraq that loomed large in Arabian eyes, and expeditions thither suffered from no dearth of recruits. Had not the Prophet himself shown the way! And now Abu Bakr had sent three more parties, said to number seven thousand tribesmen, one faction under the redoubtable Amr ibn al As, a leader whose generalship in the annals of the conquest stands second only to that of Khalid himself.

The native population of Syria, as the Arabs knew, were alienated from their Greek masters—the Byzantines. These, embarrassed by financial difficulties arising out of the Persian wars, were obliged to make economies, and one of the most impolitic was to suspend subsidies to the Beduin tribes on the Arabian borders. Disaffection was the upshot, and the victims, although nominally Christian, appear to have made common cause with the Medina raiders—an interesting commentary on the supposed proselytizing fanaticism of the invaders.

The Arabs are not credited, at this stage, with having any concerted tactical plans of campaign. Each tribe had its own banner round which it rallied, while the leader harangued his men before and during battle, urging them on to valiant deeds. The old Arab tactics of the raid had been a sudden charge, withdrawal, a return to the charge and an exchange of arrows, when the weaker side would perhaps submit in order not so to antagonize the stronger as to be utterly despoiled. But the Arabs were quick to learn more subtle and sounder tactics from the trained Byzantine soldiery. Although as bowmen they were less accomplished their skill and courage with sword and lance established early superiority in close fighting.

Compared with their adversaries, they were ill equipped; their bows, spears and lances were inferior, and even slings are mentioned as part of their primitive equipment. Only the commanders and a favoured few could at first boast a coat of mail, though each man is thought to have acquired a helmet, a breastplate and a round shield. But the Arabs had not long to wait before acquiring better arms from prisoners and the slain and from armourers of the lands they conquered. They soon learned, too, to adopt the Persian practice of digging a defensive trench around an encampment when resting for a long period. On the move the force divided itself into a main body, flank guards and advance and rear guard, the last named bringing up the baggage, war stores, women and children, possibly also flocks and herds. They seemed to have favoured a 'five' formation, and drums were beaten, the stopping of which signified a halt.

The successful early raids had the effect of attracting more and more Beduin adventurers from the deserts, so that the Arab concentrations south of the Dead Sea assumed alarming proportions, and they fed themselves by ravaging southern Palestine. The emperor, greatly alarmed, had sent his brother Theodorus south from Damascus, and he temporarily forced the Arabs back into their mountain valley bivouacs. Then a new factor came into play. This was the redoubtable Khalid.

Khalid and his Arab braves, after Hira, had marched up the Euphrates Valley, thence across to Palmyra, and then appeared suddenly before Damascus in Theodorus' rear. Eschewing what must have been a great temptation, they turned aside and marched south through Trans-Jordan to effect a junction with their Arab comrades. The combined Arabs, probably led by Khalid, now hurled themselves against the Byzantines, who had taken up a strong position between Jerusalem and Gaza, and utterly defeated them. Theodorus fled from the field and was later recalled to Constantinople, and the Arabs freely dispersed themselves over the countryside of Judæa and Samaria.

Medina awaited the return of her raiding columns that had left two years before, but she waited in vain. They had set forth to plunder, they were staying to conquer. Rich countries lay at their feet, far better blessed than their hungry Arabian home. The sight of undreamed-of prizes made of these barbarous invaders an invincible host. Success in battle was changing their outlook. They could not help seeing that a systematic occupation of these fair lands was within their grasp.

At this stage, after a brief two years of office, the Caliph Abu Bakr died in his modest house at Medina. Again a successor must be chosen, and again Ali's claims were set aside. The late caliph had taken upon himself to nominate his own successor, and the matter was thus taken out of the arena of party strife. Abu Bakr's nominee was Omar ibn al Khattab, his own strongest supporter against Ali's claims at the time of the Prophet's death. Omar was a religious zealot and a man of resolute action, a man whose sincerity won the approbation of the faithful and the esteem of even the disappointed Ali, though later his name came to be execrated by the great division of Islam that championed Ali's cause.

From the first days of Omar's caliphate news of the striking military successes of their raiding columns came trickling back to the tribes in Arabia. The effect was much like that of the discovery of a gold mine in a new country. Arabia oozed forth its peoples, the young men to join Khalid's forces, others with families to settle adventurously in the northern borderlands. The implications of these early migrations, within ten years of the Prophet's death, are significant. The Arabs were not proselytizing bands; they were not merely out for plunder. They were already colonizing expeditions.

The weakness of the Hellenized garrisons and the friendliness of the native peoples combined to bring a great rallying and reinforcing of the Arabs. Palestine, except for Jerusalem and a few coastal ports that could be reinforced from Egypt, was already evacuated. Damascus, the capital of Syria itself, became the Arab goal, and thither they marched on the heels of the fleeing Theodorus. Khalid, aided by malcontent Christian inhabitants, actually marched into the city but could not hope to hold it before a greatly superior Byzantine army that now approached from the north, and he prudently retired down the desert side of the Jordan.

In the valley of the Yarmuk he called a halt. The Byzantine army approached from the west. The two forces faced each other for a long period under the hot summer sun—a delay that favoured the Arabs, for they grew stronger by a steady accretion from the desert, while the enemy grew weaker by defection of native irregulars, and soon the numerical strength was about equal. Khalid having detached a part of his force to send it north to cut off the enemy's retreat, himself attacked from a direction that forced Theodorus into a sector of the Yarmuk where his position was tactically hopeless. Here the defenders were thrown into great confusion, and the Arabs, pressing their advantage with energy, obtained a decisive victory: this famous Battle of the Yarmuk settling in A.D. 636 the fate both of Syria and Palestine. The Arabs marched on to Damascus to invest it a second time—this time permanently. Catapults and mangonels that ejected stones, fire and naphtha, whose use the Arabs had now learned, were used against the gates in the walls of Damascus, ineffectually it would seem, for the city is said to have been taken by men who swam the moat on inflated skins, flung ropes with running nooses over the turrets and so hauled themselves up over the walls.

The Greeks suffered losses at Yarmuk from which they never recovered, and the remnants of the imperial forces retired northwards to the Taurus Mountains. The Arabs quickly following up, Baalbek, Aleppo and Antioch fell easily into their hands. A few Hellenized cities of Palestine held out for a year or two longer, but the last of these, Jerusalem, capitulated to the Moslems in 638 and Cæsarea in 640.

Consolidation of their gains was no difficult matter for the Arabs. The native Semitic-speaking peoples, Christian though they were, welcomed the Moslems as deliverers—an interesting commentary again on the supposed proselytizing fanaticism of the conquerors. Nor is the Syrian attitude to be greatly wondered at. Victims for centuries of the ravages of Byzantine-Persian wars, now subject to one power, now to another, their country had been wrested from the Persians by the Emperor Heraclius only ten years before the Moslem invasion. When at last peace came they found themselves burdened by heavy taxation and their Christian sectarianism penalized by the Orthodox Greek State Church.[1] They had risen in revolt; indeed, it had taken the emperor a year to raise the force that faced the Arabs in the Yarmuk, and, as the event showed, the Syrian irregulars had no heart for

[1]Heresy in Egypt and Syria at this time weakened the Byzantine power just as Arab nationalism weakened the Turkish power in the Great War.

fighting. The Greeks had come to be hated far more than the Arab invaders who, at this early stage, assured the country complete religious freedom.

For the Arabs the mastery of Syria soon led to the tail wagging the dog. Syria was obviously of more account than Arabia, Damascus and Jerusalem vastly superior cities to Mecca and Medina, and the Caliph Omar, shrewd man that he was, foresaw the inevitable displacement of the political centre of gravity, which in fact took place at no very distant date. The Arabs were notoriously a race of individualists, and strong men would rise among them and play for their own hands. Khalid the Conqueror was known to be a member of Ali's party, and to have permitted him to be governor would have made him powerful indeed.

After Damascus fell Omar sent a trusted companion to relieve Khalid of administrative duties. And now the caliph decided to visit his army in the field.

Omar's visit was necessary to determine the manner of government of the newly occupied territories and to decide upon the disposal of lands. The division of spoils of conquest, whether money, goods or captives, had remained in the same proportions as decreed by the Prophet. That is, one fifth went to the caliph at Medina, the remainder was divided equally between the soldiers. But spoils of land had not in the early days been envisaged. The Caliph Omar saw that the acquisition and division of land between the Arab soldiers would not only be a thorny problem, but would lead to the political ends he most wished to avoid. He wisely decreed that landed property was not the right of the conqueror but belonged to the original private holders, and that, where these were unbelievers, they must pay a special unbeliever's tax on it, the proceeds of which must be remitted to him at Medina.

He instituted another unbeliever's tax, a capitation tax. The Syrians were largely exempted from the land tax because of their assistance in the wars of conquest, so that Iraq, where the double tax was enforced, came later to be the main source of the caliphate revenues at Medina. In the light of the times the Christian Syrians must have regarded the imposts as light indeed, probably more favourable to the cultivator than the heavy war taxation of the hated Byzantines, so that Omar's decree on the land question was both benevolent and politic. On the other hand, another Omar, Omar II, half a century later imposed severe disabilities on subject peoples who would not embrace Islam. Unbelievers must not ride in a believer's presence. They might not wear the dress or the arms of a Moslem. They must abase themselves and not look to have their word believed against that of a Moslem. If they were permitted to retain their churches and synagogues they must cease using church bells or conches or any other obtrusive call to worship offensive to Moslem ears, and if they prayed they must do so under their breath. The great Omar of Medina made no attempt to upset the administrative machinery of local government as the Arabs found it, for the Arabs at this time had neither the education nor the experience to attempt reconstruction, and they wisely left well alone.

It was Persia's turn next. The Persians were staggered by the Byzantine collapse. Mesopotamia had not so far been unduly harassed since Khalid's visit to Hira, for raids in that region were not popular with the Beduin, the opposition met with being far more formidable than that in Syria. The conquest of Syria, the Persians saw, would liberate a strong force for use against them, and soon an Arab army was marching down the Euphrates to join hands with another from Arabia that was biding its time west of the Euphrates. Qadisiya, not far from Hira, was the Persian stronghold. Here the Arabs attacked during a blinding sandstorm. Rustem, the Persian general, was killed, and his force was routed. The Arabs, pursuing, swept across the heart of Mesopotamia, crossed the river Tigris to storm Mada'in, the twin cities of Seleucia and Ctesiphon, the Persian winter capital. King Yezdegird, whose hold on the throne was already precarious and who feared assassination, did not attempt to hold Ctesiphon[2] but fled, and so the wealth and treasure of yet another capital city passed into the hands of the Arabs.

The two battles of Yarmuk in Syria and Qadisiya in Iraq[3] represent a turning point in the whole Arabian movement. From now on a steady migration flowed out of Arabia, never to return. Up to this point the Arabs had been raiding columns based on Medina; henceforth they were armies maintaining themselves in the field. In the early days the raiders were adventurers picked up from tribes here and there, growing in numbers as they marched along; from now on whole tribes took part in large military operations. The idea of dependence upon Medina faded into the background; a quickening ideal of Arabian empire took its place.

The unprecedented success in Iraq led immediately to the establishment of two military camps there, one at Kufa near old Hira, the other on a site where Basrah now

[2]The old arch of the Persian palace still stands on the Tigris banks. It is the widest span of any brick arch in the world, and where the British forces under General Townshend turned back in 1915.

[3]Iraq, the Arab word, has now superseded the Greek term Mesopotamia.

stands, and these camps, designed as bases of operations against the Persians, in north and south, grew to be great cities in succeeding centuries.

After his flight from Ctesiphon, Yezdegird held on despairingly on the northern Mesopotamian-Persian border for more than two years, but his own unstable personal position, weakened further by abortive enterprises against the invaders, led him to retire into Persia. Thither the Arabs followed him and, coming up with his forces near the royal city of Nihavand, once again gained a decisive victory. Yezdegird saved his life by flight from the field, only to lose it later by assassination.

Another Arab force operating from Basrah was meanwhile overrunning the southern provinces of Khuzistan, and a sea assault was made from Oman on the islands of the Persian Gulf and on the Persian coasts, an Omani force marching inland to Persepolis, which city fell as did many others.

The capture of Nihavand in A.D. 641 gave the Arabs a strong Persian foothold, though it was not until several years more that they scaled the mountain barriers and brought about the fall of Ispahan, Hamadan and other garrisoned centres in the interior. Nor was the pacification of Persia to be the easy matter that the pacification of Palestine and Syria had been. In the Levant the Arabs met with a welcoming reception from Semitic-speaking peoples long subjected to foreign masters; in Persia they met with stubborn resistance born of a different cultural consciousness and of a proud imperial past. Indeed Persia never became completely Arabicized, as were Syria and Palestine, for her language and her institutions survived the conquests; and, indeed, Islam itself came to undergo a Persianized development that was to make Shi'ism the great dissenting sect and one to which a considerable minority of Moslems belongs to this day. 'Never has captor more swiftly and subtly been captured by his captive than Arabia by Persia,' says Dr Hogarth.[24]*

The Arabs, with astounding éclat, were conquering Egypt at the same time as they were so successfully prosecuting their Persian campaign. The inception of that conquest is the subject of a jolly Arab tradition. Amr ibn al As, most prominent of Khalid's lieutenants in Syria, conceived of the conquest of Egypt, acted on his own initiative, quickly raised a force from the Syrian garrisons and marched, without as much as 'by your leave' from the caliph. The caliph, on hearing of it, promptly sent orders after the zealous Amr, commanding him to return unless he was too far engaged in operations; and to meet the situation the intrepid general with 'his blind eye to the telescope' as it were, speeded up his braves and crossed the Palestine-Egyptian frontier before acquainting himself with his orders. On he went and abundantly justified himself. Modern authorities are inclined to view this tradition with their own blind eye to the telescope.[7]*

The conquest of Egypt was necessary to the safety of Syria at this time, for the Byzantine fleet at Alexandria was a continual menace to the coastal towns of Syria and the means of reinvasion. The Egyptians were a subject people, too, and no happier under their Greek rulers than the Syrians had been, and so were not any more likely to resent a change of masters. Whether or not, Amr, at the head of four thousand Arabs, crossed the Egyptian frontier in A.D. 640. It was a small force for so great an undertaking, but reinforcements of five thousand allowed him to march on Heliopolis, where he encountered and defeated the Byzantines. For a year or more he maintained himself in a fortified position at the head of the Nile delta and then pushed on to lay siege to Alexandria, the capital. During the long siege the unfortunate Emperor Heraclius died in Constantinople, and the Egyptian patriarch, returning thence, concluded a treaty with Amr by which the Greeks agreed to cede Alexandria, and so Egypt passed into the hands of its new Arab masters in the year A.D. 642.

The headquarters of government were moved from Alexandria to Fustat, a military camp that the Arabs had just established in Egypt after the model of Kufa and Basrah in Iraq and, like them, to grow in after years into a mighty city—Cairo. The year of its foundation was the year that witnessed the overthrow of the Persian king at Arab hands. It marked a period of amazing military achievement; for during the lifetime of these two first caliphs, that is to say, within twelve years of the Prophet's death, the untutored Arabs of the desert had defeated the armies of the two great contemporary empires of the time, Persia and Byzantium, and had wrested from them Syria, Iraq, western Persia and Egypt.

But imperial expansion meant embarrassment for the Arabian caliphate. The days of the political domination of Medina were numbered. Omar the Caliph, a man of great capacity, doubtless foresaw it, but before it came about he was able, by his edicts, to found the institutions of the Islamic state in the occupied territories on a sure foundation.

Omar's great task was completed before he fell, stabbed to death by a Christian slave of Persian origin. His successor in the caliphate was an unworthy one. Othman was an aristocrat and a man of great piety, but he was conspicuously ineffective. The high offices of state, both inside Arabia and without, were flooded by nominees of his family or faction regardless of their abilities. The followers of Ali accepted his unsatisfactory election—by a reluctant vote of a committee of six—with a bad grace and continued to intrigue against him. The new Arab world, too, fell more and more away; indeed, Mu'awiya, the governor of Syria, a gifted kinsman, already cherished personal ambitions.

The Arab conquerors, supreme on land, saw the sea power of the Byzantines still unchallenged and the Greek fleet, based on Cyprus, a menace to their Syrian and Egyptian shores. Whether the northern Arab, unlike his southern kinsman, lacked a sea tradition but now took to the sea and rapidly developed a nautical arm, or whether the Arabs used native ships and seamen to transport their armies, they were ready in 649 to launch a successful attack on the enemy's sea base, and by this single stroke Cyprus fell into their hands.

Emboldened by this spectacular success, they conceived plans for a fleet attack against Constantinople itself. In 655 all was ready, but off the Lycian coast the Arabs encountered a Byzantine fleet of superior size, and though they were able to scatter five hundred ships, themselves sustained such losses that the project had to be abandoned; and Mu'awiya was obliged to conclude an unsatisfactory peace, owing to a crisis that had arisen in Arabia.

The caliphate of Othman was tottering. The very magnitude of the Arab successes without was destined to lead to its fall, and Othman's maladministration and local unpopularity hastened the end. Hitherto the wars of conquest had brought great revenues from the Prophet's fifth and the unbelievers' taxes to the caliph at Medina. The

Caliph Omar, while refusing to have a state treasury, wisely administered these funds in characteristic autocratic Eastern fashion, maintaining civil and religious officials, providing for pensions for the old and honoured, for charitable bequests and the like, and so building up a strong personal position. Medina did well, though its new affluence had led in Othman's time to luxurious standards of living in contrast to the simplicity of the lives of the Prophet and his companions.

But now, under Othman, the wars of conquest had come to a temporary halt. No new worlds were being conquered except the remote fringes of Persia and Turkestan, and Medina revenues shrank to a trickle of their former flood. Medina suffered from a depression, and its government was blamed as better governments in more enlightened times and places have been blamed at such moments. But Othman, in feeble old age, seconded by a maliciously disloyal secretary, was not the man to face such a situation. The Arabs without, who had fought and were to fight again, had interests in such taxes as were being remitted to the caliph at Medina and there notoriously squandered on his relations and his unpopular following. Both Othman's representatives governing Egypt and Iraq were very unpopular, and the peoples wished to be rid of them. Protests grew into revolt. A body of five hundred malcontents from Egypt came on deputation to Medina to intercede with the caliph, but after despairing of satisfaction at his hands, besieged his house, broke in and slew the old man while he was at prayers.

The murder of the discredited Othman by a fellow Moslem was a blow to the Medina caliphate from which it never recovered. Ali was now to achieve his heart's desire, but only when it was too late. A week elapsed before the excitement caused by the assassination died down. Ali is represented at the hour of prayer going to the mosque clothed in a poor cotton garment and a coarse turban, for, like his master, he despised the pomp and vanity of the world. In one hand he carried his slippers, in the other his bow, and as he passed reverent onlookers would salute him as their new caliph. But to be caliph now it was essential to command the allegiance of the Arabs of Egypt, Syria, Iraq, Persia, and their support was in grave doubt.

Ali, as we have seen, was a disappointed man. He felt that his rights, based on a close relationship to the Prophet, had already been violated on three previous occasions; his followers held indeed that the three previous caliphs were usurpers and no true caliphs. The question whether the Prophet's only surviving child, a daughter, and wife of Ali, was the rightful residual legatee or not now became a major issue and split Islam into the two great divisions of Sunni and Shi'a as we know them today.

Syria, under Mu'awiya, already ripe for secession from any caliphate, promptly refused to acknowledge Ali as caliph, accusing him of connivance in the murder of Othman. Egypt and Iraq did accept Ali's representatives as governors, but if Ali were indeed to be caliph of Islam, Syria could not be permitted to remain outside the hegemony, and to win Syria the active support of Iraq was necessary. And so to Iraq Ali fled. Medina was thus left without a caliph, her treasury was empty, her voice of authority silent, and in her bereavement Arabia ceased to be the centre of the caliphate.

Islam was now divided against itself. Iraq and Syria revived their ancient feud: no longer Christian Byzantium against Zoroastrian Persia, but Moslem versus Moslem. The feud at first threatened to develop into interstate warfare but resolved itself into a fight for temporal supremacy within Islam. For a hundred years Syria triumphed under the Umaiyyads at Damascus, until the supremacy passed to Iraq under the famous Abbasid caliphs of Baghdad.

But to return to Ali. Even Iraq did not rise unanimously to acclaim him, for A'isha, the Prophet's young and favourite wife, and daughter of the first caliph, Abu Bakr, who had always been Ali's implacable enemy, had gone there before him with two other of Ali's personal enemies to raise the forces of revolt. According to one Arab tradition 'the Mother of the Faithful' rode her camel in and out among the hostile forces on the day of battle to hearten them and then took her place where the fighting waxed fiercest. 'In the heat of action seventy men who held the bridle of her camel were successively killed or wounded; and the cage or litter in which she sat was struck with javelins and darts like the quills of a porcupine.'[11]*

'The Day of the Camel,' as this battle is known in the Arab memory, went in favour of Ali and united Iraq in his favour. He now assembled an army and early in 657 moved up the Euphrates against Syria. Mu'awiya, the governor, marched down to oppose him, and the two armies met in the plain to the west of the river opposite Siffin. One tradition revels in an account of ninety battles and fabulous casualties in which both Ali and Mu'awiya performed great feats of valour and Ali displayed the quality of mercy, for his forces were enjoined to await the onset of their opponents, to spare them in flight, to respect the bodies of the dead and the chastity of female captives. Another tradition, perhaps more authentic, has it that battle was joined on one day in July, only to be broken off the very next day.

Ali's opponents contrived to avoid a pitched battle, which might well have resulted in a victory for him. On the morning of the second day the vanguard of Mu'awiya advanced with copies of the Holy Qur'an tied to their lances. Awed by this solemn appeal to the Tablets of God, their opponents were restrained from onslaught against fellow Moslems. A truce followed, the parties agreed to abandon warfare and accept adjudication a year hence, when a representative of each side should meet for the purpose on the Iraqo-Syrian frontier.

Ali had taken a fatal step. Not only had he let slip a great opportunity to achieve his ends, but by agreeing to arbitration at all he abandoned the cardinal point of his case. In the eyes of his following his right was a divine right, not a claim susceptible of argument. A considerable body of his supporters left him next day, holding that the judgment should have been God's, i.e. battle, and these Khawarij, as they came to be known, were henceforth his enemies. Ali's forces lost heart, and, conscious of his losing cause, he led them sorrowfully back to Kufa.

The conference to decide whether Ali were a true caliph or not duly assembled. Mu'awiya's representative was one devoted to his cause, no less a man than the gallant Amr ibn al As, the conqueror of Egypt. He had returned to Mu'awiya's service in Syria when Ali's representative assumed the governorship in Egypt, a post he was known to covet himself. Ali's representative at the conference was a lesser person and one whose attachment to Ali's cause was suspect. The result of their deliberations (if any deliberations took place) was interpreted by Mu'awiya as giving him a free hand. He forthwith proclaimed himself caliph at Jerusalem in A.D. 660 and thus founded the Umaiyyad dynasty of Syria, whose capital was Damascus. Ali's cup was full, and before another year had passed he was assassinated on the doorstep of the mosque at Kufa in Iraq by three fanatics who had at one time espoused his cause.

Thus ended the fourth and last of the Medina caliphs. They had all of them been early converts and companions of the Prophet; they were men of deep religious convictions, men who amid power and riches lived simple, strict, God-fearing lives. That three out of four of them should have come to violent ends is a commentary on the strong passions of their people.

With the transfer of the seat of government from Arabia to Syria a great change came over the rulers. Yezid, the son of Mu'awiya and second caliph of Damascus, was feeble and dissolute, but that did not invalidate his succession, for caliphs were in future to rule, not in virtue of piety and religion as did the early caliphs of Medina, but as Arab aristocrats in virtue of hereditary right.

The tragedy of Ali's assassination did not end there. His two sons, Hassan and Husain, were also fated to a violent end. Hassan, who had inherited his father's position in Iraq, but not his ambition, submissively agreed to retire on a pension to Medina in favour of Mu'awiya rather than be the instrument of plunging Irak Moslems into civil war with their Syrian brethren. There in Medina he lived piously and devoted himself to charitable works, only to be poisoned eight years later by one of his wives. Husain, endowed with more of his father's fervour, dreamt of wresting Iraq from Yezid. Lured by an invitation from a discontented faction in Iraq to come and lead them in revolt against the Syrian yoke, he trustingly crossed the desert, but on approaching Kufa he discovered that he had been misled as to the extent of the unrest and that his approach had been anticipated by the Caliph Yezid's representative, who had sent out five thousand men to surround him.

It is possible that Husain could have escaped into the desert and awaited a more favourable opportunity, and this course his sister spent the night imploring him to take, but his passionate belief in his cause drove him on. One tradition, doubtless apocryphal, tells of how he and his handful of supporters cut off their own retreat after the manner of the brave men of old by digging a trench in their rear and filling it with faggots. Then Husain, a sword in one hand and a Qur'an in the other, led his martyrs forward. One of the opposing chiefs, moved by the heroism, himself deserted to their side, knowing full well that it led to the immediate joys of paradise. Steeled to a supernatural strength, they were irresistible in close combat, but their enemy, greatly outnumbering them, had only to keep off and send a shower of arrows into them to achieve success. One by one they fell, till only Husain remained. Though struck in the mouth by an arrow, the grandson of the Prophet could still have been spared by a merciful enemy; but this mercy was wanting, and he fell at last, lacerated with the wounds of thirty-three strokes of sword and lance. His body was trampled on, his head was cut off and brought to the governor of Kufa, who, when he saw it, struck with his cane across the bleeding mouth. 'Alas!' burst out an aged stander-by 'on those lips I have seen the lips of the Prophet of God!'

The surviving sisters and children of Ali the Martyr were brought in chains before the Caliph Yezid at Damascus, who might have rid himself of them had he cared but instead exercised his clemency and allowed them to depart. Their posterity in later centuries grew and were especially revered. I have many times witnessed the south Arabian native holding the back of the hand of one of them to his own nostrils, to take a hearty sniff, believing that he imbibed virtue by this act. In Persia and Iraq their descendants till recent times were not obliged to work, for all would give alms to them.

But it was the imams, i.e., Ali, Hassan, Husain and Husain's nine lineal descendants, who enjoyed the special veneration of the Shi'a branch of Islam as the only rightful caliphs following the Prophet, and whose tombs, glorious specimens of Persian art, are found today overlooking the Euphrates in Iraq and in Khorasan—places of Shi'a pilgrimage. The most notable and venerated are the mosque of Ali at Najaf and the mosque of Husain at Kerbela. The twelfth and last imam of this hereditary apostolic succession of the Shi'as did not die, it is held, but disappeared into a cave at Samarra. He is alive still, after nearly a thousand years, though hidden from men's eyes, and will manifest himself some day to denounce and overthrow an anti-Christ who will appear and disturb the earth before the Judgment Day. The *mahdi,* as this twelfth imam is called, has on at least one occasion been impersonated in the Sudan with disconcerting effects to public peace and the tranquillity of British authorities.

It is the martyrdom of Ali and his sons, almost more than the doctrine of their exclusive hereditary right to succeed the Prophet, that characterizes the Shi'a faith of later times, and around these saints and martyrs the famous Passion play of the East is woven, to sadden the streets of the Shi'a towns of Persia and Iraq on the tenth day of Muharram. The growth of this movement is bound up with the conquest of the old Persian empire, for the Arabs in overcoming communities with a more advanced culture than their own themselves became Persianized, and their religion also came to undergo this Persianized development. Schism developed early around the principle of Ali's divine right to succeed, based on the belief of exclusive spiritual heirship to the Prophet, a doctrine the Persians made peculiarly their own. This doctrine of an hereditary apostolic succession by which divine virtue could pass only in the Prophet's seed came near to a doctrine of incarnation, and whatever the teachings of the Prophet, the idea could not have been new or distasteful to converts from Christianity, who were then or later to embrace the Shi'a form of Islam. As a challenge to the legality of the Umaiyyad caliphs, Shi'ism was in the course of a century to become a political weapon for ending Arab dominance in the Islamic state.

Meanwhile under the Damascus caliphate the Arab armies carried on their campaign in eastern Persia with the same indomitable spirit that had carried them there. Within twenty years of the fall of Nihavand they had overcome the two easternmost provinces of Khorasan and Seistan and were raiding into Afghanistan, undaunted by native outbreaks in the unpacified areas behind them. Hajjaj ibn Yusuf, the strong governor of Iraq, seems to have been the moving spirit of these distant activities, and when recruits for them fell off, presumably as a result of improved conditions of life in growing Arab communities, for the old camps of Basrah and Kufa were fast becoming rich cities, he resorted to compulsory levies under penalty of death. No less than twenty thousand men are supposed to have been drafted to the Persian wars from Iraq. Even then the shortage of men in the field is known to have driven Arab generals to the bold course of enlisting Persian irregulars before Persia had been properly subjugated, and the victorious army of five thousand that crossed the Oxus after the fall of Balkh in 669 is held to have been one fifth Persian.

Within a generation the invincible Arabs had overrun the entire province of Trans-Oxiana and annexed the mighty cities of Samarkand and Bokhara. At this point, a borderland between two races of mankind—the Caucusoids and the Mongoloids it is of interest to note—Arab military expansion into Asia reached its uttermost limit.[4]

[4]The expansion of Islam into further Asia, as also into inner Africa and eastern Europe, does not properly belong to these Arab wars. It came about later, either as the result of waves of conquest carried on by non-Arab peoples who had embraced Islam or from the proselytizing zeal of Moslems, Arabs and others. The starting point was this last-to-be-acquired Trans-Oxus fringe of Islam. The Emperor Mahmud of Ghazna, who had made himself independent of the Persian Samanids, invaded India, and the province of the Punjab was annexed by his son early in the eleventh century. Another wave of Iranian Moslems overran Gujerat and Kashmir, to be followed a century later by an Afghan annexation of Sind and Mooltan, and thus Islam was spread across northern India. Thence towards the close of the thirteenth century it was carried under a Turkish house through the Deccan into southern India. The Turks from the steppes of Central Asia carried Islam into southeastern Europe in the fourteenth century. Elsewhere the extension of Islam came about by peaceable means. From India it naturally spread by trade intercourse through the East Indies, Java becoming its particular stronghold from the missionary efforts of south Arabians who had settled there. From Egypt Islam was carried up the Nile into the Sudan, and at a much later time the establishment of Arab sultanates in East Africa, notably Zanzibar, led to its penetration into equatorial Africa.

CHAPTER IV

Arab World Conquest—Westwards

WESTWARDS the wave of Arab expansion along the north coast of Africa rolled more uncertainly. It was a slowed-down wave that broke over the walls of Carthage, a midway point, after caliphs had been reigning in Damascus for upwards of a quarter of a century and Arab dominion eastwards had well-nigh reached its utmost Asiatic limit beyond the Oxus.

On this western front the Arabs, after their early conquest of Egypt, had for a generation been content with plundering forays into Cyrenaica, Tripoli and latterly into Tunis—then called Ifrikiya and to be identified with our word 'Africa'—and with a light and precarious occupation of the lowlands. Authorities are prone to ascribe this delay in a determined penetration to the fierce opposition of the native inhabitants of north Africa on the grounds that the Berbers were a race not so naturally predisposed to the Arabs as the kindred Aramæans of Syria had been, and were therefore prepared to defend more vigorously their nationality, customs and language against fresh alien incursions.

Rather it would seem that the Arab hunger for fresh territory had been sated by the conquest of the Near and Middle East. The superior material rewards of the eastern campaigns as compared with those of the north African deserts acted as a stronger magnet, while the formidable obstacles that lay in the way of the eastern attainments fully occupied the Arabs at this time. It would be strange indeed if the unorganized Berbers could have stemmed a flood which was submerging the imperial Persians, a people not less proud of their own language and customs and possessing a highly developed political and military organization.

The difference in race and outlook between Berber and Arab is wont to be overstressed. Even allowing for the Arab strain in north African populations that followed the infiltrations of the seventh and eleventh centuries, the indigenous non-Arabic speaking Berbers of the High Atlas today strike the writer as being racially akin to Arabs he has met in Aleppo and the faraway mountains of Oman; in a cultural sense, too, the Berbers were made up of tribes of rude pastoralists, and their minds could scarcely have been of essentially different temper from those of the early Arab invaders.

The lowlands of Cyrenaica and Tripoli are said to have been early and easily Islamized, but traditions speak of the Berbers of Tunisia as Jews and Christians, though it is more likely that they were chiefly pagans practising animistic cults like the bulk of their brethren to the west—the Berbers of central Maghrib (Algeria) and western Maghrib (Morocco). At the time of the Arab invasion the Byzantines were masters of the coasts, a prefect of the emperor ruling from Tripoli to Tangier, but it is thought that outside the garrisoned towns the Berbers had never at any time been properly subjugated whoever the invader—Byzantine, Vandal, Roman or Phœnician.

In the year 670 the earlier spasmodic warfare of the Arabs gave place to something far more serious that boded ill alike for Berber independence and Byzantine suzerainty. This was the establishment of a regular military camp at Qairawan to the south of Tunis as a base of operations, after the model of Basrah and Kufa—a camp that was destined to grow in a few years to be the capital city of the Arab west. Its conception is associated with the Arab hero Uqba, a haughty and brave leader, who, greatly to the taste of the Arabs, was no soft-spoken diplomat but a master of the sword, and whose exploits at the head of a body of horsemen riding madly through the oases of the northern Sahara fringe, striking terror into the foe, make him a legend in north African deserts to this day. Uqba seems to have lost the confidence of his caliph, for he was superseded for a time by one Dinar, not so flashy a soldier perhaps, but a more farseeing one, for Dinar's policy of conciliating the Berbers and regarding the Byzantines as the main enemy was one that was ultimately adopted and proved successful. Meanwhile Uqba was reinstated, and according to tradition he kept Dinar as his prisoner in chains and thus took him on his raids against the Berbers. Greatly daring, he is held to have cut his way through to the Atlantic shores at Tangier in 682, but on his return was ambushed in the Atlas and slain, Dinar sharing his fate.

A temporary reconquest of Qairawan from the Arabs under a priestess (*kahina*), according to tradition a Jewess of the priestly tribe of Levi (Kahina=Cohen), was the outstanding feature of a period of resistance which lasted for twenty years, while Moslem fortunes waxed and waned so that some Berbers are said to have apostatized a dozen times. It was only when the Arabs persuaded the Berbers that their interests lay with Islam, when the Berbers saw the opportunity of joining hands with the Arabs to expel the Hellenized and Latin populations of north Africa to Spain and Sicily and of following them across the sea to plunder the treasuries of southern Europe, that the Arab path westwards was made smooth; but if the Berbers ever regarded the Arabs as liberators from a foreign yoke they were soon to find that they had only changed masters.

Carthage fell in 697–698, and with it fell the power of the Byzantines and that of their local Berber allies of Tunis and Algeria. The Arabs had obtained the command of the sea in the Mediterranean at about this time, and their fleet played an important part in the siege of Carthage, and thereafter its co-operation was to afford effective assistance in the movement westwards to the shores of the Atlantic and northwards across the straits into southern Europe.

With the investment of Tangier in 710, Spain loomed up temptingly beyond the straits, but there was neither need nor desire on the part of the Arabs for further expansion. It was the allied Berbers who seized the chance of improving their material condition by promptly setting off on piratical raids to the Balearic Islands and to southern Spain.

Spain at this time was ruled by a Visigothic aristocracy, but it was not a united country. As in Persia before its fall, the state had been undermined by internal dissensions and traitorous factions and was ready to collapse before a conqueror possessing the military prowess of the Moslems. Visigothic and Spanish-Roman antagonisms had only lately been composed; strife between Visigoth nobles themselves still continued; the Jews were utterly estranged by persecution; and the enslaved classes did not care who ruled them. For a hundred years a struggle had been in progress between king and nobility; the king, supported by the clergy, was anxious to establish an hereditary dynasty with despotic powers; the nobles, ambitious for their own aggrandisement, preferred to elect one of themselves to the throne whenever it became vacant, thus, at time of succession, causing political unrest by supporting some one candidate, some another.

The only continuity during that period had been a continuity of Jewish persecution by the king's council, in which church influence was dominant. At the outset the Jews increased and prospered under protection of the old Roman law. This, in theory, did impose disabilities; marriages with Christians, for instance, were forbidden, and Jews might not occupy public office or own Christian slaves, but in practice the law was administered laxly, and all these things had been allowed. Early in the seventh century, however, under a bigoted Visigoth sovereign, the law came to be more rigorously enforced, and Jews were offered the alternative of being baptized into the Catholic faith or suffering banishment and the confiscation of their property. Persecution ebbed and flowed under successive monarchs. It was at its height but a few years later when Jews were required to forswear their religion on penalty of death and henceforth profess and practise Christianity; an oath was devised for future kings, whereby they must undertake not to permit Jews to violate the Christian faith or allow them 'to open up the path of prevarication to those who are hovering on the brink of unbelief.' In the middle of the century the king had to bind himself to maintain the Catholic religion, prosecute all Jews and heretics, and those who refused to be converted were to be stoned to death or burnt alive. Thirty years later Jews were required to receive baptism under penalty of banishment, scourging and loss of hair.

It is scarcely to be wondered at, therefore, that in A.D. 694 the Jews were guilty of conspiring with those who dwelt in lands beyond the sea, i.e. north Africa, with a view to overthrowing the state—a conspiracy that brought upon its perpetrators penal measures by which the fortunate suffered the loss of their property, others were reduced to slavery. Within fifteen years the Moslems invaded Spain and brought the Jews deliverance.

A year before the landing the death of the Visigothic king and the ensuing struggle for the succession had the usual disturbing effects throughout the land. Roderick and Achila, two nobles, were the rival claimants to the throne; Roderick was chosen, whereupon Achila and his immediate supporters fled to Africa for refuge, as Visigoth nobles had done in 642 under similar circumstances and probably on many earlier occasions. But meanwhile the rule of north Africa had passed into Moslem hands, the ruler and representative of the caliph of Damascus was an Arab, Musa ibn Nusair, and Musa readily agreed to espouse Achila's cause.

The first invasion of Spain was undertaken ostensibly to assist Achila, in reality probably with a view rather to plunder than to conquest, for the caliphs are supposed to have regarded these later military expeditions in the distant outposts of empire with misgiving. Musa probably thought of it as just another summer raid, a means of keeping the Berbers happily occupied; three years before they had raided Majorca, and only the year before had passed on to the mainland, skirmished through Andalusia and returned to Algeciras loaded with spoils. But if he did, he underestimated his Berber general, the freed slave Tariq, who had been appointed governor of Tangier, for Tariq was now to conquer Spain.

With a force of seven thousand men, mostly Berbers, Tariq crossed the straits in the year A.D. 711 and landed near Gibraltar, a name that immortalizes his own, for it is the anglicized form of the arabic *Jabal Tariq,* i.e. the mount of Tariq. At first the force indulged in piracy and highway robbery along the coast, spreading terror far and wide. The unpopular King Roderick gathered a force to oppose the invaders, and at Salado a great battle took place. The day went in Tariq's favour, and Roderick, the victim of the treachery of his political enemies, was slain. Emboldened by this success and by the knowledge that the native populations hated their Gothic rulers, Tariq conceived the bold plan of marching on the capital, at that time Toledo. The Jews welcomed and assisted the invaders, a natural enough revenge for their long persecution, and their reward came later when Spanish trade passed largely into their hands. Cordova fell by treachery, the aristocracy and priesthood did not await the Moslems but fled, and Tariq had only one serious battle to fight during his triumphal march on Toledo, which city, again by treacherous act, threw open its gates to him.

Tariq's boldness had, by one lightning stroke, destroyed the Gothic rule in Spain, and Musa, lord of north Africa, though staggered by the event, was quick to seize the opportunity of adding Spain to the caliphate—despite the caliph—and incalculable riches to his own purse. He gathered an army of eighteen thousand men and next year himself landed in Spain at their head. Tariq's way had been the bold and dangerous one of marching through the very heart of the country to the capital, leaving great fortified cities in his rear, a plan that invited disaster, for in normal conditions his retreat might well have been cut off. Musa followed the more orthodox course of laying siege to all fortified places on his way. Seville, a former capital and the intellectual centre of Spain, was strongly garrisoned and stood his siege for many months, and other cities in which the Goths were powerful stubbornly resisted, but one by one these fell, and after two years of arduous campaigning Musa, too, reached his objective, Toledo. One of his first acts there was to disgrace Tariq, whose brilliant success had aroused his jealousy, but within a few weeks he himself was to suffer similarly at the hands of an ungrateful caliph who recalled him to Damascus.

The pacification of Spain fell to his successors, but after four years Moslem hold was already sufficiently consolidated over the whole country (except for the mountainous strip of northern coast, Asturias, which continued to be a Latin principality) to permit of raids over the Pyrenees into Gaul. In the north the France of the future was at this time in the making, but the south was divided up into petty principalities perpetually at war one with another. It was this disunity among the Franks that gave the invaders' lust for plunder the necessary provocation and opportunity. Under Samh, the fifth successor of Musa, these sporadic raids gave place to a more ambitious design. Narbonne was captured in A.D. 720, a place that served as a base for more extended operations and in which the Arabs maintained a footing for nearly forty years. But on Toulouse a Moslem attack with battering rams was easily repelled, the invaders being weakened by quarrels between Arabs and Berbers.

Emboldened, however, by the internecine warfare in which the small Frankish states continued to indulge, a large Saracen force was assembled by Abdul Rahman, one of Musa's successors, who now himself crossed the Pyrenees; Avignon fell in 730, the march was continued down the Garonne, and Bordeaux was captured—thence the invaders turned northeastwards, with the rich city of Tours as their objective. But between Tours and Poitiers they were intercepted by an army of Franks under Charles Martel, the grandfather of Charlemagne, who had marched south to resist them. The Saracens were no match for the Franks on this occasion, and after an unequal contest they fled, abandoning all their war stores.

This battle of Tours, or Poitiers as it is sometimes called, was the turning point of Arab fortunes, marking the limit of Arab penetration into France.[1] If the conquest of Gaul was ever contemplated, which is doubtful, the ambition was born of a tradition of infallible success rather than of a sober appreciation of a new and difficult situation. The Frankish soldiers were of comparatively imperturbable temper, and they withstood the light cavalry of the volatile Saracens in a way to which the latter had not been accustomed. It is sometimes heard said that had the Arabs defeated Charles Martel they would have swept through Europe, and Islam would have come to take the place of Christianity. But the importance attached to the battle of A.D. 732 is probably exaggerated, for the Arabs had by this time shot their bolt after a century of warfare; they represented but a tiny fraction of the Moslems in Spain, and thus the wars of expansion really came to an end from the inherent exhaustion of the caliphate forces.

[1]The defeat of the Arabs before Constantinople in 717 by the Emperor Leo III was the first decisive setback to Arab fortunes in the West.

After Tours they fell back on Narbonne, and for the following seven years occasional raids were made, the most impressive being that of 734 when the Rhone was crossed, Arles sacked and Avignon recaptured. For twenty years more they were content, however, passively to hold Narbonne, till the Franks rose in revolt and massacred their garrison. But if France was no longer to be molested, Spain, except for a strip of coast along the Bay of Biscay, had become a possession of the caliph of Damascus, and in the course of time was largely to abandon its Catholic faith and follow the teachings of the Arab prophet and to turn many of its churches into mosques.

At the outset Spain, with Morroco, formed the province of Maghrib, whose capital was at Qairawan. There the caliph's representative was the supreme governor, and Spain was left to a subprefect to rule, first from Seville and later from Cordova. The strong individuality of the Berbers was soon to make trouble for the Arabs. At home, in north Africa, these Berbers were a subject people of the Arabs, a condition that made them feel resentful; whereas in Spain, not only were they not a subject people, they were themselves the conquerors, or at least they had taken a major part in the conquest. All was well so long as Berbers and Arabs were actually engaged in pursuit of some common advantage, but once the objective was secured and peace came about, the Berbers were in no mood to be treated as less than equals. The arrogance of some of the officials and soldiers sent from imperial Damascus was more than they would stand, and out of their dissatisfaction grew large-scale revolts.

A rising of Berbers in Morocco in 741 was signalized by a repudiation of allegiance to Damascus, and the Arab troops sent to crush it from Qairawan were themselves vanquished. Peace was restored, but it was only a temporary peace, and the events, in any case, were bound to have serious repercussions in Spain. Another ominous feature was the declining authority of the Umaiyyad caliphs of Damascus themselves. The loss of their precarious footing in north Africa and Spain was only a question of time, for if the Moors[2] were intolerant of caliphate despotism the local Arab governors, individualists that they were, were not less ready to seize a means of realizing their own personal ambitions by becoming independent rulers. Tunis, in A.D. 745, was the first to throw off its allegiance to Damascus; parts of Morocco followed; then Spain herself, within thirty-five years of Tariq's conquest, repudiated the caliphate and asserted her independence. Ten years later a young Arab prince who had fled from Syria to north Africa after the fall of his dynasty, the famous Abdul Rahman al Mu'awiya, landed in Spain and was soon acclaimed its ruler.

In the more backward territories of north Africa conditions grew anarchic, and the caliph was powerless to prevent dissolution of his dependencies into barbarous robber states. Thus by the time the Umaiyyad dynasty was overthrown and the centre of government shifted from Damascus to Baghdad, only Qairawan remained loyal, and this final African allegiance had become little more than nominal in A.D. 800 under the ruling Aghlabids. Though the territory of these Aghlabids of Qairawan was small, they are historically notable because their fleet in 827–43 conquered Sicily and thus planted Islam at the very threshold of the Papal See.

[2]The word Moor, clearly to be identified with the word Morocco, is in fact a European term that acquired the loose usage for Spanish Moslems generally, whether of Arab or Berber ancestry; doubtless by this time they were intermixed.

From the moment the Arabs had established supremacy over the Byzantines at sea the fate of the islands of the Mediterranean was sealed, and one by one they passed into Moslem hands. In the eastern Mediterranean the first generation of Arab newcomers to Syria and Egypt raided the islands of Rhodes, Crete and Cyprus (holding the last-named intermittently for three and a half centuries till Richard Cœur de Lion came and conquered it during the crusades). In the western Mediterranean the island of Pallentaria, a steppingstone between Africa and Sicily, was early occupied, and Corsica and Sardinia were plundered. It was next the turn of Sicily. Sicily had been raided from Egypt as early as the middle of the seventh century, but the island remained loyal to the Byzantines till 826. The Berbers with a sprinkling of Arab chiefs then obtained a footing in Palermo, spent fifty years gradually reducing the western part of the island and by 962 had become its masters. They had invaded Malta at about the same time as Sicily, ruled it till 1091 and were resident for another three hundred and fifty years, when they departed, leaving behind them their dialect of Arabic, which is the language of the Maltese to this day.

From these islands and from north Africa Moslem pirates ravaged southern Europe. In the earliest days Berbers from Sicily joined with others from Tunis to raid the Italian coasts, and the savage Barbary pirates from here and elsewhere kept up the old activities. Owing allegiance to none, they were lured by the riches of seaports and monasteries, they carried off captive women and church treasures, which, according to one Arab authority, were sold to idolatrous India for gold. The terror which their swift visitations caused in Italy led to the building of watchtowers along the coast between Naples and Palermo which stand to this day. Later on the Saracens enlisted as mercenaries of one Italian state against another. On one such expedition they reached the Adriatic and seized the shipping in the Venetian roads. On another the important town of Bari fell into their hands, and, recognizing its strategic importance, they decided to keep it themselves and fortify it as a base for future operations.

The sultans of Bari threw off their allegiance to Sicily (where Moslem occupation had a very different significance, for civilization had begun to flourish there) and lived by plundering the south, their onslaughts, according to Western historians, being of the most savage kind. But it was the fabulous treasures of Rome itself that had long attracted the Barbary pirates of north Africa, and one summer morning in A.D. 840 the holy city awoke to find eleven hundred Saracens before its walls. They swarmed in to plunder the Church of St Peter and the Cathedral of St Paul and to violate the graves of pontiffs, but just as they re-embarked a violent storm swallowed up their seventy-three spoil-laden ships and every man on board; so Christian authorities record, for the pirates themselves were unlettered men who have left no records of these times.

The Saracens' next step was to obtain a footing on the Calabrian coast, where they became such a menace that the pope of the time, John VIII, was compelled, in 878, to pay tribute as the price of peace. Their depredations lasted for another generation until Pope John X was able to drive the last Moslem from Italian soil. Moslems remained in occupation of Sicily for 200 years longer until the Normans came in 1091, while their occupation of Spain continued for many centuries, though in the later period their dominance gradually declined. The small

Latin kingdoms in the north of the peninsula grew in power and little by little encroached southwards till the final expulsion of Moors in 1492, when they were driven back to Africa. The Spanish mosques were transformed into churches, though for two centuries more secret communities practised the faith of the Arab prophet till they, too, the Moriscos, were banished from the land, and Islam faded into a memory. But it was the earlier withdrawal from Italy towards the end of the ninth century that marked the beginning of Saracenic decline.

Arab military power was never again to attain the eminence it enjoyed in those first two centuries after the Prophet, the seventh and eighth centuries of our era, when the Arabs imposed their dominion from the Himalayas across Asia and Africa to the Pyrenees. The later activities of the Moslemized Berbers in the Mediterranean may seem heinous, judged by modern standards of warfare, but both robbery and slavery were probably regarded as legitimate by at least some of the maritime southern Europeans of the time, and against the sum of the injuries inflicted by the conquests must be set the splendour of the Arab era that followed, when a great civilization dawned upon the Islamic world, and Iraq and Spain, the seats of the eastern and western caliphates with connecting links of Egypt and Sicily, became great centres of learning.

This splendour had modest beginnings, as we have seen. A tiny revolution in seventh-century Arabia sent a stream of Arabs overrunning the civilized world. The ancient peoples were infused with a quickening influence, the old lifeblood invigorated by a young and strongly pulsating heart, and the Islamic civilization came into being. Thereafter for four centuries or more, while Europe lay slumbering in the Middle Ages immediately before her own

Renaissance, it was the Islamized countries—under Arab rulers at the outset—that became pre-eminent in the earth for their learning, their culture and their material prosperity.[3]

[3]Although Saracen is sometimes applied to all these Arab wars, it is a slovenly European term for the Moslems of the early period generally—Arabs, Berbers or whoever else.

Part Two

ARAB CIVILIZATION

CHAPTER V

The Medieval State and Its Society

THE original Arab warriors who poured out of Arabia immediately after the Prophet's death were for the most part unlettered and semibarbarous men. They were on a lower cultural level than the peoples they overcame, the peoples of Egypt, Mesopotamia and Persia in particular, each of them heirs of ancient civilizations—however much then in decay. If they could at first rest on their laurels as conquering invaders their descendants must adapt themselves to their new world in order to justify ascendancy among communities more cultured than themselves. That the newcomers had no learning was perhaps an advantage, for it entailed a minimum of disturbance for the lands they occupied—local administrations, for instance, went on much as they did before. The Arabs were not imposing a new civilization. They had none to impose. What time had in store for them to do was to invigorate the scattered civilizations then in decline and give them a new life and character of their own.

That revolution is most easily understood if we remember what it was they brought out of Arabia with them to a tired and distracted world, the factors that made for extension of their dominion and led to the recognition of their eminence among nations. The Arabs, in the first place, were the source of two mighty influences: a great religion and a great language; the one a creed, simple, rational and in essence democratic, that proved capable of inspiring supernational loyalties and growing to world dimensions; the other a tongue so rich and flexible that it was fitted to become the scientific and classical as well as the religious idiom of an empire, in much the same way as Latin served for medieval Europe. But it took time for these influences to pervade the earlier cultures and then prevail within them. The first wave of rude warriors spent itself to different ends. Under Khalid and Amr these original conquerors were largely Beduin, of the generation that saw the new religion's birth. The majority could only just have given adherence to the new movement, a great many from expediency, though others, of course, from honest conviction, but, as the first raids showed, they were animated chiefly by the hope of improving their material condition, rather than aflame with zeal to share with others a common salvation. Illuminating is the message of the Caliph Omar to a distant expedition. 'Pacification and tribute,' he remonstrated, 'are to be preferred to loot that soon passes away.'

The all-conquering Arabs were in the first place and for the most part hungry, brave and ruthless warriors. Their psychology was the psychology of Arabia Deserta: they inherited a belief in force; they had been reared in an environment where force was necessary and therefore acquired social justification; they were by conviction as by nature manly, militant and aggressive, and the immediate and dazzling rewards of their first easy conquests not only justified this secular creed, but fixed them in its ways. It was fitting, perhaps, that the first coin the Arabs adapted from the Byzantines, about a half century later (A.H. 70), should bear the design it did, and in place of a Byzantine emperor, staff in hand, we have a caliph holding a sword.

In Arabia they had been ranged tribe against tribe; they would naturally at first think of themselves as fighting under a supertribal banner, the enemy being the tribes outside their own allegiance and meet therefore to be spoiled. The Arab tribe, before its recent allegiance to the new larger unit, had grown out of a clan whose basis was blood kinship. Injury done to a member of a tribe from outside was regarded as injury done to the tribe as a whole, and any member of the tribe could avenge it; so, too, the original offender need not be the target; any other member of his tribe would do equally well for the purpose of revenge. Such usage had the sanction of immemorial practice and endures in tribal Arabia to this day in spite of the Prophet's reforms.

The immediate revolution that Muhammad wrought—later to grow into a great practical brotherhood—was the creation, in effect, of a supertribe whose basis was not blood kinship but a religious faith, whose sanctions were revealed by God and whose loyalties must outweigh those of either kin or tribe. Those who embraced the new allegiance became members of this supertribe, a chosen people sworn not to injure but to assist and succour one another.

Aggression had been condemned by the Prophet, and Western authorities do not believe that he planned or even foresaw the century of wars of conquest which immediately followed his death. But if the early raiding parties were tribally minded and worldly minded the caliphs of

Medina were pious and good men who sent on their heels others who had come under the influence of the Prophet's religious teachings, Arabs of high character and moral rectitude, most of them men of the settlements doubtless, so that the seed of the religious movement was sown in the outside Arab world and in the course of time came to a splendid fruition.

'In the whole history of the world, till then,' says Marmaduke Pickthall, a convert to Islam, 'the conquered had been absolutely at the mercy of the conqueror, no matter how complete his submission might be, no matter though he might be of the same religion as the conqueror. That is still the theory of war outside Islam. But it is not the Islamic theory. According to the Moslem Laws of War, those of the conquered peoples who embraced Islam became the equals of the conquerors in all respects. And those who chose to keep their own religion had to pay a tribute for the cost of their defence, but after that enjoyed full liberty of conscience and were secured and protected in their occupations.'[10]*

And so among these diverse peoples across western Asia and north Africa burst this new conqueror. In many of these lands a wide gulf had divided the alien nobility from the native populations. The social structure had been one in which luxury and culture flourished at the top; below, the common herd were in a condition not much above serfdom. The Arab invaders, unlettered men, no lovers of luxury, innately democratic, were strangers to such inequalities. The religion brought by them inveighed against colour or race prejudice, taught human equality and human brotherhood. Servility was foreign to the nature of the man of the deserts. His coming introduced to the subject peoples a sense of release from servitude. If the Arabs had much to learn, culturally, from those they conquered, they had an example of human worth to set forth, and it was this that led to the acceptance, as military prowess led to the extension, of their dominion. Hence these scattered peoples came one by one to be swallowed up in a supernational state.

The small Moslem community grew from a supertribe of Moslems within Arabia to a superstate of mixed races and religions without.

The leader of the supertribe was at first Muhammad, its creator. But in theory God alone ruled the community through his divinely revealed ordinances delivered through the Prophet's lips, and when the Prophet died Allah's guidance was stored up in the Prophet's ordinances and traditions. The Prophet's successor, the caliph, according to original intention, was not to be a ruler over his people, not a sovereign, not even a pontiff, for all believers were equal. He was merely a successor of the Prophet, to interpret the holy law and administer justice between Moslems, merely a commander of the faithful. It was a theocratic state in which the nominal head, the caliph, must guide, not by personal caprice (the tribal shaikh could not, either, of course), not even by personal right, but in accordance with the laws of God already revealed, and the faithful must obey the caliph only so long as he kept within the bounds set by the Qur'anic ordinances.

In this community, wherein rights of intertribal revenge were surrendered, an offence against an individual was to be expiated by the offender himself, though the community, as by religious duty, were interested that justice should be done.

Now the Qur'an contained legal rulings which had been revealed to meet a great variety of situations and needs. Some of the sanctions may well have been not very different from the usages of the tribe of Quraish, the Prophet's own settled tribe of Mecca, in which case they must have been admirably suited to the early Arab urban communities that sprang up around the great military camps of Basrah, Kufa, Fustat, etc., offshoots of a similar social culture. The thief, for instance, must suffer his offending hand to be cut off. The underlying principle of this law was the principle of retaliation or reciprocity, the principle of an eye for an eye and a tooth for a tooth. The *talio* was, of course, an old Semitic conception of the Jewish code, a conception quite Arabian in spirit. Under Islam there was no permission to go beyond the measure of the criminal's own deed: it must be equitable retaliation, and religion forbade making an example of punishment. Moreover it was a merit in him who showed kindliness and forgave the offender.

Shari'a, or the Islamic law, was the Code of Sanctions collated from the Qur'an. As part of the divine revelations, law and religion were thus complementary, and so to disobey Shari'a was to infringe religious ordinance. It specified conditions, for instance, about marriage and divorce, laid down how family inheritances must be divided, limited the rights of private property and those of individuals making contracts, forbade usury, defined the rights of husbands and wives, of masters and slaves and of parents and daughters. Such laws, whether or not revealed for specific cases, acquired the validity of general divine ordinance. They were applied by orthodox Moslem communities then as now.

The first collation of the Qur'an was not made before the Caliph Abu Bakr's day, and for a long time afterwards the lack of literacy and the slowness of book-copying restricted the dissemination of the written word, though learning the verses of the Qur'an by heart was a passion with the pious. Now during those first two or three decades while the Arabs were overrunning Egypt, Syria, Iraq and Persia, brushing against cultures that were different from and more complex than their own, the leaders came to be confronted with problems, political and social, for which they could remember no specific scriptural guidances, and they were thrown back on their private judgment.

Time passed, and the Arab conquerors, growing accustomed to their position of dominance in the community, not unnaturally came to regard life through different eyes. In the deserts their social structure had been simple and homogeneous. Such aristocracy as Arabia had known comprised the shaikhly families in the tribes and the rich merchant class of the settlements. Ancestry in the one case, wealth and patronage in the other, exalted certain individuals, but in spirit the Arab paid small attention to social refinements; his was a natural and easy assumption of equality; he grovelled to none and rated personal freedom over all things; it was sufficiently aristocratic for him to be a worthy scion of an ancient tribe, and the only individuals he instinctively felt reverence for were bards and warriors of renown.

His world had its depressed class of course; indeed, there were two clearly marked (and rightly enough) classes in his scheme of life: freemen and slaves. Muhammad had discouraged class distinctions among his followers. Islam, within Arabia, frowned on human claims to superiority. It counted the lowly equal with the great, recognized goodness as the only criterion of superiority. It was essentially democratic in temper and in this reflected the spirit of the desert. Had not the first caliph, indeed, gone to the lengths of dividing the spoils of the raid equally between young and old, slave and free, male and female, for were not all believers brothers? Had not the second clothed himself in coarse linen and sandals of fibre; had he not on that historic visit to Jerusalem to receive its surrender entered the city walking, while at his side his servant rode the horse that they had shared between them turn by turn, on the journey thither?

Thirty years had passed since the Prophet's death. They were thirty years of continuous fighting. The purely Arab and Moslem theocracy of Arabia had grown to become a political state of many religions and peoples. Medina had been superseded by Damascus. The old ideological conception of the caliph as the interpreter of holy law in a theocratic state, holding his office in virtue of great piety, had now given place to kingship, the rule of the sword, a hereditary dynasty. Damascus, now the capital of an empire predominantly non-Moslem, brought personal rule and political expediency. Whatever misgivings the truly orthodox felt, they were powerless to prevent what had come about by the inexorable compulsion of growth. When Islam had been a small, homogeneous, self-contained Arabian community the Prophet himself, or an early caliph, had been able to control it as its judge and guide, but the ever-widening horizons of a vast empire and the increasing complexities of its affairs led inevitably to a devolution of powers to military leaders and governors of provinces, whose problems doubtless called more for statecraft than for theology. It was an age for temporal rulers rather than for spiritual guides.

The Arabs were engaged in world war, ever conquering, ever advancing. However much heaven may condemn aggression or proclaim equality of peoples before God, there could have been no doubt in the minds of men, victors and vanquished alike, about Arab racial pre-eminence in that century of triumphant ascendancy. Across a world as yet minority-Arab and minority-Moslem ran a network of Arab military garrisons, and peoples of all nations and languages acknowledged the Arab sceptre. Within these garrisons the ordinances of holy law were observed. Outside them the Arabs with a wide toleration allowed the subject peoples to continue their own legal usages, practise their own sanctions. The 'people of the book'—that is to say, those having scriptures, namely Jews, Christians and, for some less clear reason, star-worshipping Sabians—were absolutely free to practise their own religions subject only to the two special forms of tribute, a poll tax and a land tax. It was the exception and not the rule for them to be subjected by an occasional intolerant and harsh caliph of Damascus to disabilities such as the restrictive ordinances of Omar II which we have noticed.

Still a stigma came to attach to the term 'Christian', *Nasrani,* i.e. Nazarene, which has not wholly disappeared from some Moslem lands to this day, in much the same way that the term Jew once had a contemptuous sound among Christian societies. In other ways, however, the Arabs showed what was for those days a broad toleration. They used no terrorism in their proselytizing. They did not compel apostasy to Islam, whereas, by contrast, at that very time the Christian church was compelling Jews to apostatize in Spain under dire penalties.

It is doubtful if many of the Umaiyyad provincial governors really desired conversion of the subject peoples, for it meant loss of a convenient docility as well as loss of taxes which went to support their garrisons. One governor of Khorasan is indeed known to have put obstacles in the way of his pious caliph and was recalled. The religious ends were achieved by his successor but at the expense of a weakened garrison, and when taxes came to be reimposed brought on a rebellion which lost Trans-Oxiana to the Arabs for many years.

The general absence of religious persecution by the Arabs, however, is well shown by what happened in Egypt. At the end of the Umaiyyad period the population of Lower Egypt, then Arab-ruled for nearly a century, was still predominantly Christian, and five hundred years passed before the Moslems were in a majority. Persia afforded yet another example. As the Persians were fire worshippers, they were not people of the book and, strictly speaking, were not entitled to keep their lands on the tributary terms Muhammad had laid down for Jews and Christians, or indeed to practise their faith. But in practice they fared little worse for their obduracy. True there were instances where Persians suffered the confiscation of their properties—an exceptional thing to happen in the light of Omar's liberal land decrees—but that was as punishment by military commanders where they had too stubbornly resisted the invaders, and such escheated lands were administered for the common good.

Within the purely Arab or Moslem communities the theocratic sanctions were those observed. In Islam 'religion is the law and the law is religion.' When purely practised there is no other law, for all law derives from religious principles, based on religious texts. But these were not narrowly conceived of in those early centuries when the Arabs were in the ascendant; indeed, great jurists were to arise and give the law a liberal interpretation, leading to wide development. To be a judge in the Moslem community a deep study of the Qur'an was the first requisite, so that the judge or *qadhi*—a term familiar to the reader of *The Arabian Nights*—was therefore originally a man of religion, though his office was not in itself a holy one, for Islam has no priests, no hierarchy, no consecration for sacred duties. Such officials had been first sent off by the Caliph Omar to the military camps, in later times qadhis were sent to the camps of Qairawan in north Africa and away beyond the Oxus to Bokhara and Samarkand. They were not limited to purely magisterial duties but presided at public prayers and witnessed marriages, were missionaries, too, and so played an important part in bringing about the conversion of the non-Arab populations.

These qadhis, faced almost at once by strange and complex law problems and seeking in vain for specific Qur'anic guidance, came to be guided by practices ascribed to the Prophet. These precedents were codified and, known as Traditions =*Sunna,* hence the term 'Sunni' for him who practiced them. To the Sunnis the Traditions had a validity inferior only to Qur'anic sanctions. By the Shi'as, the other great branch of Islam, the Traditions were held to be largely apocryphal, for the source of many of them was to be found among companions who supported the first three caliphs whom the Shi'as regarded as usurpers. Only those traditions attributed to Ali's camp were therefore acceptable to them. Hence in details of law the two main divisions of Islam, which, as we saw, originally split over the political issue of caliphate succession—the hereditary versus the elective principle—came to adopt in some particulars different law usages.

The non-Moslems following their own usages were at

first in a majority of the population, but soon Moslem cities appeared where the Beduin military camps had been, and mixed urban communities, with roots in alien cultures, grew up, and gradually there came about a change of religious adherence in favour of the faith of the dominant race.

The holy law under the Arabs in those first two or three centuries was essentially progressive and underwent phases of considerable development. The Moslem Laws of Evidence in those early days are said to have had no equal in Europe till the seventeenth century; so also the Moslem Laws of Contract are claimed to have been a thousand years ahead of their European counterparts. The mercantile laws of the Arabs begat bills of exchange; to their practices we owe our words 'cheque', 'douane', i.e. *diwan,* and perhaps 'tariff.' Much of the Code Napoléon and other modern Western law, also, is held to derive from the corpus of medieval Arab jurists.

For several centuries while in the ascendant the Arabs were great reformers. It was mostly after our eleventh century and during the later period of decay that their criminal and civil law came to be reduced to the rigid forms that led to stagnation. The Arabs at their best were liberal minded. Legal research and the consequent evolution of new laws was not only unrestricted but encouraged, so that criminal and civil law differed greatly, not only between one country and another, but between two periods in the history of the same country. The Arabs were not averse to adopting the law usages of other peoples, placed no hindrance to the extension of alien sanctions where these did not conflict with the sanctions found in the Qur'an. Where Qur'anic sanctions were categorically laid down, however, as for instance in the cutting off the hand for theft or flogging for fornication, the dictates of holy writ were observed.

There were periods of upheaval when godless governors took the law into their own hands and acted arbitrarily. In an age when 'strong action' was admired, strong action was usually taken, and tyrannous methods, such as imprisonment and torture to extort confession, were not unknown in Iraq. How far the spirit of holy law was abandoned at this time is shown by the conduct of the prefect of Kufa, a local Judge Jefferies, who under Hajjaj, the famous mail-fisted governor of Iraq, transfixed and burnt alive; cut off the hand of one who threatened the life of another; gave three hundred lashes to a suspected thief. Kufa, we are told and may well believe it, enjoyed long spells of freedom from any crime whatever, and its strong man was promoted to be prefect of Basrah as well.

The change of dynastic rule from the Umaiyyads to the Abbasids coincided with a widening scope for religious law. It was a tendency of the age that came about as a result of far-reaching social and religious changes. Conversions to Islam had steadily been going on to absorb a large alien element of public opinion. The decay of the Umaiyyads, as we saw, was brought about largely by the growing strength of Persian converts. Proselytism had naturally been followed by a wave of religious fervour; everywhere there was an intense interest in the Qur'an and an eager study, doubtless, of its legal aspects. Among Sunnis, who had extended the basis of holy law by the addition of Traditions, four schools of jurisprudence sprang up within the century, preserved in the names of their founders, Hanafi, Shafi'i, Maliki, Hanbali.

Such developments in the law were by no means the only or most important feature of the period which followed the change of capital from Damascus to Baghdad. The functions of the caliph were transformed, and, most radical of all, perhaps, an end came to the supremacy of the Arab, as such, within the political system. Under the caliphs of Damascus the dominant note in the state had been Arab racial superiority. Victorious wars of expansion had continued to give the imperial Arabs an unparalleled national prestige. The caliph himself was an absolute ruler in an Arab patriarchal setting; the great offices of state were held by Arabs. With the advent of the caliphs of Baghdad in the second century after the Prophet the wars of conquest, chief instrument of Arab supremacy, had come to an end, the centre of the caliphate moved east where Arab Moslems were in a minority, and Persians held the upper hand.

The Abbasid caliphs were no longer absolute Arab rulers but emperors after the old Sassanian model, 'accepting a reverence and a manner of address rightly-guided Caliphs would have rebelled against as blasphemous.'[10]* They were no longer accessible to their subjects in open court but surrounded by ministers of state, at first Persians, in whom were vested great powers. The pomp and luxury of their courts vastly excelled Damascus and was in an altogether different world from the rude simplicity of Medina.

An era of great prosperity was dawning, an age of refinement in living and an age in which the arts and sciences flourished. Rich revenues poured in from the conquered territories, the land tax was now collected from Moslems and unbelievers alike, though the latter must still pay their poll tax, too, and the national income steadily grew to vast proportions. The state treasury and the caliph's privy purse profited together, as later in times of adversity they suffered together. The most famous of the Baghdad caliphs, Harun al Rashid, a contemporary of Charlemagne, was popularly believed to have amassed a private fortune of nine hundred million dirhams—a mere twenty millions sterling perhaps!—which, even allowing for wild exaggeration, is a safe enough indication of phenomenal prosperity.

The caliph, his plentiful palaces, bodyguards and harem were supported by state expenditure, as were the army and the civil administration; all descendants of the Prophet enjoyed state pensions, and poets and musicians won impulsive and princely rewards in these spacious days of the eastern caliphate.

The form of government was a thoroughgoing autocracy. The caliph was supported by his *wazir,* at first a private and personal duce as it were, who, while in favour, had supreme powers of patronage and upon whose integrity and ability depended the just government of the times. He made and unmade governors, appointed all the principal civil officers of state and combined in his person the lucrative functions of an appellate court for the extensive judiciary of Islam. To the young aspirant, the ear of the wazir led to place and fortune, and conversely his opposition meant adversity, until the day when the caliph lost patience with that particular wazir and relieved him of his office if not his head.

The reader familiar with the pages of *The Arabian Nights* will need no reminding that the Arab-ruled country of the times was 'a man's country.' But it would be unfair to suppose that this was a peculiarly Arab contribution. The sex inferiority of women was doubtless part of the established order of the universe and man's dominance over woman a phase of sociological evolution common the world over.

Doubtless under the Arabs woman's status, though upheld by religious precepts, deteriorated in the later centuries. The common Western view, however, that the woman was at all times repressed under the Arabs, meets with a vigorous challenge by Judge Pierre Crabites, an American judge in the Cairo mixed tribunals, who, after a long experience of Moslem law as administered in the Egyptian capital, has favoured the thesis that Muhammad was probably the greatest champion of women's rights the world has ever seen.

'Muhammad's outstanding contribution,' says Judge Crabites, 'to the cause of woman resides in the property rights that he conferred upon the wives of his people. The juridical status of a wife, if so technical a term may be pardoned, is exactly the same as that of a husband. The Moslem spouse in so far as her property is concerned, is as free as a bird. The law permits her to do with her financial assets whatever she pleases without consulting her consort. In such matters he has no greater rights than would have any perfect stranger.'[34]*

Before the Propet's time Arab women's rights of inheritance were negligible, and when a man died his sons inherited his widows as well as his property. A revelation ensured her an inalienable share in a relative's estate. The divisions of inheritance were categorically laid down: to the mother one third of a man's estate unless he had brothers, in which case one sixth. If a man left but two daughters two thirds of the estate passed to them, if one daughter her share was to be one half. Where there were sons and daughters one share to a daughter and two shares to a son. A husband was to be entitled to one half of his wife's property if she died without child, otherwise one quarter, and so on. The general underlying principle was that the rewards of male relatives, in inheritance, were double those of the female—a principle by no means as inequitable as it seems, being based on the theory that the female will be supported by a husband, while the male will have to support a wife.

The right of bequest among Arabs at death was thus circumscribed. The Arab cannot will his property so as to deprive his wife or his children of their rightful share of his estate; he cannot cut his wife off with less than the share specified as her right under religious law. By divorce only will she be deprived of it.

A feature of the marriage contract which Judge Pierre Crabites singles out for special praise is its fluidity—that any wise provision may be written into it; thus the girl's father can reserve the right of the girl to divorce under certain circumstances or even the right to divorce unconditionally, e.g. in the event of the man's remarriage, or he can require the bridegroom to forego the right of divorcing his daughter. Moreover, he says, 'A wife, technically speaking, does not even take her husband's name. A Moslem girl born Aisha bint Omar (Aisha daughter of Omar) may marry ten times, but her individuality is not absorbed by that of her various husbands. She is not a moon that shines through reflected light. She is a solar planet, with a name and a legal personality of her own!'

The law of divorce required the man's utterance, 'I divorce thee,' to be said three times with an interval of a month between each occasion—the idea being to provide for a period of three months during which time reconciliation could be effected. As soon as estrangement was felt between the married couple a family council could be formed in order to bring about a rapprochement. Divorce was not encouraged by the Prophet, to whom is attributed the saying that of the permissible things it was one distasteful to God. Although there was no lifelong alimony for the divorced wife the dowry was in itself conceived as an obstacle to divorce, for the wife was entitled to a sum equivalent to the dowry paid to her at her wedding, a sum therefore fixed high when the man was in a gallant mood. It was fixed at the highest amount compatible with the social position of the contracting parties and the ability of the husband to pay. Where the dowry was small and the poor husband later acquired wealth, the qadhi in case of divorce assessed the sum on the husband's improved status instead of the original contract.

The Prophet not only conferred rights on women, he taught men to treat wives considerately and humanely, not preferring one over another: the gift of a robe to one, for instance, was to entail robes all round; and so with conjugal felicity: he brought amelioration in marriage, divorce and inheritance laws—hence early Islam 'under rightly guided Caliphs' is held to have protected her interests and given her a status which had never been hers before. In later times, however, the generous spirit waned, practice fell away from the precept, and low standards came to be the established fashion.

In the medieval state the man could take not merely the four wives which religious law permitted at any one time, but slave concubines without limit—a practice which present interpretation considers to have been a violation of Islamic canons and enlightened Arabs frown on wherever they meet with it in their midst today. He could marry an unbeliever so long as she was a 'chaste woman of the Book', e.g., a Jewess, a Christian or a Sabian, but not an idolatress, e.g., a Hindu. He could marry his slave girl if he first of all freed her, or could cohabit with her as his concubine, without marriage, so long as she was not an idolatress. The children of concubines were legitimate; indeed, many of the later Abbasid caliphs were sons of concubines, a parallel found today in some aristocratic families in Arab countries. Concubinage with free women was forbidden. First-cousin marriages were common; they are still the rule rather than the exception in many parts of tribal Arabia, where the man has the right to the hand of the daughter of his uncle (father's brother) whatever the disparity of age, she on the other hand having no corresponding right to his. The prohibited degrees of marriage were for the most part similar to those of the Old Testament, though a Moslem may not marry his niece as is permitted by the Jews, nor may he marry two sisters or even two unrelated women who, as children, had been suckled by the same wet nurse; the same stricture applied also to cohabitation with two concubines. Brother and sister marriages, forbidden by Islam, may have affected Persian practice, where, under Zoroastrianism, such unions are said to have been permissible.

The woman could not have more than one husband at a time—an inequality justified in the interests of the child—that is to say, to ensure the establishment without doubt of its male parent. Although the spirit of the law had been to give women new rights and protect those rights, practice in unenlightened circles led to abuses, and the dowry for the girl often came to be a cash payment to her parents, so that with the poor and needy a rich old suitor was probably preferred to a poor young one, the girl's inclinations—on the occasion of her first marriage—being subordinated to her interests as conceived of by her parents. A marriage contract of Morocco, quoted by Levi, is as follows—

'Glory be to God, the Lord of the Worlds!

'The honourable Kaddur, being of age and living in Algiers, a trader by calling, son of Sulayman, has contracted a marriage by God's blessing . . . with the noble virgin Fatima, now passed the period of puberty, 18 years of age, daughter of Muhammad bin Ali, weaver, domiciled in Algiers. The marriage is contracted in consideration of a dower of blessed augury amounting to 30 douros, of which half is at once due, before consummation of the marriage, and the remaining half payable within four years. The husband will only be acquitted of this debt by lawful means. The bride's father was contracted in her name, and this by virtue of the powers conferred on him by God and after obtaining her consent, expressed by silence, which is considered the equivalent to consent. The husband has appeared in person: he has accepted the contract, the offer and the acceptance have been made as required by Law.

'All that precedes has been witnessed (by two witnesses).'[9]*

The usual procedure of the Arab wedding was that on the day of the nuptials guests, male and female, were bidden to the house of the girl's father, the men forgathered in one part and the women, veiled and secluded, in another. The qadhi or imam called forth the witnesses, a male representative of the bride, another of the bridegroom, or, in the absence of one male, two female witnesses, though to have all witnesses female was not lawful, the presence of one male witness being imperative. The witnesses then signified their agreement to the terms of the marriage, whereupon the qadhi took the hands of the bride and bridegroom and held their hands together in such a way that their thumbs touched, while all present recited the opening chapter of the Qur'an.

In a polygynous society the state of lifelong spinsterhood for a girl was extremely rare. The girl was normally married for the first time at the age of thirteen or fourteen —girls reach physical maturity at an earlier age in the East than the West; she was usually given no choice in the matter of her first husband any more than she is today in backward Arabian communities—that was her father's concern. She was generally not consulted in the matter, being of tender age and without knowledge of the world. Some such procedure as this was followed. The mother of a son old enough to take a wife approached the mother of the girl she thought desirable, and if they both agreed to the match the suitor approached the girl's father, or in default of one, her nearest male kinsman to arrange matters. A marriage contract was then drawn up specifying the dowry and other legal obligations. Marriage being a civil contract, it could be performed by a qadhi (not in the mosque, however) or by any Moslem provided there were two reputable witnesses.

Another and exceptional form of marriage that came to be practised among the Shi'a Moslems of Iraq and Persia, more particularly during pilgrimage to their sacred shrines, was the *mut'a* marriage, a temporary union for a fixed term of years or months or weeks or even days, as the case might be. It did not entail reference to a woman's kin and was practised by a limited and special poor class of townswoman. It was a system that lent itself to abuse, although perfectly within the Shi'a religious law, the children of such so-called marriages being legitimate. But as we have seen, generally speaking, the female member of the Moslem family was carefully protected and honourably betrothed, and her honour, involving the family honour, was counted of the greatest concern.

Divorce under the Arabs, as we have seen, involved an outright payment based on the dowry and did not entail lifelong alimony. In spite of the difficulties which the Prophet set in the way the man could normally divorce quite easily without recourse to a court by uttering the simple formula already noticed three times. The woman could not obtain divorce so lightly, though mental disease, infectious disease, cruel behaviour and other similar grounds were recognized as sufficient; physical imperfection in either party gave grounds for annulment, as also the false description in the marriage contract of the bride as a virgin. The mother had custody of the children during infancy and thereafter the father, the age for boys and girls varying with the sect of Islam to which the parents belonged. A divorced woman must wait three months before marrying again, the widow four months and ten days. Similiarly, if a man bought a female slave he must allow the necessary time to pass before she could be his concubine, in order to obviate the risk of doubtful parenthood.

The veiling of women is thought to have been rare in the early days of the Arab period. The common Western view that it is Arab or Islamic in origin is contested by educated Arabs who are opposed to the practice today and who hold that the only veiling required in Islam is the covering of the head and neck, not the face. Be that as it may, the practice of close veiling is one that has survived only among Moslem communities and is still the rule rather than the exception in most Arab countries.

Such Arab authorities suppose that the custom was in origin Persian or Byzantine, that in the Arab period it first was adopted by the wives of Baghdad caliphs and the great ladies about the courts, so that it was a fashion of rank; hence, naturally, it spread downwards and outwards.

In the early period, they hold, it was nowhere popular and it never took root among the peasantry, where the female continued to work unveiled side by side with her menfolk in the fields as she does today—though not in Arabia—but it gradually acquired rigidity in the towns and was made law by the Caliph al Qadir Billah (eleventh century) who ordered that women must wear a veil when mixing with men and appearing in the mosque or other public places.

So it has continued down to this day. The girl born in strictest circles must, on reaching maturity, wear a veil and never again show her face to any male except her husband and those of her relatives within the prohibited degrees of marriage. For a woman to expose to the public gaze more than her hands and her feet (ankles and wrists must be concealed) came to be regarded as shameful, the rigour of veiling and seclusion increasing the higher her status in the social scale. Here the slave girl and the peasant girl were at a great advantage, braving the world with naked face and fancy free. But al Qadir Billah's proscription was a great blow to the educated class of woman who, up to this time, played a part in the life of the empire, and from the time of these restrictions in the eleventh century the position of the woman under the Arabs deteriorated.

The harem system, the practice of enforced seclusion—Persian women, it is believed, were secluded long before the coming of the Arabs—was soon established, and women were now confined to their houses by force of public opinion. They seldom went out at all; never alone and rarely by day, and of course social intercourse between the sexes was impossible. This banishment of women from the streets and from society is a noticeable feature of most oriental towns to this day.

It became the fashion for women of the wealthy classes to be secluded in a part of the house by themselves and be waited upon by eunuchs, though the practice of mutilating slaves for these duties had been expressly forbidden by the Prophet himself. These social practices led, moreover, to the gradual effacement of women from public festivities and from public worship in the Friday mosques, in contrast to the earlier days when women not only attended mosques but gave lectures in them.

Such usages which have been handed down to the backward Arabs of our day are responsible for the current Western view that women under the Arabs were throughout a lower order of creation. In those first centuries of the Arab period, however, the position of the Arab woman was very different. She was not closely veiled and little more segregated than her European or Asiatic sister of the time; indeed, in Spain she continued to mix freely with men and to pray openly in the mosques. There had been no prejudice against her education in early Islam, and the upper-class women were literate and accomplished—indeed, a millennium ago when Al Azhar University of Cairo was first opened it was attended by men and women alike; and the Arab jurist Abu Hanifa could declare in our eighth century that woman was as much entitled to practise the profession of law as man. In Iraq, in Egypt and in Spain during the enlightened periods it was the same: women played notable parts—Sukaina, Nafisat al Ilm, a great-great-granddaughter of the Prophet, Umm Salma, the wife of the first caliph of Baghdad, Zubaida, the wife of Harun al Rashid, Khadija, the sister of Saladin in Egypt, and in Spain the wife of Abdul Rahman III, to mention but a few. Some were devoted to letters, some to good works, and colleges, orphanages, hostels for the blind, the aged and the infirm, still proudly bear the names of women founders.

In these selfsame days chivalry found its way into Europe by way of Spain. To Spain it had come from the eastern lands of the Arabs. Hence it would seem that the belief which persists in the West concerning the general degradation of women under the Arabs is based on observances of later decadence; in reality the Arabs at their best were perhaps the most chivalrous people in the world.

Slavery, of course, persisted all through the Arab period. It was a recognized and legitimate institution of society. It had existed from time immemorial, was sanctioned by Judaism and survived the early Christian centuries. Muhammad himself was clearly a resolute opponent of all the evils of slavery and wrought such reforms for its amelioration as were possible in his time. Manumission of slaves was not only praised but gave atonement for small sins. 'Your brothers,' he taught, 'are they who are your servants, God having placed them under your care; and he whose brother has been placed under his care must feed him with that which he eats, and clothe him with that wherewith he clothes himself. Do not ask them to do more than they can, and if you have assigned them a task greater than they are able to cope with, then give them the help they require.'

The Arabs of subsequent generations were to take the word for the spirit and look for implied sanction in it. According to the most enlightened present-day interpretations of Islam there was never any warrant for the keeping of slaves other than prisoners of war, nor should slaves have been bought and sold. Under medieval caliphs, however, slaves were freely bought and sold, bequeathed and inherited, as they still are in Arabia. They were inferior beings, suffering certain recognized civil and social disabilities.

Yet the attitude of the Arabs to their slaves removed the stigma elsewhere attaching to slave status, for a feature of present-day Arabian slavery is the general absence of a grovelling and abject mentality, which the untravelled European may naturally suppose inevitable. 'The slave is the slave of his master, but otherwise as free as you,' runs an Omani saying. Still, generally speaking, the blood-feud scale of values ran: a freeman for a freeman, a woman for a woman, a slave for a slave.

The essential democracy of the Islamic system, however, allowed slaveborn individuals to rise to command armies, to govern provinces, to acquire great wealth. Under the Arabs slaves rose to found Moslem dynasties in Egypt and elsewhere, and many famous caliphs of Baghdad had slave mothers. But these were exceptional slaves. The vast majority of the class did the menial offices and the hard work.

The holy law provided some ways in which a slave could win freedom: a concubine, for instance, who had borne her master children became free; a slave of either sex who came into possession of an owner within a certain degree of blood relationship was automatically freed; a slave might, with his master's consent, redeem himself by purchase or labour, though in the latter case he remained under his master's protection. This was perhaps a rare thing to happen, for the master had the right to hire out a slave to work for him, as is practised in the Persian Gulf pearl fisheries to this day, or to use his slave as a pledge.

Slaves were a valuable property in medieval times, and doubtless only those masters who had religious scruples conceded slaves such rights as they were entitled to. Buying and selling slaves was a highly profitable business, not only in the Arab countries but with them—the Slavonic peoples ominously preserving in name the memory of the role they played. The Venetians are said to have had a slave market in Rome itself in the eighth century, and the slave market of the Moors at Cordova, two centuries later, was famous for its wares of fair captives from northern Spain. Thousands of white slaves from Central Asia were drawn into the eastern caliphate by way of Samarkand, while black slaves swarmed in the bazaars of Samarra and Baghdad.

Early in the Arab conquests it became an article of faith that there could be no enslavement of Moslems, though in the tenth century this rule was relaxed by the sect of Carmathians in Arabia itself on the grounds that only they were true Moslems, and as late as the nineteenth century Turcomans are known to have suffered a similar illusion. In our sixteenth, seventeenth and eighteenth centuries Turkish and Barbary corsairs hunted and enslaved Christian mariners in the Mediterranean, some, very daring, reaching parts of Ireland and the Bristol Channel; and monks who were sent on missions of ransom brought back harrowing stories of the life in the galleys.

One of the most famous victims was, of course, Cervantes, who spent thus five years of his life in chains.

But let us not be forgetful of our own record, for but a brief century ago Britain and America practised slavery in their tobacco and sugar plantations, and Gladstone as a young Member of Parliament could make his maiden speech in defense of the system. At one time Britain enjoyed a monopoly of importing slaves into the Spanish colonies, and advertisements for slaves appeared in the most reputable of our newspapers. Moreover, plantation slavery was incomparably more inhuman than the domestic slavery of the Arabs of the medieval period.

The common people under the caliphs of Baghdad enjoyed greater liberty and greater prosperity than could be found in any other country whatsoever. Personal cleanliness was a feature of the Arab world—as the lack of it was characteristic of contemporary Europe—this arising doubtless from the frequent ablutions required by Moslem prayer and other rules of life. While in Europe the serfs were bound to the lands they cultivated and the artisans still had their servile status, their counterparts under the Arabs, the smiths and the cultivators, were free men. Difference of rank and wealth existed, of course, but without the rigid distinctions of society in medieval Europe. There was no hindrance to education. Learning was held in the highest respect, freedom of thought was for several centuries encouraged and secular subjects taught in the mosques. Decay came later when the Arabs came to be satisfied with a way of life as conservative and hidebound as in earlier times it had been liberal and light-giving.

The social structure, while containing features repellent in a twentieth-century view, must in fairness be compared with other systems contemporary with itself. More depends on the spirit of a social system than the letter of its regulations, and in the Middle Ages Eastern enlightenment was pre-eminent in the world, and the religion of the Arabs insisted with the greatest emphasis on humanitarianism.

To conceive of the Arab system as being in the likeness of our own, with a grafting onto it of its less pleasant features, is wholly misleading; it had another and wholly differing *ethos:* it was in essence as in origin patriarchal. The approved relationships between man and woman, parents and children, masters and servants approximated to the ideals of Abraham rather than to those of Lenin. It is not so much that one was four thousand years behind the other as that they were products of two differing environments and two utterly opposed philosophies.

If under the Arabs women as a sex enjoyed less of the social and political liberties than they enjoy under modern European civilization—mixed dancing, mixed bathing and the like are still objectionable, of course, to the orthodox—yet no woman went unmarried and was thereby unnaturally debarred from motherhood, and motherhood was held by Arabs of all time in the profoundest respect. If slaves were deprived of all political privileges there is still less difference by far in the material rewards of life between the freeman and the slave in 'subsistence cultures', such as in Arabia today, than between the 'haves' and 'have-nots' in our European civilization. This is said in no way to slur over those features of the medieval Arab way of life which in a twentieth-century view are repugnant, but as an indication that in practice it had a humanity of its own, a humanity untainted by the worst features of our modern economic industrialism. Without a wide humanity, indeed, the old Arab system could scarcely have displaced the earlier systems of so many different peoples across the medieval world from the Himalayas to the Atlas, and survived in a large measure down to this day.

'What struck me even in the decay and poverty,' wrote an Englishman a few years back, 'was the joyousness of that life compared with anything I had seen in Europe. These peoples seemed quite independent of our cares of life, our anxious clutching after wealth, our fear of death. And then their charity! No man in the cities of the Moslem Empire ever died of hunger or exposure at his neighbour's gate!'

CHAPTER VI

Arab Civilization: The Arts

In the Middle Ages art was first and foremost a religious expression. We instinctively identify the great orders of medieval art with the creeds that shaped them, for however clearly certain elements in their composition and technical procedure may unite them in common ancestry, they were moulded into distinct entities by religious influences.[12*]

A. H. CHRISTIE

THE INSPIRATION of Moslem arts owed much then to the Arabs—an odd thought when we remember that the Arabs were an artless people. For the desert hosts that vanquished Greeks and Persians originated, as we saw, in a culture conspicuously devoid of any artistic tradition. Indeed, as they swept across the civilized world of their time they carried with them a suspicious attitude towards art if not an aversion to it, for was not the graven image anathema and a decoration in the likeness of man or bird or beast an affront to the true faith, did not silken apparel and vessels of gold, proper enough for the mansions of the hereafter, come under religious interdiction here below?

Now in the lands the Arabs overran they came upon arts highly flourishing, arts with a long local history going back to the civilizations of the Nile and the Euphrates.

In the former, Christianity had arisen a few centuries earlier and remoulded a new and beautiful Byzantine art; in the latter the Eastern genius still survived among the Persians. But the arts of unbelieving Greeks and Persians, however superb, were little better than heathen abominations to the rude puritan invaders in the seventh century. Yet it was Islam, borne by these unlettered desert men, that was destined to set the world aflame, fuse the great artistic inheritances of the ages and bring in a new and splendid tradition.

The Prophet's ban on the portrayal of human and animal forms was of course scarcely propitious. Indeed, it atrophied the fine arts from the first. Under a newborn vigorous Islam there could be no great statuary in a Greek or Roman sense, no more sculptures like those of ancient Susa and Persepolis, no great painting such as that of the later Italian, Dutch or Spanish schools. Islam not only discouraged the fine arts, it forbade them in God's name, and its first rude votaries were active iconoclasts, so that our later Western schools of both painting and sculpture were not able to profit from any Moslem inheritance but grew straight out of the classical tradition. One shining exception brightens the period of Arab civilization, and that is architecture. Here there was no ban. Indeed, the ritualistic requirements of the new faith called into existence new needs, while glorious examples of cathedrals and temples enshrining Christianity and other rival religions stood before rising generations of Arabs, provocatively challenging. Thus it was that Saracenic architecture came to have its birth and development in the Moslem congregational place of worship, the Friday mosque.

The first callow invaders from the deserts could scarcely

COURTYARD OF THE MOSQUE OF AL AZHAR, CAIRO.

(*From* L'Art Arabe, *Presse d'Avennes*)

have remained unimpressed in the face of the architectural splendour they encountered. Beyond the Euphrates, Sassanian palaces stood near the sites of ancient Babylonian cities, some but recently decayed, some still inhabited; over the Jordan, the Greco-Roman Decapolis formed a group of cities of arcaded streets and marble pavements, colonnaded forums and splendid amphitheatres and temples; Alexandria, a great Greek seaport already famed for close on a thousand years, possessed one of the architectural wonders of the world, the Manara, a famous lighthouse built by Ptolemy Suter, which was destined to give the word 'minaret' to the mosque tower. But a still greater wealth than these had fallen to the Arabs, namely, the inherited artistic traditions at the back of such monuments—the accumulated technical skill of the conquered peoples.

The Arabs, before their emergence from Arabia, had raised a mosque at Medina after their own rude fashioning, an unpretentious building with a roof of palm branches covered with mud and supported on palm trunks. Under the immediately succeeding caliphs of Medina the first mosques outside Arabia sprang up at Jerusalem, Fustat and Kufa, still, doubtless, simple and chaste, in keeping with the puritanism of the times, but necessarily more elegant from the excellence of ready-made columns and other building material taken from the ruins of classical temple or palace and from the skill of competent local craftsmen who raised them.

By the time this first spiritual phase of the caliphate had run its course and an imperial Arab dynasty had risen at Damascus a generation of Arabs had grown up amid alien cultural influences who had become conscious of great architecture, conscious of their own deficiency, and were persuaded that Islam must have worthy shrines, fitting, too, for her votaries as men of the dominant race. Already the Arab conquerors of Damascus had annexed for their own use one half of the magnificent Christian church of St John the Baptist, in origin a Roman temple, and before very long acquired the whole of it, a precedent to be followed at Cordova in Spain within the century; for where the subject peoples came to give up Christianity in favor of Islam old churches were automatically changed into mosques. The faithful thus became familiar with architectural splendour associated with religion and formed standards which they came naturally to adopt in their own new religious buildings.

The main features of the mosque, as it is known today, had already appeared by the time of the first Damascus caliph. The building was oriented towards Mecca, the direction indicated in the appropriate wall, facing which the worshippers lined up in a long row; this wall formed the long axis of the sanctuary, and midway along it was the *mihrab,* a praying niche corresponding somewhat to the apse of a Christian church. The mosque had its pulpit; its screen or grill (within which the caliph worshipped), recalling a chancel screen; its minaret, the parallel of a church tower, where the *muezzin*—the Moslem precentor, as it were—ascended to chant the call to prayer—this a distinction from church bells or the clappers which preceded them in Christian usage; and its font in the courtyard for the necessary Moslem ablutions before prayer.

These ritualistic needs were gradual developments. The first mosque in Egypt had no mihrab, but a stone was set up in the direction of Mecca; indeed, in the first mosque of all at Medina the worshippers, led by the Prophet, at first faced Jerusalem after the manner of the

Jews. So, too, the mosques built in Mesopotamia during the next century did not adopt the praying niche of rival Syria but had their own device of three arched openings. The Egyptian mosque was the first to have a pulpit, an innovation which, by elevating the preacher, provoked the democratic wrath of the Caliph Omar, so that its adoption came only after his day. If the screen is rightly ascribed to his successor, following the lesson of Omar's assassination, it belongs to Medina, while the first minaret to be built is believed to have appeared only at the end of the century, its function having presumably first been suggested and served by one of the four Roman towers of the temple-church-mosque of Damascus.

At first it was the conquered peoples who alone could provide the architects, masons, paviors and all the subsidiary craftsmen which fine building entailed, yet it was the Arabs who, by creating the needs and supplying the will and commandment, brought about a great architectural renaissance and, in the course of time, a new school. It was, indeed, the very vastness of their conquests that brought together the two great classical building traditions of the time and so led to the new synthesis.

These two traditions were the stone-building tradition of the West and the brick-and-plaster tradition of the East. The former, belonging naturally to the stony countries of the eastern Mediterranean and beyond—Egypt, Syria, North Mesopotamia, Armenia—was exemplified in the solid, stately, naked masonry of Egyptian temple or Byzantine cathedral; the latter was a tradition rooted in the mud plains of Mesopotamia, extending eastwards through Persia and across the Oxus to Samarkand, the old Babylonian-Sassanian brick tradition, the appeal of which lay in its lighter shapes under a mantle of exquisite ornamentation of glazed tiles and mosaics, sumptuous interiors of stucco, carved and painted panelling, coloured glass and similar features of a richly decorative oriental art.

The earliest Arab architecture of the Umaiyyad period —the Great Mosque of Damascus which was the remodelled church of St John, the Dome of the Rock in Jerusalem and the Mosque of Uqba at Qairawan—belonged to the stonework tradition, proper both to their geography and the prevailing political influence of the day. With the change of government to Baghdad, under the Abbasids, the brick-and-plaster tradition of the Persians came to be the dominating influence and continued to be so for the next four centuries. Not only did the first great mosques built in eighth-century Mesopotamia belong to this tradition, but also those built in the immediately succeeding centuries in Egypt and north Africa.

This wave of oriental tradition, sweeping westwards to invade the stone-building countries, was a natural consequence of the diffusion of Islam. Autocratic governments sent bodies of craftsmen skilled in the arts of one tradition to the lands of the other; the common language and religion encouraged enterprising craftsmen on their own account to move to courts and cities whose star was in the ascendant; the annual pilgrimage brought men of wealth and taste as well as craftsmen from the remotest corners of the Arab conquests through countries and cities having different building traditions, and what they saw to be novel or attractive was carried back and adopted in their own lands; and finally, the great Asiatic inroads of Turks and Mongols later drove craftsmen westwards from lands that were the source of so much artistic inspiration. Thus across the world from Merv to Marakkesh a continuous permeation of common ideas brought about an architecture of that distinctive shape and quality by which we now recognize it.

The foreign visitor cannot but be impressed by some of the beautiful and arresting features of Moslem architecture, notably, perhaps, massive domes and lofty minarets that raise themselves above flat-roofed cities. If he has travelled as far afield as Egypt or the Holy Land, Persia or India, he will have experienced the effect of dome and minaret in combination—an entrancing outline against a brilliant Eastern night. If north Africa and Spain are the limit of his wanderings he will have missed the great domes and the circular minarets, though horseshoe arches with a characteristically exaggerated pinch forming the portal of mosque and city wall will have struck a novel and pleasing note. If he has been privileged to enter the walled seclusion of a great mosque (intolerance will have thwarted him in Morocco and Persia) and passed by way of arcaded cloisters across the spacious courtyard, scene of ritualistic ablutions, to the roofed sanctuary, he will there have met with a luxuriance of interior effect he may not have expected in the service of the puritanical religion of the Arab Prophet.

But it is the exteriors of the famous mosques, particularly the domed ones, which are at first so impressive. The dome became, from the first, a favourite device of the Arabs. As a traditional tomb form—it is met with in earlier buildings, the Church of the Holy Sepulchre in Jerusalem, for instance—it was well known, of course, in the lands of the conquests as far back as Roman times. The Arabs at first placed it in the mosque over and just in front of the praying niche. Later on it became, in Egypt, the central feature of the smaller tomb mosques of the caliphs, some mosques being given twin domes. The building of these domes, the transition from a square substructure through an octagonal phase and thence to the circle, effected by arches across the corners, led to the development of brilliant devices of corbelled masonry with pendentive carvings, a feature for which Moslem architecture is distinguished. In the tomb mosque of Egypt one minaret later came to be the fashion in place of two or even four, and this was usually built over the doorway, as had been the custom in Iraq.

Domes under Islamic development became infinitely various. 'In Cairo the dome form was usually stilted, in Persia and Turkestan bulbous or ovoid domes were preferred, while in Constantinople the mosques had low Byzantine domes. Externally the stone domes of Egypt were decorated with lace-like patterning in the fifteenth century: in Persia they were covered with dazzling glazed tiles. Stalactite pendentives supported them, and indeed stalactites were used everywhere, often in excess, and sometimes hanging from the ceilings like the "pendants" of our English fan vaults. But whereas the Saracen dome had little influence on our Renaissance domes in the West, it seems possible that Muhammadan minarets of the graceful type, found especially in Cairene buildings of the fourteenth and fifteenth centuries, may have influenced the design of the later Renaissance *campanili* of Italy, and hence some of Wren's fine city steeples.'[13]*

One of the notable characteristics of the Persian tradition was its roundnesses. The minarets were round in contrast to the square type of north Africa and Spain; the corners of walls were rounded, too, this a relic, of course, of a mud-brick ancestry when sharp corners, being most susceptible to damage, must be avoided. But with the

THE TOMB MOSQUE OF SULTAN BARQUQ
from a drawing by Martin S. Briggs.

By permission of the artist. *(Fisher Unwin.)*

spread of the round and chamfered forms to the stone countries they were copied in stone and so persisted and became characteristic of the later stone buildings of Islam. This feature of Arab architecture is credited by scholars with having begotten a notable line of developments which were to flourish, too, in Europe. 'It is not a long step,' says Ernest Richmond,[22]* 'to evolve from a rounded corner the conception of an engaged shaft, and from an engaged shaft to conceive the device of an independent corner column, both of which are features of Moslem architecture from very early times, first appearing in brick as in the engaged shafts at the corners of the brick piers; then in the form of independent shafts in stone or in marble placed at the angles of entrance recesses . . . or at any corner where their appearance might be considered pleasing, as, for instance, on either side of a *mihrab* or on either side of a window in a minaret.'

And to this introduction of engaged shafts at the angles of piers and edges of columns the system of vaulting so important in our later Gothic architecture is held to be under a great debt. Vaulting, based on intersecting arches, may originally have evolved in Armenia or Persia, but it seems to have found its way into the ecclesiastical architecture of Europe by way of Spain, where examples of it belong to immediately preceding centuries. Gothic architecture is held by some to have derived its pointed arch, its multifoil windows and ornamental battlements from the East, while its tracery patterning on surfaces is also a feature of the earlier Arab period. The horseshoe arch, suited best perhaps to low squat buildings and supported on the slenderest of pillars, both features so characteristic of Arab buildings, made no appeal to contemporary European architects with their desire for

SANCTUARY SCREEN AND LAMP OF THE MOSQUE OF SULTAN BARQUQ: *extra muros.*

(*From* L'Art Arabe, *Presse d'Avennes*)

perpendicular forms. The Moslem architects paid the penalty for their too-slender supports by having to fortify them with straight timber rods extending from column to column—to us an eyesore even in some of their most famous monuments.

Bright and garish decoration, a characteristic of Moslem architecture in Africa and Spain as well as in Asia, is of Perso-Mesopotamian ancestry. It sprang from the need of a mantle for inferior surfaces of naked brick and timber. Mosques everywhere, the mosque of the Dome of the Rock in Jerusalem, as well as the Mosques of Ali at Najaf and Husain in Kerbela, are thus clothed in a luxurious Persian dress. In Jerusalem, for instance, the dome is covered with glazed tiles, the substructure of glass mosaics, edged with dados of marble with windows of coloured glass or filled with intricate traceries; elsewhere domes are often completely covered with gold. For devices so splendid the crafts of wood carver and metalworker, of workers in plaster, mosaics and marble, makers of glazed earthenware and tilers must have been at a high degree of perfection, indeed one that has perhaps never been surpassed.

In the matter of decorative design the craftsmen, forbidden by religion to copy naturalistic forms, were driven to seek expression in other channels. Thus came a prolific invention of new patterns, at first geometrical, later in floral traceries, patterns of great intricacy, delicacy and charm which were used in stucco, in glazed tiles in mosaics, in wood and metal and every other medium. This ornamentation gave its most characteristic imprint to the Moslem minor arts. By its name, 'arabesque', it is most familiar to us. The Arabic character, an exquisite ornament in itself, susceptible of angular *Kufic* and other variation, was another favourite design. The craftsmen of medieval Europe flatteringly imitated it and so came unwittingly to adorn the coin of a Christian king and the cross of a Christian country with a characteristic Islamic text from the Qur'an.

Persian influences continued to survive in Egyptian architecture under the Fatimids even after the Abbasid yoke had been thrown off. One of the great monuments of the period, the Al Azhar Mosque, famous today as the Theological University of Cairo, shows this with its tiled bands of Kufic inscriptions round the minaret, gilded bands of stucco inscriptions in the interior and pierced arabesques in the stone grills of the window openings. But when a Kurdish dynasty succeeded and the Seljuq invasion of Asia Minor drove stone-building craftsmen, both Christians and Moslems, to take refuge in Egypt, there was a gradual creeping back to the ancient stone tradition.

Two new mosque forms were thence to appear, the theological school mosque and the tomb mosque. In the tomb mosques the façade came to undergo architectural treatment; stone entrances in the form of giant archways were recessed in the walls, the roof of these being beautifully shaped in corbelled stonework. While in the school mosque the old flat roof on rafters gave place to the vaulted roof of stone ancestry. This school-mosque innovation, associated with the short-lived dynasty founded by the famous Saladin, was intended to teach Sunni rites and to purge Egypt of the Shi'a tenets of its late Fatimid rulers. The visitor to Morocco will doubtless also recall the famous *madarsas* of Fez and Marakkesh. The long axis of the building was now aligned differently, the shrine being subordinated to the courtyard, around which students' cells were placed, and another feature, the barrel vault of the school mosque, came henceforth to be associated in Islam with education.

Under the next dynasty Egypt came to build entirely in stone, turning the ornamental designs of the brick-and-plaster traditions of the Persians into the new medium. It was this age—when for two hundred and fifty years Egypt was ruled by the slave dynasty of Mamlukes of Turkish and Circassian blood—that oddly enough constitutes her age of greatest architectural splendour. The final expulsion of the crusaders, who for centuries had driven a wedge between Egypt and Asia Minor, brought the Mamlukes into touch both with the Christian architecture of Palestine and Syria and with Seljuq architecture beyond, where the splendid stone-building traditions of Armenians and Byzantines survived. And this, together with the great wealth which the Mamlukes derived from the control of all trade between Europe and the East—for the Cape of Good Hope route had not yet been discovered—provided the means of raising in Cairo (A.D. 1250–1500) a series of monuments which, according to the brilliant analysis of a great authority,[22*] is unsurpassed in Moslem architecture. The glory of Cairo came to an end with its conquest by the Turks, and hence an army of medieval craftsmen turned for a livelihood, as by Islamic precedent, to the new court that had arisen—Constantinople.

In Palestine and Syria the crusades brought the building of fine mosques to a complete standstill. From the end of the ninth to the end of the twelfth century military architecture monopolized the scene, the only notable exception being the reconstruction of the mosque of the Dome of the Rock in Jerusalem, a work of the tenth century. But defensive walls and solid fortresses kept the masons fully occupied, especially during those next two centuries when the Holy Land was being overrun by Christian invaders from the West.

If the Frankish builders, brought by the crusaders, made contributions in the form of churches and military works, they also learned a good deal from the monuments of the Saracens, and they carried back novel ideas and practices to Europe. One such feature was machicolation. The *machicoulis* consisted of a platform projecting out high in the wall of a fortress or city rampart in which was a trapdoor through which boiling oil or arrows could be dropped on an enemy. This somewhat inhospitable device seems first to have appeared in a gateway tower of the city walls of Cairo, when constructed anew of stone, by the famous Armenian general, Badr al Jumali (eleventh century), but it was too neat and effective a feature to be missed by the crusaders and soon was to make its appearance in the medieval architecture of Winchester and Norwich, where it survives to this day. Another borrowing found in our medieval castles is the crooked entrance inside the gateway, designed to curb the attackers' onslaught when they had gained the gate, a feature the visitor to the citadel of Aleppo (ascribed largely to Saladin) will have seen the prototype of and the visitor to the Alhambra at Granada may recall.

Domestic architecture during the Arab period, judged by its relics, does not seem to have been particularly noteworthy. The first Arab camps of Kufa and Basrah had been made of reeds, probably a collection of local *madhifs,* a thatched tunnel of hayrick-like proportions such as are met with nowadays as guesthouses among the marsh Arabs of the lower Euphrates. But later peacetime generations of Arabs soon took to the manner of living of their better-housed urban subjects. The second Abbasid caliph, in A.D. 762, founded the capital city of Baghdad, a city of yellow brick, which grew to be one of the most splendid metropolises of the world and remained so for nearly five hundred years till the Mongols came and utterly destroyed it. Mesopotamian domestic architecture was naturally Asiatic in feeling, whereas the houses of Syrian and Egyptian Arabs were of east Mediterranean type. But rich men in the spacious days of the Abbasids in Mesopotomia, the Fatimids and Mamlukes in Egypt and the Umaiyyads in Spain built palaces for themselves which developed common features.

The typical Moslem house of the more pretentious sort was built round double courtyards, the outer a public one where only men foregathered during the day, the inner a private one reserved for domestic life. In origin this arrangement is thought to have been Persian and to have been introduced into Egypt during Abbasid times when Persian influence was paramount and Cairo went in for Persian fashions. But if the prototype of this house is found in old Sassanian palaces it was a design eminently suited to the social organization of the times with its segregation of women. The women's part of the house was devoid of windows in the exterior walls, thus screening them from outside attention. Their windows opened on to the interior courtyard and even then must be filled with lattice woodwork or plaster or metal grills to ensure a maximum of privacy. In the decoration of the house glazed coloured tiles in bright designs were a favourite feature, as they still are in Persia and Spain, for facing the fronts of houses, garden seats and fountains and for paving courtyards. The Moorish palace of Alhambra, one of the few remaining worthy monuments of the Moslem era in Spain, but a very precious one, preserves in grandiose form some of the elements of the domestic architecture of the Arabs: the severe, unimpressive exterior, the lavishly ornate interiors, open tiled courtyards enclosed by arcading carried on slender columns, walls in exquisite stucco panelling, timbered ceilings, carved, coloured and gilded, window openings filled with stone slabs of pierced traceries.

Offshoots of Moslem architecture are found today in such differing idiom as that of the National Spanish School and that of the palaces of many ruling princes in India. Regional influences have naturally brought about variation in a school of architecture that has persisted for a thousand years and well-nigh half encircled the globe. In India the glorious Taj Mahal has closer affinities with Persia than with Egypt and yet is different from both; in Turkey the influences are largely Armenian and Byzantine; in Morocco and Spain the two glorious square minarets, the Giraldo Tower of Seville and the Qasbah of Rabat, are obviously close kindred, as are cusped and horseshoe arches. Thus comes about the fivefold Saracenic building forms—Syro-Egyptian, Hispano-Moresque, Persian, Ottoman and Indo-Saracenic.

As regards the minor arts of the Arab period, these, in a large measure, were linked up with fine architecture, so that the early indifference of the first Arabs was a phase that quickly passed. Within a generation of the conquests a kingly court of Damascus, as we have seen, had risen to take the place of the simple dwellings of the Medina caliphs; a century more, and the palaces of Baghdad had as greatly excelled the courts of Damascus. Thence an affluent leisured class of Arabs grew up with a taste for the ancient refinements of their un-Arabian surroundings. A 'court art' was already in being before the Dasmascus caliphate decayed, and luxurious banqueting vessels and rich textile furnishings had come to be regarded with a friendly and tolerant eye.

But it was the removal of the seat of government from Arab Damascus to Persian Baghdad, in the second century after the Prophet, that marked the establishment of a real tradition. Moslems henceforth adopted the luxury of the Sassanian inheritance and delighted in exquisitely wrought gold and silver plates, vessels of bronze and brass and copper inlaid with precious metals, painted pottery, sumptuous silks and brocades, carved and painted ivories, inscribed manuscripts with water-colour miniatures and the like. The Arabs had embarked upon a new and great adventure, which the puritans among them must have regarded a little dubiously, for they were shaping a course close hauled to the winds of early orthodoxy. The inspiration for that adventure came from the Persians, for the Persians were a nation of artists as the Arabs had been a nation of warriors.

Carpet weaving, a cottage handicraft among the Persians, was to attain world eminence. Beautiful examples of the art came in time to be made for the great mosques. There, their colours mellowed with age, and their smooth sensuous quality was enhanced by the naked feet of multitudinous worshippers. In the diwans of the well-to-do the walls were hung with carpets of shimmering silk, infinitely various in colour and design, though carpets of wool served the commonest ends as floor coverings; there were tiny prayer rugs, too, that were drawn out of their closets and unrolled five times a day, these more chaste and sober, as suited their sacred purpose.

Among the minor arts that Europe came earliest to admire, perhaps, was the metalwork of the Moslems. Luristan, with its mysterious bronzes, must have enjoyed ancient fame, the Mosul school, too, shaped by Armenian and Persian influences, had flourished from very early times. It continued to prosper under the Arabs until the Mongolian invasion scattered its craftsmen westwards and led to the promotion of a school at Damascus and an Egyptian revival at Cairo. The most characteristic product of these schools was an inlay work of gold and silver in brass or bronze, a process which Europe learned late from Damascus and chose to remember as 'damascening.' Domestic utensils of the house of the Arab period, such as vases, candlesticks, writing boxes, were commonly made in this work. The common metal had first to be cast to the shape; it was then incised with delicate traceries of floral designs, geometrical arabesques, possibly a familiar couplet in ornate Arabic lettering, and these were filled in with black mastic and a thread of the precious metal. Metal enamelling with colours, however, such as the cloisonné work of the Chinese, was not a Moslem handicraft. Schools did spring up later both in India and Spain, but too late in the day to be regarded as traditional Moslem art. Spain, however, like Egypt, shared in all the other Moslem arts: the swordmakers of Toledo were famous, and goldsmiths and silversmiths enjoyed European renown in the Middle Ages; even today the designs of earrings and suchlike jewelry in gold filigree seen in the Spanish shopwindows are strongly suggestive of oriental affinities.

If enamelling on metal found no favour in the Arab period, enamelling on glass had been an old industry both in Syria and Mesopotamia, and beautiful specimens continued to be made throughout Islamic times.[1] A notable

[1]Glass mirrors, too, are thought to have found their way into Europe from the Arab East.

MOSLEM MINOR ARTS: GLASS LAMP OF FOURTEENTH CENTURY, IN THE MAUSOLEUM OF TAKI–UD–DIN.

(By courtesy of the British Museum)

use was in the giant hanging lamps of the mosques. These hung on massive chains from the ceiling, candelabralike, a circle of coloured bowls, faintly illumined from within, which gave to the sanctuary its dim religious light. Bottles and beakers were other popular forms of enamelled glassware. The Moslem nobility were accustomed to emblazon their heraldic arms in coloured enamels on these. 'Their use of such figures influenced the development of Western heraldry which, during the crusades, evolved into a systematic science with a peculiar nomenclature of its own. In this the technical term for blue, *azure,* is derived from the Persian word denoting the blue stone called lapis lazuli. There are other interesting links between European and oriental heraldry, such as that curious figure the double-headed eagle, which makes its first appearance in remote antiquity on Hittite monuments. It became the badge of the Seljuq Sultans early in the twelfth century, and in the fourteenth was adopted as the blazon of the Holy Roman Emperors.'[12]*

Painted earthenware and pottery were other crafts, long famous in Egypt and Persia, that underwent their own Islamic development. Centres sprang up from end to end of the Arab conquests, devoted especially to tile-making to satisfy the demands of religious and domestic architecture. Beautiful faience appeared, too, an elegant floral design making Damascus work celebrated, though Persian work, in which draughtsmanship and colouring reached their highest excellence, was still more famous. The realistic representations of tulips, lilac and other flowers on Persian pottery is said to have been the means of their introduction into Europe. Rayy was the famous ceramics centre in Persia, the home perhaps of that exquisite vase handle, in the form of gold-winged ibex, familiar to European students. Rayy made famous wares in blue, green, red, brown and purple, until the Mongols came in the thirteenth century and destroyed it.

One of the most widespread forms of Moslem pottery was lustreware with its shimmering quality of gold lustre that came from a process of painting a metal salt on a glaze and firing in smoke. It is still made in southern Spain and, although not to everybody's liking in these times of severer taste, enjoys local favour. Blue-and-white pottery and porcelain, such as Europe later drew from China, was being imported from the same source by the Abbasid Arabs in the ninth century; indeed, the characteristic cobalt colour, known as muhammadan blue, is thought to have been of Persian origin and to have been copied by the Chinese orginally for the Arab market. Faience in perfect taste, objets d'art such as lapis lazuli jars beautifully inscribed, silver- and gold-encrusted bronze vessels and the like, found in museums today, give some indication of the taste in domestic furnishings of the wealthy under the Arabs.

The divine disapproval of the wearing of silk—a taboo still faithfully observed by the Wahhabis of Arabia—was beyond the endurance of the non-Arabian Arabs cradled in the lands of the conquests. Indeed they became the great silk mercers of the Middle Ages. Beautifully woven silk fabrics, such as had been sought after by Roman emperors, and rich brocades—for the textile arts of Byzantines and Persians were at a high pitch of excellence at the time of the Arab invasion—continued to be made in new Islamic designs.

Europe, in later times, when oriental trade came to flourish, became an enthusiastic purchaser of these fabrics, at once technically and artistically perfect. Even chasubles and other church vestments and canopies for Christian altars were commonly made of them. The tombs in the larger mosques were draped, too, with these exquisitely woven coverings of coloured silk and gold. Spanish silk shawls with designs suggestive of Chinese influence enjoyed a vogue which has not disappeared to this day, and Persian designs were similarly much earlier affected. Not only did silk in the first place come from China—and the caravan route between China and Persia existed from early times—but the Mongolian conquests of China and of Persia in the twelfth to thirteenth centuries (towards the close of the Arab period) established kindred hegemonies across Asia and so greatly facilitated trade and cultural influences from end to end of the Continent.

Chinese motifs were woven into silk fabrics by the Moslem weavers, side by side with their own, so that exotic birds and beasts and figures enjoyed popularity at times when orthodoxies were relaxed and perhaps at all times with the non-Moslem elements of the population; for tradition was too deeply rooted, human inclinations too strong to prevent it, and despite religious discouragement the human and animal figure never utterly disappeared from Persian works of art. When we read of the gold throne of an Egyptian Fatimid caliph, of carved trees set with precious stones and hoards of other art treasures, it clearly testifies to the mundane taste of the Shi'a elect as well as to their wealth.

At a time when the courts of Baghdad, Cairo and Cordova were resplendent with unparalleled collections of art treasures, Europe, in her Dark Ages, was deficient in such arts as these. Specimens which formed presents from Moslem caliph to Christian monarch (tradition makes Harun al Rashid send presents to Charlemagne), objets d'art brought back by travellers to the Orient and novelties that appeared from trade contacts following the crusades were soon to minister to Europe's growing inspiration. Oriental canons came to be studied, oriental technique to be adopted. Spain and Sicily, where Latins and Moslems lived side by side, were natural contact points by which Moslem arts became known, but it was the port of Venice, as the flourishing port of crusade times and after and the home of rich and enterprising merchant princes, that became the gateway by which they were introduced.

The Italian aristocracy had already acquired a taste for Moslem arts, and oriental craftsmen and oriental guilds were soon installed in Venice. Italian workmen were the first in Europe to learn from Persian carpetmakers how to make pile carpets, learn inlaid metalwork and Moslem ceramics from Persian and Egyptian craftsmen and to master the art of weaving precious silks on a loom of Moslem origin introduced from Sicily. From Venice these arts and crafts passed into pre-Renaissance Europe.

As with architecture and the lesser arts, so with music, the original Arabs could only have been familiar with forms of a very rudimentary kind. Swarming out of Arabia, they immediately came into contact with the more developed music of Byzantines and Persians. A century and a half later the translation of Greek musical theorists, adapted to the taste of the leisured and artistic class that was growing up in Abbasid times, created an Arab musical tradition.

In the deserts we may suppose the Arabs, like the Beduin of today, to have possessed a full repertory of camel chants and not much else. These they sang lustily as they went about special occasions, much as our sailors of another day used their sea chanteys; the loading up of camels, the march, the trot, the halt over a water hole —each had its appropriate chant shouted in unison to familiar words endlessly iterated.[2] Of instrumental music they had none, unless it was a crude shepherd's pipe made from the horn of an antelope, and near the settlements a drum and perhaps an instrument of a rudimentary fiddle-banjo kind, strung chiefly with animal gut. But simple vocal music was their stand-by, and poetry, which they loved, was doubtless often intoned to some simple chant.

To the original militant zealots of Islam music was associated with impiety and levity and was therefore to be frowned on, as it is to this day by the very orthodox among peninsular Arabian communities, among whom drums are suspect as instruments of Satan, and no decent girl with a thought for her good name would dare to sing aloud. As with other arts, so with music, a sharp line divided the Arabs of Arabia from the Arabs of the conquests. Arab music belongs to the latter, both in time and place.

The Umaiyyad Arabs in the early part of the eighth century favoured a musical mode based on the Pythagorean scale, the scale at that time in use in Europe, where it was, of course, an inheritance of the Greeks but was here coloured by both Persian and Byzantine influences; and this continued in common use in Islam for five centuries to come, till it was superseded by the quarter-tone scale which is the one found throughout the East to this day.

Arab music was essentially different from the music to which our modern ears are accustomed. Melody, not harmony, was its chief feature. It was rudimentary—a horizontal one-dimensional music incapable of the struc-

[2] I have set down in European musical notation, not a very satisfactory medium, all those I heard in Arabia. See *Arabia Felix.*[36]*

tural developments of our vertical, as well as horizontal, form. Its 'gloss' was a sterile substitute for harmony, without which there was no room for that development through which European music grew and still grows more complex. Development in the Arab mode lay through subtle intricacies of melody within the fractional intervals of their scale. These melodies they wailed in what to us would be a very coarse quality of voice, and, judging from the progeny which they have begotten and which issue brazenly forth from gramophones of an Arab bazaar, it would have been extremely melancholic and unpleasant to our ears. Harmonization in vocal music was unknown and in instrumental music restricted to an occasional intrusion of an undertone making some simple interval—an octave, a fourth or a fifth. A strongly marked rhythm, however, was a feature, deriving doubtless from an ancestry of poetical setting, for Arabic is a stressed and rhythmical language.

Songs came to have instrumental accompaniment of lute, psaltery, tambourine and drum, and though musical notation was known early in the ninth century most musicians played by ear. Caliphial palaces had their staff of court musicians, male and female (the male singers often evirate, doubtless owing to the popularity of the boy's voice), while wealthy notables kept also their singing and dancing girls, recruited doubtless from Jewesses and Christians and other suchlike unveiled and low-class grades of society, as has been the way down to recent times. The 'party' of the age took the form of a gathering of men, at the invitation of one of them, in his cool open courtyard. There, after the evening meal, the guests formed an intimate circle. The singing and dancing girls sitting in a row, came, one at a time, tripping into their midst, the scene lit up by lanterns. Here by their wheedling arts they soothed or charmed or excited, the audience now and again moved to an occasional loud sigh as by some note or gesture an emotional impulse was stirred. Sargent's famous picture, "El Jaleo" (in the Isabella Stewart Gardner Museum at Boston), depicting a Spanish girl dancing with castanets, backed by a row of squatting male musicians sweeping the strings of their lutes, is doubtless a fair representation of its begetter—the scene of the chamber music most popular in the Arab period.

If the puritans condemned music as a lure of the devil, the mystics, more often, of course, Persians than Arabs, regarded music approvingly as a means of revelation through ecstasy.[3] As the *Arabian Nights* has it: 'To some people music is meat, and to others medicine.' 'This conceit,' says Dr Farmer, 'grew out of the doctrine of the "influence of music", which, with the belief in the principles of the *ethos*, the harmony of the spheres, and the theory of numbers, attracted unusual attention. This doctrine of musical therapeutics had a fairly wide acceptance!'[14]*

The musical theorists and devotees, generally mathematicians,[4] carried Arab musical theory in the eastern caliphate a step beyond the point at which the Greeks had left it, and in its more advanced forms music naturally found its way across the Arab world to Spain. There it flourished throughout the half a millennium more of Moslem occupation to leave its mark to this day, as I was startlingly reminded when first hearing the humming of maids in an Andalusian household. Arab music came into Spain doubtless as the handmaiden of Arabic verse, and

[3]For a learned discourse on Islamic mysticism see Professor Nicholson's *The Idea of Personality in Sufism.*[82]*

[4]Notably al Kindi, Avicenna and most notably of all al Farabi.

from this seed sprang our strolling minstrelsy of the Middle Ages; indeed our word 'troubadour' may well derive from the Arabic word for minstrel. This class of artist affecting painted faces, gaudy costume and long hair under a cap with jingling bells, a tabor in one hand, a pipe in the other, disseminated the practice of music through medieval Europe. They gave us, too, our Morris dancers, a verbal corruption of Moorish dancers.

Europe had also its intellectual contacts with Arab music when wandering scholars went to Spain in the twelfth century to acquire the new learning, but in this there was small profit, for very little of the Arabic literature on music, in contrast to that on philosophy and science, seems to have been translated into Latin or Hebrew. The troubadour was a better advertising medium than the theorist, and he brought into Europe the lute, the guitar and a one-stringed fiddle said to have been a favourite of the poet Chaucer. Seville was the centre of the manufacture of such instruments. Those most favoured by the Arabs were of the string or percussion sort, such as lutes (of which the mandolin was one), guitars, harps, psalteries and dulcimers; cymbals, castanets, drums and tambourines, the last named sometimes square and 'unsalvationist' in shape. Reed and metal wind instruments were also made and, not improbably, the first harmoniums. The earlier European stringed instruments, such as zithers and harps, had been tuned by ear, but the finger boards of the Arab instruments were mathematically marked by frets (Arabic =*fard*) and it is supposed that to the fretting of the Arabian lute European music may have owed the major mode. Mensural or measured music seems, however, to have been the greatest contribution that the Arabs made to the art.

The musical literature of the Arabs records some famous names of both composers and theorists, but in Spain, as in Baghdad, much of it is work of religious jurists and devoted to the issue whether music is permissible according to religion or not. The argument had already been won by the 'antis' in the East in the thirteenth century, after which time no great composer appeared. In Spain, however, Arab music flourished for a century longer, though its greatest exponent, Avempace, belonged to the tenth century.

But in Islam music was, clearly, always under suspicion. And thus, whereas in the West, Christianity was later to inspire some of the immortal masterpieces of Handel, Bach, Brahms and the rest, the religious system of the Arabs so discouraged the musical art that their music remains, by European standards, a crude thing indeed. Certainly such encouragement as it enjoyed brought no comparable development, and this may well have been because music was never permitted in the mosques to become a medium of divine worship.

CHAPTER VII

Arab Civilization: The Sciences

Civilizations, like individuals, spring from two parents, and in all civilizations we can trace, the heritage from the Civilized Mother has been more important than that from the barbarian who violated her.[26*] ARNOLD TOYNBEE.

OUR MIDDLE AGES rang with the fame of the Arab sciences, an interesting thought when we remember that but a century or two earlier the Arabs had not yet emerged from an agelong desert obscurantism. The Arab sciences were, of course, a flower of the Arab world outside Arabia. They owed neither seed nor soil to the Arabian peninsula. Religion, language, social system—all these elements of Moslem civilization were of peninsular origin; not, however, the arts and sciences. Still, it was in the Arabic tongue that the scientists and the philosophers of the age wrote, irrespective of their nationality. Arabic was, as it were, a torch, no sooner lighted in a corner of the eastern caliphate than beacons flared across the new Islamic world, whose radiance Christian Europe called Arab.

The evolution from the conquering Arab raider to imperial ruler, the change from penury to affluence, from tents of hair to palaces of marble, was the miracle of little more than a hundred years. The revolution that the Arabs stood for stirred the world to its depths. Racial and religious loyalties were soon in the melting pot. The world became convulsed with intellectual unrest, ancient philosophies and sciences were haled forth and rejuvenated, and out of it all grew the civilization which the Middle Ages knew and bequeathed as Arab civilization.

The seed of the new learning was the legacy of Hellenism, the soil was first and foremost ancient Persia, but the stimulus that quickened life and induced the first vigorous growth came from the religion of the Arabs. They burst in upon societies intellectually more advanced than themselves and possessing developed religious systems that had come under the influence of Greek philosophic thought; they soon had to look to their laurels. In the early days of the conquests the Arabs could listen to that strong inner voice that assured them possession of a God-revealed and utterly true religion, based on a book that was not man made but a revelation of the eternal verities. Erelong they heard many voices, the most insistent, perhaps, that of foreign learning. They had come armed with a religion at once authoritative and satisfying, one which, moreover, bore all the recent marks of divine blessing. Worldly wisdom must have seemed to the religious zealot either heretical or unnecessary. When philosophical speculation first came to dawn on their intelligences the narrowly orthodox doubtless felt antagonism for it as so much dubious foreign wisdom. For them, as yet, Allah's revelations, through Muhammad, were enough. Time was to shatter their sufficiency. As the first century wore on and they acquired a wider knowledge of the universe, as they came into contact with other systems, religious and pagan, and with men who continued to live under them, men who intellectually were their superiors or, at least, admittedly not less rational than themselves, and yet could not accept the Islamic faith despite the inducements of escape from taxation and social disabilities, the conviction that Islam embraced all knowledge worth knowing met with a serious challenge.

Now these rapidly changing Arabs of the outside Arab world were, for their times, not religious bigots; there was room outside the circle of narrow orthodoxy, especially in a world as yet predominantly non-Moslem, for men resolved to pursue knowledge wherever found. Was there not warranty, indeed, in abundance in the Qur'an itself and in the Traditions, which besought men to search for knowledge? Why should there be apprehension lest 'foreign science' should upset divine truth—how could it? Rather the tokens and wonders of creation would be all the more manifest, the Omnipotent proclaimed, the faith vindicated. It is due to the enlightenment of some of the early Abbasid caliphs of Baghdad, notably Mansur and Ma'mun, that official Islam, cast off from the moorings of narrow and intolerant orthodoxies, was swung into the wide stream of classical learning.

Religious arguments between the rival imams of Islam and the leaders of other faiths doubtless early took place around the familiar issues, of the nature of God and of the universe.

> *. . . and reason'd high*
> *Of providence, foreknowledge, will, and fate,*
> *Fix'd fate, free-will, foreknowledge absolute;*
> *And found no end, in wand'ring mazes lost.*[1]

Intellectually the classicists must have been at an advantage, and the Moslem doctors could only hope to confound or win them by demonstrating the rational basis of Islam in the terms of the ancient wisdom. This, it is sup-

[1]Milton, *Paradise Lost,* ii.

posed, was at the root of the new and eager study of Greek philosophy.

The intermediary between the ancient masters and the Moslem pupils was at the outset the Nestorian Church. It was this Christian sect, exiled in Persia, that first translated Aristotle into Arabic, and once translations had begun they did not cease for a century and a half, during which time nearly all the Greek literature in the natural sciences passed into the thought of scholars professing Islam. Hellenistic traditions had naturally survived in parts of the lands wrenched from the Byzantines, notably in Egypt, but the Greek spirit, curiously enough, had best been kept alive in Persia. There, in tolerant Sassanian times, the 'heretical' Nestorian Church had for some centuries found refuge. Old Hira, on the Euphrates, was the seat of a Nestorian bishop.

But the real centre of Greek learning was Jundeshapur, a city in southwest Persia. It had been so for a century before the Arab conquest and remained so during the century that followed. There a famous academy attracted wandering scholars of the East—a meeting ground for the learning of Greece, Persia and India. Scarcely less famous was its hospital which sent doctors successively to the courts of Damascus and Baghdad. Christian medicine enjoyed pre-eminent prestige in these centuries, and that medicine was founded largely on Greek medical science, that is to say, the works of Galen. Greek physicians, often Monophysite priests, when taken prisoner in the old Greco-Byzantine wars, had been well received in Persian court circles and their skill and knowledge put to use, so now, under the Baghdad caliphs the translation of Galen into Arabic early came to be desired and accomplished.

But it was not in Jundeshapur, the centre of Hellenistic

thought, not even in Baghdad, the new city of the caliphs, that Moslem scholarship first blazed forth. The great figures of the new learning sprang up in northeast Persia and beyond, in an area that embraced the provinces of Khorasan and Trans-Oxiana, familiar to us as Bactria and Turkestan—territory which today is in a very backward state. Here, not far from the borderlands of India, a land already at this time with a considerable scholastic tradition, the old Persian spirit lived on. But the new learning was not long to be confined there. The common Arabic tongue and the brotherhood of Islam rapidly diffused it across the Islamic world. Political disintegration—Spain and Egypt soon achieved independence—was no impediment to its spread from east to west, and from Spain the Arab sciences passed into Europe. It is this role of intermediary played by Spain that makes her contribution loom large in European eyes, but her greatest figures, most notable in medicine and philosophy, did not appear till the third century of Moslem occupation, so that in some ways the Spanish period was but a reflection of the earlier glory of the Moslem East.

To resume. The first century of the Arab period was not a time of great learning. It was a period of racio-political supremacy. The Arabs were too busy with their world conquest and their internal dynastic upheavals to concern themselves deeply with books. Doubtless the dawn of a coming glory was looming; indeed some Umaiyyad caliphs are thought to have had a taste for philosophical subjects, but the fact remains that we have no books in Arabic at all, except poetical diwans, from these Umaiyyad times. Such secular learning as existed in the caliphate would appear to have been an inheritance of the lettered classes among Christian, Sabian, Jewish and Persian communities and the Persianized-Arab aristocracy of Iraq.

The rise of the Abbasids, the change of the seat of government from Damascus to Baghdad and the accession to office and influence of those who cherished learning brought about the new era of scholastic splendour in the East. Philosophers, mathematicians, astronomers, medical scientists, scholars of world reputation in the science of the Greeks, passed in a continuous procession during the ninth, tenth and eleventh centuries across the stage of the eastern caliphate, lending it a glamour which is the pride of the Arabs to this day, and if few of its principal figures were men of wholly Arab blood[2] it is fair to remember that the Arabs formed but a small minority in their huge empire.

Before the coming of the Arabs scholars of Jundeshapur had known their Aristotle and their Galen as well as

[2]A list—by no means exhaustive—of some of the great names in Arab civilization with their respective origins is given by Baron Carra de Vaux[15]* as follows—

al Khwarizmi was a native of Khiva.
al Farghani of Trans-Oxiana.
Abu'l Wafa }
al Battani } were of Persian origin.
al Biruni }
al Kindi was of pure Arab stock.
Farabi was a Turk by origin.
Avicenna (Ibn Sina) hailed from near Balkh.
al Ghazali }
Nasir al Din } came from Tus in the east of Persia.
Omar Khayyam was a Persian.
Averroes (Ibn Rushd) }
Alpetragius (Al Bitruji) } were Arabs of Spain.
Arzachel (Al Zarkali) }
Non-Moslems {
Hunain bin Ishaq }
Ishaq bin Hunain } the translators were Christians.
Qusta bin Luqa }
Thabit bin Qurra }
al Battani } were Sabians.
Masha'allah was a Jew.

miscellaneous Indian masters, these having been long ago translated into Syriac, the language of the Nestorian Church, and to some extent into Pahlevi, the contemporary language of Persia. The earliest translations of the Greek learning under the encouragement of the caliph-founder of Baghdad were thus made into Arabic from Syriac. With the extension of the fields of knowledge under succeeding caliphs translations at Jundeshapur came to be made, however, direct from the Greek, the movement reaching its greatest activity half a century or so later.

The Caliph Ma'mun, under whom this took place, held a view—the first caliph ever to have done so—that the Qur'an had been created in time, in opposition to the orthodox tenet that it was eternal before all worlds, co-existent with God, so that he took a long step forward towards giving a caliphial blessing, as it were, to the validity of reason in matters of faith. A school of liberal theologians had already sprung up in Iraq, antagonistic to those bigots who condemned the new learning as being inconsistent with the Qur'an and the Traditions, and who preferred to occupy themselves with such issues as whether horseflesh did or did not come under the religious taboo. Two movements were thus active. On the one hand the intellectuals were devoting themselves to the Greek sciences, which indeed were becoming their overmastering passion; truth must be pursued for its own sake and traditional beliefs modified where they were not reconcilable with scientific fact; on the other hand the religious leaders of the many bemoaned the heresy or even atheism to which the love of pagan wisdom must lead. It thus came about that under the enlightened ægis of the early Baghdad caliphs an unfettered spirit of inquiry existed side by side with narrow dogmatism.

A great library in Baghdad called the House of Wisdom was founded by the Caliph Ma'mun, an example to be followed a century and a half later by a Fatimid caliph of Cairo. The grandees of the court vied with each other in collecting books, and every mosque of the times was encouraged to do the same. A school of translation was established in Baghdad at the same time, Hunain ibn Ishaq, at once a great Christian physician and the most brilliant and prolific of the translators, being appointed to direct it. The remaining scholars and physicians of Jundeshapur were transferred to the courts at Baghdad and Samarra under the Caliph Mutawakkil, and hence its own famous academy and hospital fell into decay.

The new library of Baghdad now enjoyed even more munificent royal patronage; staffs of translators, most of them Christians and Sabians, who, as yet, alone had the scholarship, were sent to Alexandria and other ancient libraries of the Near and Middle East to hunt out old Greek manuscripts and bring them back to Baghdad for translation. Thus before the ninth century had run its course not only Galen and Aristotle, but Plato's political works, and the geographical, mathematical and astronomical works of Ptolemy, Euclid and Archimedes had all been turned into Arabic. It is curious that classical poetry, classical drama and Greek history should have been passed by. But no translation of them was made, and so the Arabs missed the more intimate touch with the inner spirit of the Greeks. Whether this neglect is to be put down to utilitarianism or not, the Arabs were doubtless by nature realists and attached importance chiefly to knowledge that served practical ends—medicine, mechanics, geography, arithmetic.

One of the greatest tools of civilization which we owe

to the Arab period is the zero—the foundation stone on which all our arithmetic and mathematics rest—and our everyday numeral system. These are almost certainly an Indian invention and are, in fact, called Indian by the Arabs themselves. The other peoples of antiquity, including even the Greeks, had no numbers; they used the letters of the alphabet in their order as numerals. Our earliest trace of numbers is found in the Arabic works of the tenth century. Numbers 1 to 5 are represented by a corresponding number of strokes ligatured; 6 to 9 by simple conventional signs; the nought by a dot or a circle, thus:

1	2	3	4	5	6	7	8	9	0
١	٢	٣	٤	٥	٦	٧	٨	٩	٠

The introduction of the nought or zero—the Arabic word is *sifr, f*rom which our word 'cipher' may ultimately derive—simplified and revolutionized arithmetic. It had previously been necessary to keep separate columns for units, tens, hundreds, etc.—the abacus system still met with in shops in China. But the introduction of the nought allowed figures to be kept in a row, in the series of units, tens, hundreds, etc., familiar to us and so did away with the need for a separate column for each. This discovery, under the name 'algorism', found its way into Europe in the twelfth century, after having been current among the Arabs for two hundred and fifty years. Such terms as 'algorism', 'cipher' and 'algebra' bear witness to the part played by the Arabs in our systems of calculation.[15]*

The algebraists under the Arabs made advances on the knowledge of the Greeks. The works on the solution of cubic equations by Omar Khayyam is held in high estimation, and Omar was no mean astronomer, too, though we prefer to think of him in his minor role of poet. Measurements on plane and spherical surfaces were developed quite early in the Arab period, the greatest geometer of all being a Sabian named Thabit bin Qurra, who improved on Euclid's *Elements,* who translated into Arabic seven of the eight books on conic sections of Apollonius and wrote the earliest known work on the sundial. Trigonometry owes the discovery of the secant to Abu'l Wafa, though it is sometimes attributed to Copernicus; trigonometrical ratios, as we use them today, were the remarkable discovery of the unbeliever, al Battani, while logarithms came within an ace of discovery by al Farabi in his work on musical intervals. Infinite quantities were dealt with by the great Avicenna among others; measurements were made of equilibrium and specific gravity, al Kindi already experimenting in the ninth century with the object of discovering the laws governing a falling body.

In mechanics astronomical instruments were of major importance. New forms of astrolabes, improvements on Ptolemy's, were invented both in the East and the West. For land purposes they were generally designed for a particular latitude and served to find the position of Mecca and so the direction of prayer; while at sea their use for navigational purposes continued down to the seventeenth century. Spanish astronomers devoted attention to the construction of armillary or celestial spheres, making them as big as possible to minimize error. In major engineering the Abbasid times produced extensive canalization of Tigris and Euphrates for irrigation purposes; a tradition is also cherished by the Arabs that one of the caliphs planned to make the Suez Canal and was only prevented by the danger it entailed to the holy places at the time of the crusades.

The Arabs were particularly well placed to make contributions to geography. The pilgrimage to Mecca early led to the compilation of books that set forth the journeys to the holy cities from the uttermost ends of the Islamic world and gave detailed descriptions and names of cities and villages en route and the distances of the various stages.

The early Arabs conceived of the world as disc shaped, its interior a land mass of which Arabia was the centre; without was an encircling ocean having two deep intruding arms—presumably the Indian Ocean and the Mediterranean. They do not appear to have had any geography in a scientific sense till the translation of Ptolemy, and this led, among the scholars at any rate, to an acceptance of Greek conceptions. By the end of the tenth century their geographical knowledge had far outgrown that of contemporary Europe, and if their maps of the Mediterranean represent it as a circular or elliptical shape, this doubtless was a cartographical convention of the times, for they knew better from Ptolemy's maps.[16]* Ptolemy's methods, which they used as their model, had been scientific. He used parallels of latitude and parallels of longitude, as in a Mercator's projection, the former based on the equator, the latter measured from the westernmost meridian then known, the Island of Ferrol. He plotted his point of latitude and longitude from data obtained by the rough methods of his day—the logs of sea captains, the diaries of army officers home from campaigns, distances obtained by dead reckoning and other data such as the duration of the hours of daylight and the times of the rising and setting of heavenly bodies.

The Arab astronomers, al Farghani, al Battani and al Biruni, were soon producing their own tables of latitudes and longitudes. But astronomers and geographers at first worked independently. The land mass of the world had been conceived of as divided by the equator into a habitable northern part and an uninhabited southern part. The habitable part was further divided into seven climes, a series of parallel zones running east to west and lying one beyond the other northwards, diminishing in extent as they went. A literary geographical school sprang up in the tenth century. One of its luminaries, al Mas'udi (he was a widely travelled author who had visited China but possessed little astronomical knowledge), held the opinion that all cities in one clime must necessarily be in the same latitude. But Idrisi, who followed him, co-ordinated the scientific with the descriptive aspects of the science. The Norman king of Sicily commissioned this brilliant geographer to write a geographical description of the world—an interesting light on how Europe regarded Moslem scholarship. Voluminous writings of travellers (one of the most important was Ibn Batuta, a Moor who had visited Ceylon and Africa as well as every part of the Islamic world) were inspired perhaps by the earlier encyclopaedic works of Abu'l Fida and Yaqut, the latter a particularly notable contribution to knowledge.

The Arabs had a great sea tradition, too, particularly in the East, which is reflected in the popularity of sea literature at the time, and of which we get a glimmering in the voyages of Sindbad the Sailor in the *Arabian Nights*. It was indeed an Arab mariner named Ibn Majid who is believed to have piloted the Portuguese explorer, Vasco da Gama, on his historical voyage of discovery around the Cape of Good Hope (A.D. 1492), thus opening the ocean way to India, and a legend makes Ibn Majid the actual inventor of the mariner's compass. That the compass was in some way an Arab contribution is logically within the tradition, but the compass was already known in France and Italy, and Majid's own ascription of it to King David, the great ironmaster of antiquity—in which role I have many times heard of him from Arab Beduin—suggests a much earlier knowledge of the compass. The Chinese indeed claim to have used it continuously from the second century, and this may suggest that Arab mariners introduced it to the West from their Far Eastern voyages.

It was Arabian astronomy, however, rather than Arabian geography, that exercised an enduring influence on European thought. Although we owed much of our earliest specialized knowledge of Eastern countries to the geographers their half knowledge and rudimentary map making came in time to be superseded and the debt due to their pioneer contributions forgotten or underestimated. To the Moslem astronomer is due the credit of accepting the roundness of the earth, however unenthusiastically, at a time when it was as yet too big a pill for Europe to swallow. Accompanying the conception of the earth as a sphere was a curious theory that somewhere in the centre of one hemisphere was a summit, 'the cupola of Arin,' and Christopher Columbus three hundred years later held the quest-provoking belief that in the opposite hemisphere, the Antipodes of Arin, must be another and still more elevated summit, giving to the earth a pear-shaped form. 'It is highly probable,' says Kramers,[16]* 'that it induced Dante, whose indebtedness to Muhammadan traditions has been established in many respects, to localize his *Purgatorio,* in the shape of a mountain, in the western hemisphere, by combining with it, in an ingenious way, the ancient Christian belief that the terrestrial Paradise was situated in the extreme east of the world, behind the sea.'

As did the Hebrew scriptures, the original Arabs had doubtless conceived of our earth being the hub of the universe. Within two centuries of the conquests Moslem scholars had accepted the Ptolemaic conception. In the tenth century they speak of the planets—of which they regarded the sun and the moon as two—each with its hollow concentric sky; the outer sky of all contained the fixed stars and turned round and round like a water wheel on two pivots, or celestial poles, thus keeping the inner skies of the planets revolving in their several motions. Two centuries earlier a Hindu astronomer brought to the new court at Baghdad an Indian work on astronomy which was soon translated, and the astronomical tables of the Caliph Ma'mun, who set up an observatory at Baghdad fifty years later, were prepared according to the Indian method. At this observatory the great Thabit took altitudes of the sun to discover the length of the solar year, and his fellow Sabian, Battani—the astronomer most admired during our Renaissance period—calculated the first appearance of the moon, the inclination of the ecliptic, the length of the tropic and sidereal year, and parallaxes.

The passion for astronomy spread to Spain, where, in the eleventh and twelfth centuries, it flourished exceedingly, the Spanish school calculating its longitudes in relation to the meridian of Toledo. Al Bitruji (Alpetragius) in the twelfth century was developing his own original views on planetary movements. He boldly criticized the complexity of Ptolemy's theories and looked for a simpler explanation of the entire stellar system. Al Biruni had already in the eleventh century had glimmerings of what Aristarchus of Samos and Seleucus of Babylon had intuitively felt more than a thousand years before, a belief sometimes ascribed to Indian savants, namely that the phenomena of the skies may be explained by the rotation of the earth on its own axis and its progress on an orbital path around the sun.[15]* But that thesis and its mathematics had to await the Renaissance and the Pole, Copernicus.

Arab civilization is scarcely less distinguished in the domain of medicine than in mathematics. Arab medicine was rooted in Greek medicine, and the original centre of medical learning was, as we saw, Jundeshapur in southwest Persia. The famous hospital there produced seven generations of a celebrated family of physicians known to the East as Bakhtishu, i.e. Fortuna Jesu. With its decay medicine ceased to be a Christian and Sabian preserve, Moslem doctors were trained in the new hospital at Baghdad, and in the course of a century or so thirty similar hospitals sprang up in the principal cities throughout the Moslem world.

Hunain, the physician and translator, had written several original medical works in Arabic, including ten treatises on the eyes, and Thabit, also physician-translator, is credited with a big work on hygiene. But before this first century of Arab science had passed a Persian Moslem was born near Teheran who became one of the greatest figures of the era. This was Rhazes, a pupil of Hunain, who surpassed his master in the prolixity of his works. One on smallpox and measles gave the first clear account of these diseases; it found its way into many languages, including English, and was still being published in East and West a thousand years later. Rhazes's masterpiece, called *The Comprehensive Book,* brought together the knowledge and treatment of Greeks, Arabs, Persians and Indians, respectively, for every known disease, together with the author's summing up, a stupendous piece of scholarship which was later to influence European practice.

There were many other medical scientists, the most notable of them Avicenna, whose *Canon of Medicine* was at once an encyclopaedia and pharmacopoeia. It was translated into Latin, and it is still used in the East. At about this time a medical school was springing up in Spain which was to achieve eminence in surgery. The *Materia Medica* of Dioscorides had, at the outset, been translated for the Cordova court by a Jewish doctor, and Abulcasis, another famous court physician, soon afterwards produced his treatise on surgery, illustrated with drawings of instruments. This work had a wide vogue; it was translated into Spanish, Latin and Hebrew, and some experts claim that it laid the foundations of European surgery.

Optics reached their highest development under Alhazen, who, at the beginning of the tenth century, was in the service of the Fatimid caliph of north Africa. Alhazen rejected the theory of Ptolemy and Euclid that the eye sends out rays to the object beheld and asserted the reverse process, a discovery that is at the bottom of photography. He examined the refraction of rays through light and water, estimated that the atmosphere around the earth was ten miles high and came very near to discovering the magnifying glass; his researches carried Arab optical science far beyond the limits of Greek knowledge. All this time the Arabs were becoming highly proficient in the practical treatment of eye diseases, and their methods of A.D. 1000 were being followed in Europe down to the beginning of the eighteenth century.

The decline of the Eastern sciences coincides with the revival of narrow religious orthodoxies in Islam, which dated from the early part of the twelfth century, and the work of the great religious teacher, al Ghazali. If a pious caliph of Baghdad was to burn the works of Avicenna, Spain was free to advance for a century longer. Indeed at this very time she produced two of her great figures, Avenzoar and Averroes. But by the fourteenth century Arabic writings had so far declined that magic and superstitious practices were appearing. Not that these were ever entirely absent, even in the halcyon days of the tenth to twelfth centuries, for both astrology and alchemy were widely believed in. Quite competent astronomers accepted the influence of the heavenly bodies upon terrestrial affairs, and despite the Traditions which forbade belief in omens Mas'udi, among others, was a believer in them. The popular mind associated astronomy with astrology, so that astrolabes came to be suspected by the vulgar as partaking of the magical, whence at the end of the tenth century, one pope, who was an enthusiastic astronomer, was held to have 'dealings with the devil at Cordova.'

The case for alchemy was stronger. It was founded on the theory that all metals are fundamentally the same—a basis not incompatible with the Aristotelian theory that everything ultimately is composed of four elements: moisture, dryness, heat and cold. Transmutation from one metal to another was therefore held to be not impossible. Gold was the purest, silver the next purest, and the desire for them was, of course, in order of their preciousness. Alchemy postulated a substance that was capable of turning a base metal into a precious one, and it was the hunt after this elixir that occupied some of the best thought of the age. Even such eminent scientists as Rhazes and al Farabi were enthusiastic experimenters, though others, notably al Biruni and Avicenna, were in a nonbelievers' camp, holding by a theory that metals were fundamentally different (elements?). An interesting feature of Rhazes' book on alchemy is his division of substances into vegetable, animal and mineral, a verbal usage that has passed into our modern speech, while the so-called father of Arab alchemy, Jabir, is supposed nowadays to have been a secret company that was at work not earlier than the tenth century.

'The legacy of the Islamic world in medicine and natural science,' says Dr Max Meyerhof,[17]* 'is the legacy of Greece, increased by many additions, mostly practical. ... But the additions of the Islamic physicians refer almost solely to clinical and therapeutic experience. The theory and thought of the Greeks were left untouched and treasured up after careful systematization and classification. It must be remembered that the Moslems were strictly prohibited from dissecting either human bodies or living animals. Thus experiment was practically impossible in medicine, so that none of Galen's anatomical and physiological errors could be corrected. On the other hand, they received some impetus from the experience of Persian, Indian, and Central Asian scholars concerning particular lines of treatment, operations, and the knowledge of drugs and minerals. ... In other sciences some of the best Greek works were unknown to the Moslems, as, for example, the botany of Theophrastus. Their own share in this branch is a considerable one, but, again, of purely practical importance. The Moslem scholars, although acute observers, were thinkers only in a restricted sense. It is the same in zoology, mineralogy, and mechanics. The glory of Moslem science is in the field of optics. Here the mathematical ability of Alhazen and Kamal al Din outshone that of Euclid and Ptolemy. Real and lasting advances stand to their credit in this department of science.'

Original Arab contributions in the field of philosophic

thought are often belittled by Western authorities, who indeed have dubbed them negligible, in opposition to some modern Arab authorities who think that during the golden age of the caliphate a system of philosophy flourished which was peculiarly Arab or Islamic and which profoundly affected European thought and achievement. Professor Guillaume, in his brilliant essay on *Philosophy and Theology*[18]* to which the present writer acknowledges a deep obligation, holds that while the Arab addition to Greek philosophy was not substantial, it seems unfair to deny to the Arabs a 'peculiar synthesis of philosophic thought' which gives Arab philosophy a definite meaning. During our Middle Ages it was the world under Arab domination that rediscovered Greek philosophy, devoted itself to a rational interpretation of God, man and the universe, and arrived at intellectual standpoints that greatly influenced the teachings, not only of Islam, but also of medieval Christianity. We have seen that the first Arabs accepted the Qur'an much in the same way that fundamentalists accept the Bible—a literal acceptance through faith. The impact of Greek philosophical ideas on the increasingly enlightened generations following the conquests brought intellectual questionings. Soon a school of Moslem thinkers arose, the Mu'tazilite or Secessionists, who held 'that God could not predestinate man's actions because He was a moral being who was bound to do what was righteous' and who demanded that 'theology should be subjected to investigation by the mind.' To this society the Caliph Ma'mun himself belonged, and its activities in pressing the translation and study of the ancient thinkers were such that its influences are thought to have spread across the Islamic world into Spain, to survive there after its own suppression in the East as a heretical body.

While the orthodox were suspicious of innovations of foreign origin—and was not philosophy 'wisdom mixed with unbelief'?—the Arab philosophers took the path of intellectual approach. The earliest distinguished name among them is that of al Kindi, whose theories of the soul formed, with some modifications, the basis of later Arab philosophical thought. His conception of the universe was akin to that of Aristotle: 'The divine intelligence is the cause of the world's existence: its activity is mediated through the heavenly spheres to the terrestrial world. The world-soul is intermediate between God and the world of bodies. This world-soul created the heavenly spheres. The human soul is an emanation from the world-soul. There is thus a duality in man: inasmuch as the soul is tied to the body it is influenced by the heavenly spheres, but in so far as it is true to its spiritual origin it is free and independent. Both freedom and immortality are only attainable in the world of intelligence, so that if man would attain thereto he must set himself to develop his intellectual powers by acquiring a right knowledge of God and the universe!'[18]*

The philosopher, al Farabi, who followed al Kindi and was also a commentator of Aristotle, argued 'the impossibility of an infinite chain of causes and the postulate of a first cause necessarily existent in and for itself.' Al Farabi was an enthusiastic exponent of the theory that the world had no beginning, a doctrine which was an offence to Islam and Christianity.

The philosopher whom the West regarded as the greatest exponent of Arab philosophy—till Averroes arose in Spain two centuries later—was Avicenna. His lucid interpretations of his predecessor's philosophy were indeed translated later by the Christian archbishop of Toledo. Avicenna, following Plotinus, laid down the principle 'that from the one and indivisible only one being can originate. . . . Therefore it is not permissible to assert that form and matter spring directly from God for that would involve the assumption that there are two different modes in the divine essence. Matter, indeed, is not to be thought of as coming from God, because it is the very principle of multiplicity and diversity. Again, argued Avicenna, we may not suggest that a necessary being which has no final cause is influenced by a purpose in the sense that he acts for the sake of something other than himself. For if he did he would be dominated in his actions by regard for a being inferior to himself. It would then be necessary to distinguish within the divine nature: (*a*) the good of the thing which made it desirable; (*b*) the divine knowledge of that good; and (*c*) the divine intention of acquiring or producing that good. Therefore something intermediary between God the "necessary being" and the world of multiplicity must be postulated. The problem, therefore, was how to account for the fact of a complex universe and a simple creator.'[18]*

The philosophical thought of the East passed naturally across the Arabic speaking world to Spain, where, however, for the first three centuries religious orthodoxy resisted Mu'tazalite doctrines. The great thinkers of Spain do not belong to the centuries of the Arab rulers at Cordova but to the later ones of political upheaval under Berber rulers. These, though inclined to fanaticism and narrow orthodoxies, seem to have connived at the speculation of the philosophers so long as it was kept out of the reach of the common herd.

The Christian Church in Spain, unlike the Nestorian Church in Persia, was not in contact with Greek philosophic thought, so that whereas in the East Greek philosophy had come to Islam through a Christian link, in the West it was to come to Christianity through a Moslem link. Three great Spanish thinkers arose, Ibn Musarra, Ibn al Arabi, and Ibn Rushd (Averroes), whose ideas were to exercise great influence in Europe during the succeeding centuries, as did those of a Jewish school whose principal figure was Avicebron (Ibn Gabirol). Many of the Moslems had been mystics. The greatest Moslem mystic, a man of wonderful erudition and deep piety, was al Ghazali, called the St Thomas Aquinas of Islam. His arguments in favour of the 'creatio ex nihilo', proofs that God's knowledge comprises particulars and the dogma of the resurrection of the dead commended themselves to Christian scholars. Al Ghazali had passed through a stage of scepticism to set himself the task of exploring the four ways which claimed to lead to the truth, namely Scholastic theology, belief in an infallible teacher, Aristotelian philosophy and Sufism, i.e. the way of Persian mystics who held that God could be mystically apprehended in ecstasy. He emerged a mystic.

The philosopher who had the most pronounced influence on the West was Averroes of Cordova, though he does not appear to have occupied a corresponding position in Islam, for at one stage he was accused of apostasy to Judaism and banished to Africa. By the orthodox, Averroism was indeed generally equated with rationalism. Averroes, however, did not argue that philosophy and revealed religion were irreconcilable but held like St Thomas Aquinas that when they appeared to conflict the error lay in the interpretation. For Averroes the interpretation of the Qur'an by the ignorant was not possible. Better they be left with their crude ideas while 'the philosopher interpreted the sacred text in the light of reason.' Such ideas and others came from the East by way of Moslem Spain to colour Christian outlook. 'The resemblances between Averroes and St Thomas Aquinas indeed are so numerous it is only natural to conclude that Averroes has bequeathed something more than a commentary on Aristotle to Christian scholarship.'[18]*

Thus European scholars hold that 'however small the Arab contribution to pure philosophic thought may have been their service to theology was of considerable extent.' 'We may be sure,' says Professor Guillaume, 'that those who accuse Moslem scholars of lack of originality and of intellectual decadence have never read Averroes or looked into al Ghazali, but have accepted second-hand judgments. The presence of doctrines of Islamic origin in the very citadel of Western Christianity, the Summa of Aquinas, is a sufficient refutation of the charge of lack of originality and sterility.'[18]*

The influence of the Arabs on medieval civilization was clearly very considerable, the term 'Arab' being used in its broad cultural connotation; for Arab civilization, as we have seen, was not the civilization of the Arabs as a race, still less of Arabia as a country; it was the civilization that sprang up among the heterogeneous peoples of the Arab-conquered world in the early centuries of Islam. Its great figures, indeed, seem to have been mostly of Persian blood, and not a few were outside the allegiance of the Arab faith. Still, for all that, without the Arabs it probably would never have taken place.

One very striking thing about these scholars was their amazing versatility. Thus a philosopher of distinction like al Farabi could be eminent in music and in mathematics. Rhazes seemed equally at home in theology, in astronomy and in the natural sciences, and al Biruni had the time and talents to be physician and physicist, geographer and astronomer, and still write learnedly about arithmetic. The Arabs may 'not have had the same gift of scientific imagination, the same powerful genius as had the Greeks',[15]* but they made themselves masters of the Greek heritage and kept alive the higher intellectual life.

Europe, as yet backward, profited from intercourse with this civilization particularly through Moslem Spain. In the tenth century Cordova was the most civilized city in Europe;[19]* Seville, a hundred years later, was to rival, but only Toledo was to excel her and in the eleventh century become the first seat of learning in Moslem Spain. Wandering scholars from Europe now came to acquire, through the medium of Jewish interpreters, a taste for Aristotle. Others, following in succeeding centuries, came to study Arabic, the eminent among them, like Robertus Augustus and Adelard of Bath, making translations of their own. As the conflict between the Latin and Berber kingdoms led to the gradual withdrawal of Moslem power Spain became more congenial to European taste, and more and more of those with a bent towards scholarship turned to her.

Just as the Arabs had profited from the Greek translations in the eighth and ninth centuries, so in the twelfth and succeeding centuries Europe profited by these Latin translations from the Arabic. And so Greco-Arabic learning spread across Europe, and the first universities sprang up in response to the demand for it—Bologna, Padua, Paris. The Christian West was awakening. She had already inherited a large part of the Moslem legacy when the crusades brought her into closer contact with the Greek Church of Eastern Christendom. She had become fully aware of the legacy of the Greeks bequeathed through the Arabs, and as time passed she abandoned Arabic to go straight to the Greek originals.

The Arabs had meanwhile forsaken their Greek idols, had in turn become conquered peoples and so sank back into obscurity. Their work was done. They had held aloft the torch of Greek civilization and after four hundred years passed it, still more brightly burning, to the Christian West. That heritage contained the seed of the Renaissance, and out of the Renaissance grew European civilization and European ascendancy.

Part Three

THE DECLINE

CHAPTER VIII

Disintegration and Decline

FEW PEOPLES have left their impress on the world as the Arabs have left theirs. At this day in a vast sweep of territory across north Africa eastwards into the heart of Asia the religion, the dress, the habits, the very outlook of the peoples, the Arabic tongue, the written character where the tongue is not Arabic, are all living monuments to the great medieval empire of the Arabs.

Yet, strange though it may seem, the Arabs were a people without taste for discipline, without capacity for organization, lacking stability. The marvellous expansion of the seventh and eighth centuries that carried their sway over an area as vast as the Roman Empire was followed immediately by a period of disintegration almost as rapid. There was scarcely any marking time at the top of the hill, scarcely any sustained imperial dominion. Political unity crumbled from the moment the soldiers stopped marching; the conquered territories split up, regional dynasties followed one after another; and within three centuries political ascendancy had virtually passed almost everywhere to men of non-Arab blood. Within another century or two foreign invaders were thundering at the inner gates, the crusaders from western Europe, heathen Mongols from Hither Asia. The Arabs knew no peace. As they had lived by the sword, so must they perish by it. And thus for five centuries the sword was seldom sheathed. Yet despite the clashings, latterly of three races of mankind, despite the political submergence of the Arabs themselves, their faith emerged from the contest a world faith; their social culture, inextricably bound up with that faith, had laid hold of the ultimate victors. If the Arabs suffered political eclipse, yet they triumphed in the Arabization of their masters.

The new Arab world that had come to exist at the end of the expansionist wars was not predominantly Arab in blood. For colonization and conquest are ultimately two very different processes, and while the conquests were almost world wide in extent, as the world was then conceived, Arab colonization was not. It well-nigh exhausted itself in the Fertile Crescent, the lands half encircling Arabia's northern confines—Palestine, Syria, Mesopotamia. Here more than anywhere else the proportion of Arab invaders to indigenes stood high and grew to be dominant. Egypt and Persia, on the other hand, were conquered rather than colonized, the Arab minority element ultimately dominating the one, being submerged by the other. In the outward extensions, north Africa and Spain to the westwards, Trans-Oxiana to the eastwards, the Arabs were still more thin spread, these outermost conquests having been achieved indeed only with the aid of allies. Most notably was this the case in Spain where Tariq's original conquering army of seven thousand contained a mere handful of three hundred Arabs,[19]* and the backing-up force of eighteen thousand commanded by an Arab the following year was a composite one of Berbers, Arabs, Egyptians and Syrians, doubtless again preponderantly north African in personnel. Marriage with Spanish women rapidly multiplied the newcomers' stock, but it still must have represented but a tiny fraction of the entire population of Spain, while its blood in the second generation was for the most part half Spanish and grew more diluted with succeeding generations; indeed the more local generations a Spanish Moslem could boast of, the less Arab blood he was likely to have in his veins.

Disintegration not unnaturally started in these remote fringes. Spain was conquered in 711; it threw off the Damascus yoke and asserted its own independence in 746, after a brief thirty-five years allegiance. Tunis had repudiated the contact a year before. Parts of Morocco followed rapidly. It was a state of affairs arising not from native discontent with local Arab rulers, however, for these continued to maintain themselves for hundreds of years, such was Moslem military prestige. The root cause was the strong individualism, the overmastering ambition of the local Arabs themselves to carve out independent kingdoms and found personal fortunes. Indeed those very qualities which had been the strength of the expansion when distances from headquarters daily grew greater and communications across a slow-moving world made dependence upon central authority impossible—qualities of independence, of opportunism, of courageous initiative—were, when peace came, to be the undoing of imperial unity. Arab world dominion had been brought about by independent local action of brilliant individual leaders rather than as the result of a clearly thought-out and coordinated policy vigorously prosecuted by a general staff.

Do not the traditions tell us that the invasion of Egypt was made despite the opposition of a caliph of Medina, Spain invaded despite a caliph of Damascus?

When the expansionist phase ceased the Arab leaders in the field did not change their spots. The farther removed they were from the central government the less dependent they were upon caliphs who often were jealous of them. They were impatient of interference; they were opportunists still. If the first Arab coins minted at Damascus omitted the caliph's name, those issued a year later in Iraq bore the name of his provincial governor who struck them. Among a people of individualists—so prone to self-assertion—peace had the effect of diverting energies into disruptive channels.

Disagreement between caliphs of Damascus and their provincial governors in eastern Persia, Khorasan and Trans-Oxiana soon led to rifts, and although the native populations steadily embraced the Islamic faith the authority of Damascus dwindled so as to be almost nonexistent ten years before the Umaiyyad dynasty came to an end. Representing the Arab caliphs as loose-living, wicked and dissolute tyrants, the Persians were already espousing another cause under the banner of a rival claimant to the caliphate, a Persian-born descendant of the Prophet's uncle, Abbas. Rebellion came to a head, the Umaiyyad garrisons were expelled first from Persia then from Iraq, the last caliph of Damascus was defeated in the Battle of the Greater Zab, pursued to Egypt and there with most of his family exterminated.

The Abbasid caliphs thus owed their throne to Persian and Khorasan levies and must shape their rule accordingly. As time went on Eastern influences continued increasingly to dominate the affairs of the new caliphate. But later

Turkish mercenaries—recruited from beyond the Oxus as the caliph's bodyguard—climbed to supreme power at the expense of Persians and established a military ascendancy within the state, the most powerful Turkish amir of the day becoming the de facto ruler.

Away beyond Egypt, north Africa had never properly been subjugated, had indeed already started crumbling when the Spanish buttress fell away, so that at the time of the removal eastwards of the caliphate capital from Damascus to Baghdad, Qairawan alone of Barbary was in allegiance. To assert Abbasid authority, Aghlab, an Arab general, and native of eastern Persia, was sent to north Africa. Aghlab found Qairawan a far cry from Baghdad. He succeeded only too well, identified himself with local disaffection or at least profited from it, so that in A.D. 800 he ruled as an independent prince and founded a north African dynasty.

Seventy years later Egypt was to travel the same path. Ibn Tulun, a Turkish viceroy of the Baghdad caliph sent to Fustat, became virtually independent while carrying out his mission, and Egypt, ripe for independence, now achieved it under him. Thus within a century and a half after the Arab conquest of Spain practically the whole of north Africa as well as Spain had become independent of the great Arab caliphate of the East and had broken up into many independent states.

But Qairawan was the scene of a new movement that was destined to unite north Africa again under a single ruler of Cairo and to give rise to a caliphate that in its heyday was to rival the prestige of the contemporary Abbasid caliphate of Baghdad. The Fatimids, as the rulers of this African caliphate came to be called, owed their name to a blood claim of descent from Fatima, the daughter of the Prophet, wife of the martyr Ali, and mother of the saints, Husain and Hassan. They were of Shi'a sect; indeed the first Fatimid caliph claimed to be the Madhi himself, though his Abbasid traducers represented him as an impostor of Persian origin and with Jewish blood in the female line. The genesis of the movement which brought him to power is thought to have been a secret society started by his grandfather some half-century before. This man, Abdullah ibn Maimun, is said to have been a Persian oculist, a rationalist who had conceived a violent hatred for orthodox Arabian Islamism. In origin the movement stood for rational belief, requiring none too high a code of personal behaviour judged by orthodox standards, though it had a religious veneer in a cult of Mahdism. The imminent expectation of a great teacher was proclaimed; not, however, the occluded member of the twelfth generation of the Prophet as in the Shi'a cult of the East, though like him a Mahdi who would sweep away false caliphs and usher in an age of peace and justice. The movement had at its head Sa'id ibn Husain, the grandson of the founder, when it attracted to its ranks one Abu Abdullah, the Shi'ite, a native of Basrah. Aghlabid rule was in decay at this time, and Abu Abdullah put himself at the head of the rebellion to dethrone the last of the line. Sa'id was thereupon proclaimed caliph at Qairawan and assumed the name of Ubaidallah the Mahdi. But caliph and popular leader were soon quarrelling. The former proved, in the event, to be a pious and orthodox Shi'a Moslem, and, whatever the indulgences asssociated with the movement of his grandfather, early made it clear that he was not going to stand for 'free love, pig's flesh, and wine-bibbing.' The ladder by which he had climbed to power could now be kicked aside,

Abu Abdullah was accused of casting doubts on the Mahdi's credentials and so was put to death.

Fourth in this Fatimid line came a great caliph, Mu'izz, scholar and statesman, to whom is ascribed a knowledge of the Greek, Slav and Berber tongues. Mu'izz rose about the middle of the tenth century at Qairawan to make himself master of the Islamic world about him. His iron hand extended westwards to subject the whole of north Africa; his ambitious eye looked still more eagerly eastwards to Egypt, with her appanages of Palestine and Syria. And thither Jauhar the Sicilian, his great slave general, was dispatched at the head of an army. Fustat, the capital, fell, and where the victors encamped on its outskirts rose the new Fatimid capital of Cairo. (Arabic = Qahira.)

'And,' says Maqrizi, 'it is said that the origin of the city's name was as follows: When the Commander-in-Chief Jauhar desired to build the city, he summoned the astrologers, and told them that he wished to construct a town outside the city of Misr (i.e. Fustat) in order that the army should abide in it, and he ordered them to choose an auspicious moment (a happy rising) for laying the foundations, with the object of insuring that the place would never be lost to them and their successors: and the astrologers chose a moment for laying, and a moment for excavating the foundations; and they placed timber poles round the circuit of the site, and between the poles a rope was strung, and on it bells were fastened: and they said to the workers, "when the bells ring, throw down (into the already completed trenches) what is in your hands of stones and mud" (i.e. mortar). Then they stood watching for the happy moment. Whereupon it happened that a crow alighted upon one of the ropes whereon the bells were hung, so that all the bells rang: and the workers thought that the astrologers had rung them; therefore they threw down (into the trenches) what was in their hands of stone and mud (mortar) and began to build; and the astrologers shouted "Al Qahir (the victorious) is rising." Thus it happened that they missed what they had intended, and it is said that it was the planet Mars, victorious at dawn, that was in the ascendant when the foundations were begun: and so they named the city Al Qahira (Cairo) (the victorious): and their insight is justified, for the city has remained under (subject to) conquest till this day.'[22]*

Two centuries later the crusaders were to come to find the 'insight' still working. Meanwhile the fortunes of the Fatimids of Egypt waxed and waned, the ties with Syria and north Africa were not always and everywhere maintained, the arts and sciences flourished, the spiritual orthodoxies flagged. One mad and cruel caliph, the notorious Hakim, believed himself to be the incarnation of the divine wisdom till a religious zealot assassinated him on one of his lonely night rides, while the capital, Cairo, was the home of a secret society that aimed at the undermining of religious orthodoxies. Initiates came to learn —towards the end of the nine degrees of initiation—that religious beliefs were fundamentally a means to secular ends, to wit, the preservation of public order in a regimented state; they were a soporific for keeping the common herd in subjection. European modernism was thus having a vogue in Islam before the coming of the crusaders, but whether or not as a result of their challenge to Islam, dogmatic religion was soon to be enthroned again, a reaction which not only damped the ardour of the libertine but dried up the sources of scientific inspiration.

Before this set in, however, the Arabs were to suffer politically in the general subjugation of western Asia by a new power which had risen in the East—the Seljuq Turks. The eastern caliphate had for long been virtually ruled by a Perso-Dailamite family, the Buwayhids, the Arab caliph of Baghdad himself being little more than a religious figurehead. Its influence waning, Baghdad had lost hold of its eastern borderlands; Trans-Oxiana threw off the Arab yoke in the tenth century under the Persian Samanids and was seized in turn by the rising Seljuqs. These were a tribe of Turks who just before this time (circa 960) had settled in the Khorasan-Trans-Oxiana empire and embraced the Sunni branch of Islam. A century more, and they were not only masters of the local situation but had moved west to Baghdad, superseded the power of the Buwayhids and secured, at the caliph's hands, the title of sultans. Twenty years later these Seljuqs were streaming on westwards in two main lines, one in the north to invade the Byzantine Empire, annex Armenia and Georgia and lay the foundations of the Asia Minor kingdom of Rum, the other to sweep southwards through the Arab lands of the Egyptian Fatimids, capture Damascus and annex Syria and Palestine, sending Shi'a refugees flying before them to the more congenial atmosphere of Egypt; for medieval times had a way of being unkind to those who persisted in officially branded heresies, and religious sectarianism and dynastic loyalty were closely connected, as they still are in Arabia. The Fatimid general, the famous Armenian, Badr al Jumali al Juyushi, was forced to fall back on Egypt where he became, in turn, the great wazir.

Weakness meanwhile grew in the Seljuq ranks, for their vast conquests soon split up and fell to ambitious generals, so that in place of a solid empire, western Asia was dotted over with small principalities under tributary chiefs. Fifty years later Egypt was ready to advance again under Juyushi's equally famous son, Afdal, who marched into Palestine and reconquered Jerusalem from its Seljuq ruler. In the north the Seljuq invaders of Asia Minor who had originally driven the Christian Byzantines westwards against the Aegean coasts had similarly grown weak by disunity, but the cry for help from Constantinople had been heard in Western Christendom, and towards the end of the eleventh century the crusaders were girding on their armour.

The Arabs of Syria and Palestine whose lands had within half a century been thrice overrun by Seljuqs and Fatimids now found these inter-Moslem wars dwarfed by a menace far more terrifying. A strange and incalculable invader was coming out of the West, an invader imbued with a hatred of the Arab faith and resolved to expel it from Jerusalem and the Holy Land and impose its own religious and political dominion.

During the two centuries that followed, the lands of these Arabs were the main battlefield of that epoch-making struggle between Christianity and Islam which the West remembers as the crusades. The Arabs formed the bulk of the inhabitants. They had done so for four and a half centuries, since, indeed, their armies had wrested the land by the sword from the Christian Byzantines. Christianity and Islam had since then learned to live side by side, and whatever the rivalries between the two faiths, a spirit of considerable tolerance had normally existed. The traditional view that the original Arab conquerors were religion-inspired zealots who came to trample on other peoples' religion with a fiery mission analogous to the crusaders' own is doubtless exaggerated. For in Palestine, Syria and Egypt the native Christians offered no determined resistance to these first rude Moslem Arabs but welcomed them as deliverers from their Greek imperial Christian rulers. It seems more probable that the coming of the simple Arabs promised to bring religious toleration for native Christian sectarianism which had been the object of persecution by an orthodox state church, promised a less burdensome taxation—however invidious it might be—than the old imperial exactions, while the simple Moslem slogan 'There is one God' involved no fundamental contradiction of Christianity. It was only in later times when Islam became intellectual and contentious, eager to assert her supremacy, when proselytism sapped the walls of the rival religion and carried dissension into the family household, that religious antagonism sprang up. All through these early centuries of Arab occupation the Arabs not only permitted the practice of Christianity within the Holy Land but had allowed Christians from without to perform the pilgrimage to the Holy Sepulchre of Jerusalem. This pilgrimage, which the pious believed carried with it a remission of sins, brought Christians not only from Syria, Egypt and Iraq, but from Europe, in a regular annual invasion. Such special European interests had indeed grown up as induced the Caliph Harun al Rashid—according to some Western authorities—to recognize the title, Protector of Jerusalem and Owner of the Holy Sepulchre, assumed by his great Christian contemporary, Charlemagne.

It was an age when the rulers of Islam were passing through an enlightened phase, were much more interested in scientific speculation and Greek philosophy than in hindering the pious exercises of 'The people of the book' coming from dark western Europe. In Europe, on the other hand, the times were shaping for a religious revival. The public conscience had been deeply outraged by the act of the mad Caliph Hakim, who, in 1010, destroyed the Holy Sepulchre; the violent unrest caused by Seljuq-Fatimid wars had greatly interfered with peaceful pilgrimage to the Holy Land; the clarion call for help from Eastern Christendom, following its loss of territory to Moslems in Asia Minor, yet another provocation to Western Christendom.

Europe was emerging from her Dark Ages and, if not fully conscious of her destinies, had reached a stage of concerted self-assertiveness. Religion was all powerful. The authority of a single voice in Rome could suspend old feudal antagonisms, old private wars, and send warriors, recently hostile to one another, to wage war across the seas in a common cause. Fighting instincts sharpened by want, by famine, by overpopulation, by greed, could be consecrated to the establishment of Christian rule in the Holy Land; the bellicose spirit of the younger son without a heritage could be legitimately directed to the ambition of an estate or principality in the East at the expense of the infidel. This cure for Europe's growing pains had the blessing of religious authority. Western Christendom was swept by a fever of religion and war. 'It was an age which was dominated by the spirit of other-worldliness, and accordingly ruled by the clerical power which represented the other world,' says Professor Barker,[25]* 'a new path to Heaven, to tread which counted "for full and complete satisfaction" and gave forgiveness of sins . . . the foreign policy of the Papacy, directing its faithful subjects to the great war of Christianity against the Infidel. As a new way of salvation, the Crusades connect themselves with the history of the penitentiary system; as the foreign policy of the Church, they belong to that clerical purification and direction of feudal society and its instincts, which appears in the institution of "God's Truce" and in chivalry itself.'

If commerce had not attained the significance it has in modern statecraft, yet the growing maritime ambitions of Venice and Genoa were, even at this early stage, not an entirely negligible factor. The Mediterranean had virtually been an Arab sea all down the early Islamic centuries. Its shores on three sides, south, west and for a large part east, were still Moslem; on the northern shore the Italian ports of Bari and Amalfi as well as the Mediterranean Islands had for centuries been Moslem footholds too.

At first there had been no direct maritime commerce between the Christian and Islamic worlds. It had been opposed on both sides, wherefore Tunis, the midway point between Spain and Egypt, had risen and Alexandria declined. Moslem shipping dominated the Mediterranean, Moslem ships traded only between Moslem ports, visitors to European shores at this time being Berber pirates on plunder bent.

But in the tenth and eleventh centuries the disintegration of the Islamic world and the relative weakness of its dismembered western parts was an encouragement for southern Europe to be up and doing, and Christian ships began to multiply upon the seas. Moslem and Christian sailors served side by side in the same ships, not, let it be supposed, because they had become animated by a new and tolerant religious spirit, for both were no better than pirates when occasion offered. But isolation had gone. Venetian and Genoese shipping came to grow and share the eastern trade, and by the twelfth century Ibn Jubair, the Arab traveller, can tell us that he travelled from Ceuta to Alexandria in a Christian ship.

Europe was shaking off her sloth. It is true that in the century before the crusades the heart of Asia Minor had expelled the rule of Christian Constantinople. But at the same time Christian rulers had been driving the Moslems of Spain out of their capital of Toledo and farther towards the south, driving the Moslems of Italy out of their Italian footholds and expelling their rule from Sicily. These wars against Moslems in Europe, prosecuted by Iberians in Spain and Normans in Italy, had naturally produced an exacerbation of religious feeling, and this, with the events taking place in the East, nourished that spirit of hatred for the infidel which animated the early crusaders. In Europe the Saracens were on the run; in the Holy Land they were fighting one another under Seljuq and Fatimid; it seemed a propitious moment for the eastern adventure. Thus in the year 1096 there assembled at Constantinople a hundred and fifty thousand armed pilgrims ready to embark upon the first militant pilgrimage into the lands of the Arabs.

Marching southwards under the banner of the Cross, they first encountered the banner of the Crescent in Asia Minor. There the opposition of Seljuq Turks was brushed aside and a trail of Christian garrisons left in many principal cities, Edessa and Antioch, among others, to form Latin principalities. Southwards, in the lands of the Arabs, authority vested in Fatimid governors of Egypt. Before the clash Afdal, the Egyptian wazir, had been prepared to come to terms with the crusaders as a means of alliance against the Seljuqs; for the invaders, however, in the first flush of their religious fervour and strength, there could be no trafficking with the infidel. By the year 1099 the

Fatimids had been expelled from the greater part of the coasts of Syria and Palestine; in the following year, 1100, the Latin Kingdom came into being with Baldwin as king of Jerusalem, and so the Arabs passed under the rule of the 'Ferenghi.'[1]

The initial successes of the crusaders turned ambitious eyes eastwards to Baghdad and southwards to Cairo, but presumptuous dreamings were soon shattered by Seljuq successes in Asia Minor. The crusaders profited from the lack of co-ordination between the two Moslem fronts. The rival Sunni and Shi'a divisions of Islam split Cairo and Baghdad. Arabs had recently been at war, one with another, for the mastery of the land that had now passed to the stranger and the unbeliever. But this did not heal their divisions, and the Latin Kingdom was thus able to maintain itself for eighty years to come. Before a third of that time had passed the kingdom reached its greatest development, exceeding in size present-day Palestine, for it extended northwards to Beyrout, eastwards over the Jordan and southwards to the head of the Red Sea.

Divisions within the Seljuq ranks enabled the Frankish principalities to maintain themselves the more easily, and Christian princes made alliances with one Moslem leader

[1]The term 'Ferenghi' is a corruption of the word 'Frank.' It is commonly used by Arabs today for any European, and so bears witness to the supreme part played by the French, particularly the Norman French, in the crusades. The first crusade was preached on French soil by a pope of French descent and was largely French in personnel. All through the Holy Wars for two hundred years to follow the French played a major part. The Latin Kingdom of Jerusalem was French in body, soul and mind. The language was French, and when Latin rule was finally extinguished at the end of the thirteenth century, French fleets still harried the coasts of Syria for a century afterwards, and French influence in the Levant has continued down through the centuries. Whatever the result of the crusades for Christendom, the part France played in the wars, and her colonization of the Holy Land, exalted her prestige in contemporary Europe.[25]*

against another. Aleppo and Damascus were held by rivals, and the alliance of Damascus with Latin Jerusalem was a source of great strength to them both. Seljuq rulers, known as *atabegs* or regents, were in many cases emancipated slaves who had held high positions under the military founders and in time had passed from regency to rule. One of these, the famous Zangi, atabeg of Mosul, rose in the year 1127 to extend his power westwards, absorb some of his weaker atabeg neighbours and carry war into the Christian camps. He captured Edessa, marched on Damascus and invaded the Latin Kingdom, reaching the walls of Jerusalem and Acre. Oscillations of political fortunes led to a union of the Christian Antioch and Jerusalem, and with it the Greek Church's influence increased at the expense of the Latin West; for Christendom had its two divisions no less than Islam, and Constantinople held a rigid view of its historical rights and interests to which the West must conform, however irksome it found that conformity.

Dissensions within the ranks of both Christians and Moslems brought greater toleration as between representatives of the two religions. A generation of Franks had grown up in the East whose zeal to fight the infidel had given place to a desire to live on terms of amity with him, who preferred to trade rather than to fight and was not averse to adopting Arab dress and customs. On the other hand renewed zeal for prosecuting the Holy War came with fresh blood from the West, the new arrivals not being always welcomed since they antagonized the infidel. A contingent from the Low Countries and from England that came by the long sea route and put in at Lisbon to succour coreligionists had captured the city from the Moslems and so laid the foundations of the kingdom of

Portugal—a close friendship between that country and England surviving to this day. But the maintenance of Christian political domination in the Holy Land remained the supreme object of crusading policy.

To the north of the Latin Kingdom Zangi's mantle had fallen upon his powerful son, Nur al Din. To the south the Fatimid caliphate was in decline, and Egypt was torn between rival ministers contending for power. One sought the aid of the Seljuqs, another of the Latins, till Nur al Din, sending an army into Egypt, carried the day for his protégé. In this force was a young Kurdish officer named Saladin, a man of destiny, who was later to shake the crusading movement to its foundations and send the Latin kings of Jerusalem into a forty years exile. Saladin's uncle, the general of this force, soon after his arrival himself became the caliph's wazir in Egypt, and when the caliph died, Saladin, who had succeeded his uncle, seized the power and made himself ruler. Thus the Shi'a caliphate of the Egyptian Fatimids was brought to an end after two hundred years, and prayers were once more said in the Friday mosques for the Abbasid caliph of Baghdad. But this allegiance was not a permanent one, for Saladin was to entrench himself, become absolute and found a dynasty.

He first turned north to make himself master of the Syrian Moslems. Damascus and then Aleppo were conquered, and, by bringing about the fall of Nur al Din's successor, he achieved his object. On all sides but the sea the Latin Kingdom of Jerusalem was thus faced for the first time by a united Moslem front. Its days were numbered. Saladin marched south from Aleppo at the head of an army that was animated by a militant religious spirit akin to that of the early crusaders themselves. He swept everything before him. Jerusalem capitulated after a fortnight's siege, and so, in 1187, the kingdom fell, all that remained of it being the seaports of Tyre, Tripoli and Antioch.

The Christian West was roused again, and France, England and Germany mustered crusaders to restore the shattered position. The immediate objective, Acre, the sea gateway to Jerusalem, was shortly attained, but forty years passed in continuous struggle, as crusade after crusade poured forth its zealots, before Jerusalem again came under Christian rule. The first fine flush of religious frenzy under the inspiration of the papacy had meanwhile faded, and a new spirit of compromise and adjustment had come to colour the counsels of the movement. To us the most picturesque, if not the greatest, of the crusaders who was to measure his strength against that of Saladin was England's gallant King Richard, Cœur de Lion. His journey out was memorable by his capture of the island of Cyprus, and though he promptly sold it to become a Latin kingdom, he had nonetheless founded a base of future operations against the enemy in the Holy Land. But for all Richard's exploits, the great prowess of Saladin could not be humbled, and a truce was made, and the two great and opposing protagonists spent a year in trying to find a peaceful solution. The clerical domination of the crusades had been passing. The movement had been growing secular. Richard could enter into friendly negotiations with Saladin, who, like himself, was the chivalrous soldier rather than the religious fanatic. He arrived to find the mere vestiges of a coastal strip representing a Latin kingdom; he would have been content with the addition of Jerusalem linked by a corridor of the port of Acre. For this he strove and to achieve it went to the lengths of offering his own sister in marriage to the brother of Saladin that they might jointly rule the kingdom, but Saladin was unyielding.

Saladin's death threw Egypt into a turmoil, and this gave a stimulus to fresh crusading activity. Cairo, as the capital and centre of the enemy's power in the West, was now the target. The fate of Jerusalem was seen to depend not on overcoming the local Arab opposition but on vanquishing the Egyptian masters of the land, and throughout the remaining phase of the crusades, lasting through the thirteenth century, this remained the crux of Frankish strategy. Egypt became the crusaders' battlefront if Jerusalem remained their goal.

Thus the crusade, which followed the death of Saladin, became a sea crusade. The fleet was got ready for sea, the crusaders were ready to embark when at the last moment the plans were changed and a new and different campaign was launched. The deciding factor might have been the maritime interests of Italian ports, which are said to have been enjoying advantages under trade agreements with Cairo, but whether or not, the fleet sailed for Christian Constantinople, its ostensible object being to wrest the throne from the hands of a usurper. The upshot was that Constantinople, not Cairo, was stormed, and so Constantinople, the original begetter, became the victim of the crusades. France and Venice shared the spoils between them. The new empire emerged. Baldwin of Flanders became the first Latin emperor of Constantinople, while the coasts and islands of the archipelago passed to the Venetians. But the new empire proved a source, not of strength but of weakness to the crusades, for it drained the resources of the Holy Wars for years to follow.

The projected crusade against Egypt took fifteen more years to gather strength. In the West there had been an attempt at reviving the religious stimulus, and a cardinal accompanied the expedition. The Frankish fleet appeared before the port of Damietta, which fell to a siege, a landing was made and the march on Cairo begun. Saladin's successor offered terms the half of which would have satisfied Richard of the Lion's Heart, namely the cession of Jerusalem, the surrender of the Cross (Saladin had captured it in 1187) and the liberation of prisoners. But the crusaders wanted more. They wanted an indemnity, and when this was not forthcoming war was resumed. Nemesis now flung them back to the coasts, and they were content to evacuate Damietta in exchange for the Cross.

When the crusaders came again they did so under Frederick II of Sicily, a great man if a freethinking monarch of a lately oriental state whose title to the throne of Jerusalem was based on a wife's inheritance. Frederick was no religious zealot. He came not to fight the infidel but to treat with him, and the papal blessing had been withheld. Frederick's was a calculating peace crusade, and it succeeded. The caliph of Cairo in 1229 was ready to yield what Richard had pleaded for in vain. The treaty between Egypt and Sicily conceded the holy city, Nazareth, Bethlehem and a way to the sea at Acre, and thus Frederick entered Jerusalem as its king without having to strike a blow. Political bargaining had succeeded where arms had failed for forty years, and the outcome was that Christian authority was enthroned for another fifteen years. This success, however, proved to be the last gasp of the Latin Kingdom.

Egypt was stirring again. The caliph's authority had been undermined by the rivalries of Mamlukes. One of these rose in course of time to absolute power and founded a dynasty, figured in the final Moslem conquest of Syria and reduced Latin authority to the point of extinction. Baibars' first step on the road to dominance was as general of the force which marched against Frederick. The latter's authority was crumbling amid the internal dissensions of the Latin nobles, so to Baibars the Latin Kingdom looked an easy and tempting prey, and at Gaza in 1244 he routed the Christian forces so completely that Jerusalem passed once more into Moslem hands. Cairo had again become its master. The cry went up for help, and western Europe again took measures to respond. Under St Louis the crusaders attacked Damietta as they had done before. History repeated itself by the launching of another march on Cairo. But this time there was no Egyptian attempt to buy off the invader. A force marched out and utterly routed him. St Louis was able to escape only by payment of a large ransom, and the stricken army fell back to Acre. There, as in other coastal towns, a Christian governor maintained a precarious existence for another half-century, aided at first by Moslem allies in Syria who had broken away after Saladin's death. Still Egypt, aided by Baibars' military prowess, would doubtless have swept it into the sea but for the appearance of a new menace looming out of the East—the arrival of another great non-Moslem invader. The Mongols were coming.

Just as the Arabs had swarmed out of the Arabian peninsula across the known world in the seventh to eighth centuries, so now in the thirteenth, armed bands of Mongols from Central Asia swept east and west under Chingis Khan to strike terror from Pekin to Persia. Next they ascended into the plains of Iraq, and so it came about that while the Arabs of the West were delivering themselves from the Frankish yoke those of Iraq were swept by an avalanche of Mongols. The year 1258 saw the conqueror Hulagu, Chingis Khan's grandson, swoop down to the destruction of Baghdad and put the last Abbasid caliph, Musta'sim, and his family to death. Two years later they swarmed westwards through Syria and Palestine, subjecting the Arabs to devasting destruction, and only the prowess of Baibars at Gaza again prevented their invasion of Egypt.

If to the Arabs these pagan Mongols (they were Shamanists) brought pandemonium, the crusaders saw in their victories a new hope. The idea of converting these heathen to Christianity fired their imagination. This would, so it seemed, be a means of achieving for all time the crusaders' goal and of driving Islam back into its Arabian home. The existence of a sprinkling of Christians within the Mongol ranks—a backwash of Asiatic Nestorianism—the fact that Kilboga, the leader of the Mongol invasion of Syria, was himself a Christian, lent fair ground for hope. Eagerly the pope sent off missions to the Mongols of Russia and to those of Persia; Christian missionaries penetrated Asia and established themselves as far east as Pekin. The historic military contest between Christianity and Islam now seemed to depend not a little on the conversion to Christianity of the Mongol invaders.

But the prestige of the sword rather than the persuasions of preachers was decisive. Again the fundamental distinction between conquest and colonization was to influence the issue. The Mongols were too thin spread to be colonizers. They were but a whirlwind army that swept down and as quickly veered away. How thin spread they were is clear to an observant visitor to the Middle East who today will look in vain for survivals of the telltale slit eye, the round head and stubby hair. If the Mongol invaders of the Arab lands were Mongols in a racial sense, they came and went.

The Latin hope of establishing a permanent kingdom in the Holy Land, solidly supported by Mongol allies, vanished with the vanishing Mongols. Egypt, galvanised into activity under the energetic Baibars, marched in to occupy the vacated spaces. Jaffa and Damascus fell easily, and the Mongols retired to Asia Minor, where they were able for a brief time to usurp the power of the Seljuq Turks.

Syria and Egypt were now again united as they had been in Saladin's time, but Baibars was no tolerant chivalrous Saladin; he was as uncompromising a religious zealot as the fieriest crusader, and he resolved to drive Christian rule from the East, propitiously starting by taking Antioch, one of the remaining four Christian principalities.

A final and pathetic throw to restore shattered crusading fortunes was made by the English Prince Edward, who in 1272 landed at Acre and strove in vain to court Mongol succour. His departure in despair was followed by ten years of precarious peace between Franks and Arabs, when Baibars' successor rose to expel the Christians from their final footholds of Tripoli and Acre. And thus, in 1291, after nearly two hundred years of incessant warfare the last vestige of Latin rule was extinguished. Military success had increased Moslem prestige throughout the East; the apathy of the West—for Europe had, in those two hundred years, grown to be secular, legal, scholastic—was reflected in the long-drawn-out, losing, rear-guard action. By the end of the century the western Mongols, the crusaders' last hope, had themselves embraced Islam, the religion of the dominant power, and Asia was thereby lost to Christianity.

The military offensive passed from the Cross to the Crescent. The battlefields were thereafter to lie a full month's march to the north of the Holy Land. The Islamic standard-bearers were no longer Arabs but Ottoman Turks—a tribe of Turks that had established itself in Asia Minor during the Mongol upheaval and had since then inherited the sceptre of their Seljuq kindred. Turkish aggression against imperial Christian neighbours to the west had already provoked a landing of Cypriots and Venetians who, anxious to protect their Aegean interests, came to occupy Smyrna. But they were in the long run powerless to stem the Ottoman tide which, in 1363, swept across the Hellespont into Europe, overrunning the countries of the southern Balkans—Thrace, Bulgaria, Macedonia, Serbia. A check came to the Ottomans, but only at the hands of another Asiatic invader who fell upon their rear. The Tartars, under Tamerlane, king of Trans-Oxiana, invader of India and conqueror of southern Russia, reached out at the beginning of the fifteenth century to strike at the Turkish province of Asia Minor at Angora. This was, however, only another lightning Asiatic stroke that lacked continuance. The Ottoman adventure in Europe was only momentarily affected by it, and under the next ruler Ottoman pressure was resumed, and Constantinople itself fell into the hands of the Turks in 1453.

Strong in their European possessions, the Osmanlis[2] turned their faces back on Asia. There were forty independent Turkish principalities in Anatolia at the beginning of the fourteenth century, but by the end of the fifteenth

[2]Osman was the eponymous ancestor.

these had all been united, and this great and growing Moslem power in the north was now a menace to the Arabs of the Holy Land and, indeed, to Egyptian independence. The Arab peoples of Syria and Palestine, tributaries of the Mamlukes, had already been mustered to defend themselves against the attacks of Tamerlane, had marched on two occasions northwards against Turcoman states. But there was to be no rest for them under the threat of Ottoman aggression. In the early sixteenth century the Sultan Selim, after defeating the Persians, turned south to invade the Arab states. North of Aleppo the Egyptian forces gathered to fight a decisive battle. It went against them, the Ottoman way was open into Syria, and early in the following year (1517) Selim marched triumphantly into Cairo. The rule of the Cairo Mamlukes thus came to an end; the caliphate passed to European soil and to men of Turkish blood, the Ottoman sultans of Constantinople.

The Arabs had changed masters once again. Yet they remained, in a sense, the victors, for they belonged to the Moslem empire that within a quarter of a century that followed extended its European conquests eastwards through the Crimea, westwards through Hungary. Thus was the religion of the Arabs carried to the gateway of Vienna and maintained there for a hundred years.

The duel between Cross and Crescent reached the end of a definite phase. It had been waged for four hundred years. For the first two hundred the crusaders had waged an offensive war, for the last two hundred Christendom was on the defensive. When the crusades opened, Europe (if Spain, which ultimately came to be wholly Christian, is excluded) was under Christian rule, and western Asia Minor too. During the first two crusading centuries more of Asia Minor as well as Palestine and Syria were in part and at times added. By the end of the next two centuries Christian rule had not only been expelled from the lands of the Arabs and from the Asiatic continent, but Islam had penetrated deep into eastern Europe and established itself on the shores of the Danube. The Arabs, during those four centuries, were in turn the subjects of Seljuqs, Fatimids, Franks, Mongols, Mamlukes and Ottomans, but if the history of the period in the Near East is conceived of as a duel between the civilization of East and West, they emerged exalted, they had lived not in vain, for in spirit they had made captives of their captors and witnessed the extension and triumph of their Arab faith.

CHAPTER IX

The Arabs of Arabia

The Najdian spirit leads the oasis dwellers to reject all but the simplest doctrine of Islam, and to regard expansions or interpretations of this by any society, living under other conditions than theirs, as offences, against the God they have made in their own image. Such a spirit (not, of course, unknown elsewhere in the histories of other creeds), remains passive in stern self-righteousness till reminded with sufficient force that man's responsibility to the One God of the Universe cannot be acquitted by securing Him less than universal honour![24*] DAVID HOGARTH

THERE ARE two Arabs. There is the Arab within Arabia; there is the Arab without; broadly speaking, the one representative of a patriarchal culture, the other the product of a medieval civilization; the one cut off in a little-known backwater of the world, the other borne upon a restless tide amid the interplay of world currents.

It is the second Arab, the historical Arab, whose fortunes we have been following down to the sixteenth century. And now, at the risk of breaking the continuity of his story, we must turn aside to consider, for a brief chapter, how it has fared with the other Arab, his stay-at-home brother, the Arab of Arabia. It is, moreover, necessary to distinguish between the two cultures in order to understand the respective parts 'the Arabs' played, and did not play, in the Great War, their varying outlook and the several roads they are now travelling. For the single term 'Arab' on Western lips is responsible for much misunderstanding and confusion of thought. When, for instance, our newspapers talk of the political aspirations of 'the Arabs' they are almost invariably referring not to the Arabs of Arabia, but to those outside, to wit, the Arabs of Syria, of Iraq or of Palestine. The danger of equating Arabs and Arabia is seen in the journalistic tag used in connection with the late T. E. Lawrence, 'The Uncrowned King of Arabia,' for, with the exception of the western coastal fringe from Mecca northwards along the Pilgrim railway that saw his gallant doings in 1917, his brilliant exploits during 1918 were performed outside the Arabian peninsula, into which country indeed he never had occasion deeply to penetrate, and at the time of the early peninsular adventures most of the Arabs of Arabia could scarcely have known of his existence, while the suggestion implied of Arabian unification under a foreigner and a non-Moslem is, of course, a myth. This is not in anyway to be understood as detracting from Lawrence, for whose masterly and heroic achievements on the Arab front the writer has the greatest admiration. But we must get the terms 'Arabs' and 'Arabia' clear.

Before the rise of the Prophet Arabs and Arabia may have been complementary and co-extensive terms. But in the seventh to eighth centuries the great exodus took place. Those who went forth grew mighty, prosperous, secular; those who stayed at home remained poor, unlearned, orthodox. The second generation of colonials threw off allegiance to the mother country. They became a world power. The rule of Medina patriarchs was no longer acceptable to them. At the time of the coming of the Turks these Arabs had had seven centuries of seeding amid peoples that had inherited the cultures of ancient Mesopotamia, ancient Persia, ancient Egypt. They had acquired a different psychology from that of the Arabs of Arabia. Theirs had been the Arab civilization, the arts, science, philosophy, all of which passed Arabia by; theirs the experience of crusader, Mongol, Tartar, impacts which Arabia never knew.

The Arabs of Arabia, the peninsular Arabs, on the other hand, remained inviolate by their poverty, their remoteness, their unwillingness to change, their hostility to foreign intrusion. Their deserts and their dogmas remained, for them, the warp and woof of life. In pre-Islamic days there had been Jewish and Christian colonies in Arabia, but a fanatical insular spirit had within fifty years of the Prophet largely driven them forth. The peninsula today inherits the same spirit. Throughout Islamic times Arabia has been forbidden country for the foreigner and the infidel. The cause of this is not purely political, as I for one, in spite of official connections, have found opportunities of making many journeys of exploration. But such opportunities for Europeans are rare. Indeed no European (T. E. Lawrence excepted) has ever been permitted to visit the holy places of Mecca and Medina who has not professed himself a follower of Islam, nor may one go except in peril of his life. An intolerance survives which is almost without parallel in the world today and explains why so few European explorers have penetrated deep into the peninsula—scarcely twenty throughout the ages.

The Arab of the desert is instinctively suspicious of the man who does not look like himself, dress and talk like him and worship his God. This dislike is not born of fear, for he considers himself to be a superior person. He believes he is superior in most things but two. For some inscrutable reason Allah has given the infidel a temporary superiority in arms and money, and if you travel in his country it is well to be wise to these things. You must make very solid payment for his services, a generosity on your part, which, be assured, has little to do with your own volition; it is ascribed to the bountiful and the compassionate.

From the age of the Prophet to the age of Vasco da Gama the greater part of Arabia remained veiled in its old mystery. Doubtless regional groups of Arabs followed their simple and primitive ways of life as they continue to do to this day. The barren wastes supported wayward nomads, oases and mountain valleys a sparse, hungry, unlettered people; the coasts sailors and fishermen. Only along the western fringe of the peninsula had a great change taken place. Here, as Islam grew to be a world religion, came Persians, Turks, Kurds and Afghans, Iraqis, Syrians, Egyptians, Berbers and Spanish Moors in an annual pilgrimage. Mecca attained world eminence. The Mother of Cities and the City of God, the birthplace of Muhammad under the shadow of the Mountain of Light whence came the first astonishing revelations from the Infinite, became a cosmopolitan city. This old place of pilgrimage of the pagan Arabs before Muhammad's day was transformed into a place of pilgrimage for a world religion. Mecca's sister city, Medina, the city that gave Muhammad refuge in the years of persecution, the city of his later-day preachings, his burial place and the first capital of Arab world empire, had also become a place of world pilgrimage. Thus Mecca and Medina, the

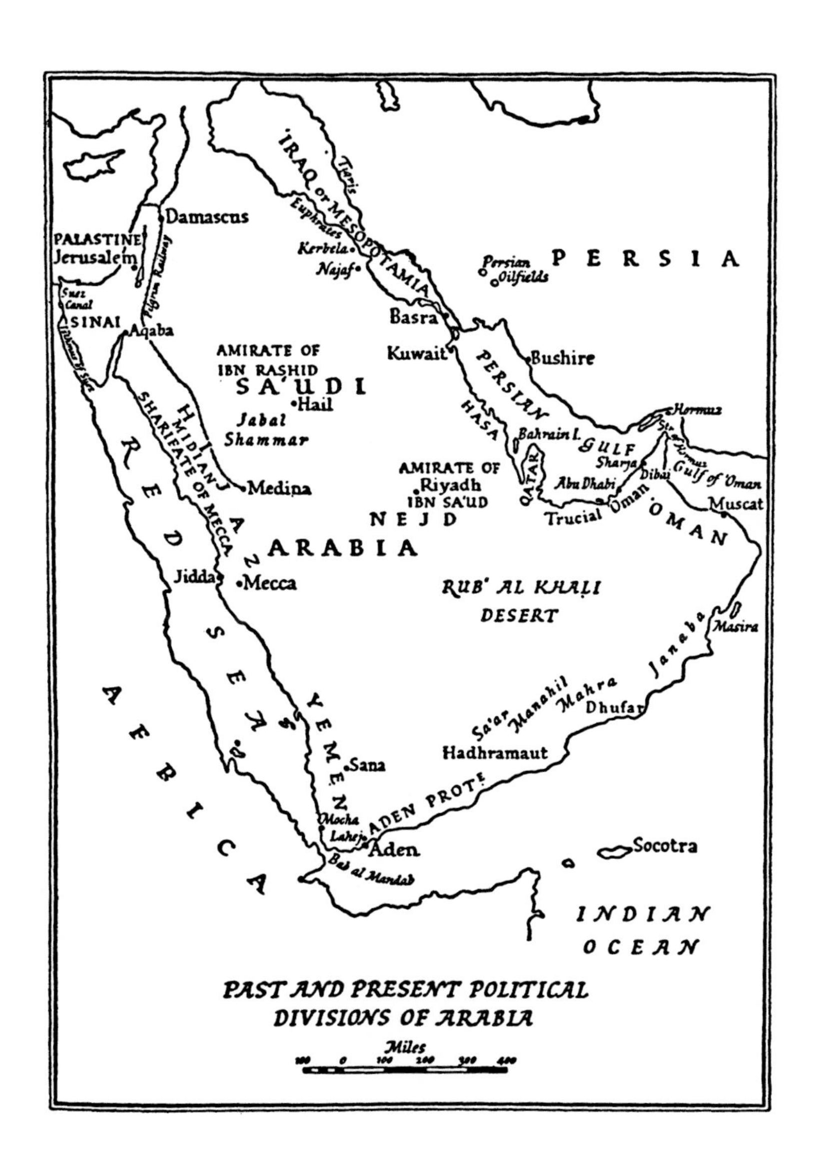
Damascus
PALASTINE
Jerusalem
Pilgrim Railway
Suez Canal
SINAI
Aqaba
'IRAQ or MESOPOTAMIA
Tigris
Euphrates
Kerbela
Najaf
Persian Oilfields
PERSIA
Basra
Kuwait
Bushire
AMIRATE OF IBN RASHID
SA'UDI
Hail
Jabal Shammar
HIDJAZ
MIDIAN
SHARIFATE OF MECCA
Medina
PERSIAN GULF
HASA
Bahrain I.
QATAR
Hormuz
Sharja
Dibai
Abu Dhabi
Gulf of Oman
Trucial Oman
Muscat
OMAN
AMIRATE OF Riyadh IBN SA'UD
NEJD
ARABIA
RED SEA
Jidda
Mecca
RUB' AL KHALI DESERT
Masira
Janaba
Mahra
Manahil
Sa'ar
Dhufar
Hadhramaut
YEMEN
Sana
ADEN PROTE
Mocha
Lahej
Aden
Bab al Mandab
Socotra
AFRICA
INDIAN OCEAN
PAST AND PRESENT POLITICAL DIVISIONS OF ARABIA
Miles
100 0 100 200 300 400

holy cities of Islam, acquired world significance under the new dispensation, and if Meccans of old time valued the commercial side of their city's sanctity (limited as it then was to Arabia), Mecca, Medina and the surrounding tribes came to have a deep sense of a harvest increased fortyfold now that the Prophet had worked in the vineyard. The townsfolk profited by catering for pilgrims, the rulers by taking a toll of their gifts, the tribesmen by the wages of transporting visitors come in pursuit of salvation, or by plundering them, whichever was more profitable.[1] Without much other wealth of its own the Hijaz became assured of an eternal livelihood.

This blessedness derived from the visiting subjects of outside caliphs, who must therefore be recognized as overlords. But caliphs, content with the prestige attaching to such association, generally allowed local rulers a large measure of autonomy, if not complete freedom, so long as pilgrims could come and go without being unduly fleeced. The caliphs, first of Baghdad and then of Cairo, were obliged at times to assert more than nominal suzerainty and send a representative to rule the holy places, but they never thought it worth while to extend their domination, so that Arabia was virtually detached from the caliphates in the great days of the Arab period. There was a lack of identity of interests, political, cultural, economic, between the Arabs within and the Arabs without, and even sentiment waned as the real power behind the caliphs passed out of Arab keeping into the hands of Persians or of Turks.

The Arab rulers of the holy places were jealous of their natural priority at the Arabian end of things, were resent-

[1]Under the enlightened aegis of Ibn Sa'ud this state of things exists no longer.

ful when the mastery, even nominal, passed to those of alien blood. These were grounds for friction.

Outside Arabia the Islamic world was divided into its two great historic divisions, Sunni and Shi'a, but the secular aspects of civilization at its height overshadowed the religious. With the primitive Arabs of the peninsula, on the other hand, religion remained a dominant interest, and there was space and leisure for cultivating all the refinements of a divided and subdivided Islam. The southern half of the peninsula was quite early the site of two principalities, the Yemen and the Oman, each with a theocratic form of government such as had disappeared in all but name from the Islamic world without. They were both anti-Sunni peoples, the Yemenis practising a brand of Shi'ism known as Zaidism, the Omanis practising Ibadhism, dissenting from Shi'a and Sunni alike.

Shi'ism, of course, originally found its main support in Iraq and Persia, but with the advent of the Seljuq Turks a Sunni domination established itself in Baghdad, whence Sunni representatives came from time to time to control the holy cities. Thus in southern Arabia of those times 'Sunni' came to be associated with 'alien.' It was natural that Mecca should look for alliance with the Yemen, the historic province lying to the south, and the legitimism of the Yemen—that is to say, the religious principle that true succession vested only in the seed of the Prophet—was a helpful counter to the claims of the Baghdad caliphs. The preachings of a Yemeni mystic named Hamdan Carmat, in the ninth century, led to the spread of legitimism through eastern Arabia, too, and during the tenth century the Carmathians, as they called themselves, swept into the holy cities, removed the sacred Black Stone of the Ka'ba (it remained in eastern

Arabia for twenty years) and eliminated Sunni domination from Mecca for a century.

When Carmathian ardour at length grew cold and Arabia split up again into its normal scattered autonomies, legitimism still remained the religious principle of Mecca and the Yemen, and the two together continued to resist any encroachments by the caliphs. Cairo at first had filched Mecca's allegiance from Baghdad, as Shi'ism spread westwards from Iraq to take official root in Egypt under the Fatimids. The ruler of Mecca was not as yet ruler of the province about it, the Hijaz, and his authority was weakened by internal divisions and by the old rivalry between the holy cities. In the dynastic struggles for power the house that looked to the Yemen for support was often opposed by a party with Medina contacts, and Medina, from geographical considerations, leaned towards Egypt; but Meccan rulers steadfastly cultivated the friendship of the imam of Yemen as a counter to the influence of Baghdad or of Cairo, and this went on into Ottoman times. When, in the twelfth century, the crusades drove Shi'as and Sunnis in the north into a common camp under Saladin, legitimist Mecca felt the pressure and must again offer prayers for a Sunni caliph. Indeed Sunnism was soon its established creed, though subservience to Egypt was thrown off for a time by the rise of Qatada, a local soldier ruler, who extended Mecca's dominion to embrace the whole Hijaz province and bequeathed the enlarged legacy for all time. When, however, the Mamlukes arose in Egypt, the link was renewed. Baibars, the founder of the new dynasty, came on a pilgrimage to the holy places, left behind an Egyptian garrison, and so in time the Hijaz became again an Egyptian appanage. Thus it came about that when the Turks took Cairo the keys of the

Ka'ba, with Mecca's homage, were carried to Selim the Grim.

Ottoman overlordship of Mecca (the holy places had known Turkish governors in Abbasid times) in no way implied overlordship of Arabia. Arabia was not then a political entity any more than it is today, and virtually only the Red Sea littoral provinces of the Hijaz and the Yemen were affected. In the Yemen, where the people regarded Sunnis as heretics, the yoke was light and for centuries nominal; the Yemen mountains, a difficult terrain, peopled by a hardy fighting stock, with an Arabian reputation such as is enjoyed by the frontier hillmen in India, allowed no secure foothold for intermittent Turkish garrisons. In the Hijaz, however, conditions for the new masters were easier. Yet the ruling Arab *sharifs* enjoyed long periods of freedom from control, particularly in the seventeenth century, at a time Egypt and Syria achieved a measure of autonomy, though Shi'a heresies were no longer tolerated, and the sharifs must henceforth be Sunni coreligionists of the Ottoman Turk, their master.

Arabia, outside these two provinces, remained unmolested, independent, able to cultivate regional sectarianism to its heart's content. The sects of Islam, the subdivisions of both Sunnism and Shi'ism, besides the dissenting sect of Ibadhism, even where not indigenous, all seem to have found the soil of Arabia congenial. There was, as there still is, an identity between sectarianism and dynastic government.[2] For Islamic sectarianism

[2]Zaidism, the state religion of the Yemen—a name derived from Zaid, the grandson of the martyr Husain—is a theocratic form of government in which rule can only vest in the seed of the Prophet. The field thus circumscribed, the theory allowed democratic election; the practice brought a hereditary religious office with a tradition of personal sanctity.

Ibadhism, the state religion of Oman, has resemblances to Wahhabism in

is a more vital thing than Christian sectarianism; it is legal rather than religious. Our nonconformists, for instance, while divided by academic differences, all live under a common law, whereas religion and law are so closely identified in Islam, where practised in its purity, that the difference between two sects assumes an important difference between the civil and criminal sanctions under which they respectively live. In the Islamic world outside Arabia, as we have seen, a liberal interpretation of holy law early took place, an adaptation, in communities at first predominantly non-Moslem, to more secular forms, but in the primitive societies of the peninsula holy law, varying with the sect, is followed to this day. Zaidi canons differ in some particulars from Ibadhi canons, while Sunni canons are different again.

To take, by way of example, a few differences between the four schools of thought of Sunnism, the orthodox half of Islam—sects known as Hanafi, Maliki, Shafi'i, Hanbali—which as we saw arose round about the second century over conflicting interpretations of Qur'anic law. The Hanafis stood notably for the validity of private judgment in doubtful cases, provided the judgment was based in inferences from the Qur'an—a system of analogy or derived sanctions. For instance the Qur'an provided for theft but not for burglary. By analogy that the motive of burglary is theft, the Hanafis agreed that the burglar

its puritanism. A very ancient sect, the Ibadhis, are the successors of the Secessionists who overthrew Ali, the fourth caliph, and between whom and the Shi'as there is therefore the greatest antipathy. The Ibadhi imam need not be of the seed of the Prophet as with the Zaidis, nor need he be accepted on grounds of political expediency as with the Sunnis. The theory is that he should be democratically elected on grounds of piety and learning, though practice led to temporal and spiritual offices vesting in the same individual. For the past two centuries, however, the roles have been separated and still remain so.

should suffer the same punishment as the thief, that is, his hand should be cut off.

The Malikis reacted against this emphasis on the principle of private judgment and stood for a greater importance attaching to the Traditions, that is to say, to precedents ascribed to the Prophet. If no Tradition could be cited to meet a case, then, said Malik, 'the consensus of opinion' of the theological doctors of Medina must be followed.

The founder of the Shafi'i sect next arose and, having studied in both earlier schools, evolved a compromise avoiding their extremes. Thus in the matter of the consensus of opinion of judges he held that this need not be confined to the doctors of Medina alone; he attached great importance, moreover, to the principle that local canons and long-established usage could not be overlooked in doubtful cases. South Arabian tribes belong predominantly to this sect.

The founder of the last school, Hanbali, was a pupil of Shafi'i but differed from his master's teachings, disliking the emphasis on 'private judgment' and 'theological benches' alike, and declaring for 'back to the Qur'an.' Hanbalism was the most reactionary and rigidly traditionalist of the four schools of thought, and after the sixth century, Hijra, found a lasting footing only in the Arabian peninsula itself, where in the Nejd, i.e. north central Arabia, the Wahhabis are its principal strength today.

The most latitudinarian school has traditionally been the Hanafi, to which the most advanced Sunni communities of today belong in Egypt, Turkey, Syria, Iraq—in short, the old Ottoman Empire. Only the Hanafi, for instance, held it permissible for prayers to be said in tongues other than Arabic. While all four schools agreed that within Islamic territory Jews and Christians might not erect places of worship in towns and villages at will, the Hanafis qualified the restriction under licences to a one-mile limit from the city walls; while usury was forbidden by all schools, the Hanafis allowed from the first the practice of mortgage and also that of hiring labour against a share of the produce; they also provided that a murderer should pay the extreme penalty—death or blood money as the next of kin may prefer—even if the victim was a Christian, Jew or slave; with them, too, a male may suffer the extreme penalty for the murder of a female, and an old woman for a young one. By Shafi'i and Maliki codes, on the other hand, a Moslem could not be slain for the murder of an unbeliever, or a freeman for a slave. The Hanafis did except the cases of the man murdering his own son or his own slave; the extreme penalty in such cases was not imposed.[9]*

Between Shi'a and Sunni differences in domestic usage were along the following lines. In the matter of custody of children after divorce the mother in Shi'a practice retained the child while it was at the breast, i.e. until two years old; after weaning the father had the right to it. In the Shafi'i sect the mother kept the child till it reached the age of seven, when it could choose which parent it would go to. In the Maliki sect the boy remained in the mother's custody till puberty and the girl till marriage. With them all a son's apostasy from Islam in later times excluded him from a right to his share of inheritance, so also an unbeliever or a slave could not inherit from a believer. Bastardy with the Sunnis excluded inheritance from the father but not the mother; with the Shi'as from both.

Outside Arabia the distribution of Islamic sects is almost geographical; west of Egypt the Maliki sect of Sunnism runs, as in times past, throughout north Africa and during the Moslem period (eighth to fifteenth centuries) extended over into Spain; eastwards Shi'as predominate in Iraq and Persia, a few are found in Afghanistan, while in India they form a small minority. But among Moslems of this outside world the criminal sanctions of holy law have disappeared, and even some domestic aspects have been superseded by alien-derived practices. In Arabia itself, however, the legal sanctions of sectarian practice are still in many parts de rigueur. State law is the complement of state religion and is administered by state qadhis. In the most liberal states there are qadhis for each of the Islamic legal codes; in others religious intolerance forbids any but the particular law of the state sect; while in many tribal areas the ancient usages, running counter to holy law, have survived. The Arab is born into one or other of the many sects after the manner of Gilbert's England, where

> Every little girl and boy alive
> Is born either Liberal or Conservative.

For in peninsular Arabia the strong religious prejudices of his environment make it extremely difficult or unwise for a man to change. Sectarianism is not a matter of intellectual persuasion; it is a tribal or family escutcheon. And as for our modern Western secular sectionalisms—Liberalism, Conservativism, Socialism, Communism, Capitalism, Fascism—these are not even dimly apprehended and so create no problems in the peninsular mind. The Arab of Arabia is a Wahhabi of Nejd, an Ibadhi of Oman, a Shafi'i of Hadhramaut or the like. These are the realities.

Arabia is not a political entity in spite of its common blood and tongue and social culture—Western criteria of nationalism. Its patriarchal tribal culture and the Arab's waywardness and love of individual freedom are agents perpetuating disintegration. Its thin-spread population, not as large as the city of Greater London, and dotted about a country half the size of Europe, makes for want of cohesion; the means of livelihood of its various parts is mutually exclusive, so that there is no economic advantage in unity; and, finally, historic tradition of opposing political and religious divisions is strong. Arabia is made up of numerous governments, each with its own dynastic ruler, its official religious sect (law), and each jealous to maintain its own traditional independence. Some in the Hadhramaut and the Persian Gulf are little bigger than city-states—such as Lahej, Bahrain, Qatar, Abu Dhabi, Dibai, Kuwait; others are loose tribal confederations whose paramount chiefs owe allegiance to none—such as the Janaba, Mahra, Manahil and Sa'ar that lie continuously across south Arabia; the comparatively big territorial divisions are today three: the Yemen, the Oman, and greatest and most dominant, if most recent, Sa'udi Arabia, lying to the north of them.

In a thinly populated, hungry country geographical size is not a necessary criterion of importance. The little state of Bahrain,[3] for instance, a British-protected group of

[3]Shi'ism is the chief sect of Bahrain, though, as in Muscat, other sects, notably Maliki, Shafi'i and Ismaili elements, are present. The last named are the followers of the Aga Khan, so well known in European circles. As the present-day imam of the sect he is an almost sacred figure with his followers not only in the Persian Gulf but parts of western India and East Africa too. These Ismailis, like the Zaidis of the Yemen, are historically a branch of Shi'ism, though now nonconforming and distinct. They are in agreement on the fundamental principle of succession in the Prophet's line but stop at the seventh generation (hence they are known as Sevenites, too) instead of the twelfth as do the Shi'as. They do not believe in a living concealed imam like the Shi'a Mahdi. With them there is an alternation of imams in public and in concealment; all, however, dying in due course.

islands off the east coast has a world importance: to the fair sex for its pearls; to commerce for its potential oil—this struck quite recently by some American concessionaires; to Persia for a shadowy claim to suzerainty; and to Britain as an air and naval station near the source of its Persian oil supply and on the air route to India.

The Yemen, lying across the left-hand bottom corner of the Arabian map facing Abyssinia, and Oman, lying across the right-hand bottom corner facing India, each inherits great traditions of Arabian prestige; the Yemen being the soil of the ancient south Arabian civilization; the Oman—a maritime state famous before and after Sindbad the Sailor!—little more than a century ago still exercised a hegemony over the Persian littoral, held sovereignty in Zanzibar and the neighbouring African coast and was the object of Napoleon's interest. Pre-eminent today is Sa'udi Arabia, lying to the north of them, an amalgam of three separate Arabian principalities, viz. the sharifate of Mecca and the two central Arabian amirates of Ibn Rashid and Ibn Sa'ud—the Hijaz, Nejd, Hasa and Asir constituting the entire northern half of the peninsula.

At the time of the outbreak of the Great War these enjoyed separate existences. Indeed, among all the princes of Arabia, Husain, the grand sharif of Mecca, stood foremost in the eyes of the outside Moslem world, this not in virtue of personal prestige, for he was the nominee of the Turks, but by reason of controlling the holy cities of Mecca and Medina. It was the custom of Turkey to recognize the head of the Hashimite family of Mecca, the family from which the Prophet sprang, as ex officio the Keeper of the Holy Places. This by no means meant that he was paramount among the princes in Arabia. These, in their various states, were rulers by hereditary right and would not have regarded him as in any way their superior, for, as a client who might be removed by a principal to make way for another member of his family (his own was a fortuitous appointment), he was in a way less than a dynastic ruler.

The other two principalities of what is now Sa'udi Arabia, northern Nejd (dynasty of Ibn Rashid) and southern Nejd (Ibn Sa'ud), were both comparatively recent, neither more than two hundred years old, but they had had time to become hereditary enemies, and at various times each, in turn, had dispossessed the other to rule the combined territories for a generation or so. Thus at the beginning of the century Ibn Rashid was in possession. At the outbreak of the Great War the two amirates were of about equal strength and existed side by side, Ibn Rashid being on friendly terms, Ibn Sa'ud at enmity, with the sharif of Mecca.

Periodical ascendancy of the Sa'udi house has mainly resulted from their championing the cause of a periodical religious revival which has come to be known by the name Wahhabism. The founder of this movement, Muhammad ibn Abdul Wahhab, was a religious reformer and revivalist who, exactly two hundred years ago, returned from theological studies in eastern Islamic countries to set his native central Arabia aflame with his eloquence. An ancestor of Ibn Sa'ud married the preacher's daughter and so strengthened still further the connection between the ruling family and the religious movement. Thirty years later the sword and religious fanaticism had extended the puritanical message and Sa'udi dominion over a greater part of the peninsula (the Yemen excepted); the holy cities fell into Wahhabi hands, and the gold ornamentation of the

Prophet's tomb was torn off as an offense to God. Bands of Wahhabis invaded as far north as the grazing grounds of Iraq, to the west of the Euphrates, spreading terror and intolerance, until one day they fell upon the beautiful shrine of Husain at Kerbala, sacred to the whole Shi'a world, and stripped it of some of its artistic splendour.

Turkey was alarmed at the sudden rise of power that was a constant menace to her borderlands and, conscious of her responsibility in the eyes of the whole Moslem world to keep open the Pilgrim route, would have moved against the desert but was too weak to do so and in any case found it politically prudent to allow the initiative to pass to the self-appointed, ambitious viceroy of Egypt, the Albanian, Muhammad Ali. This strong man sent an army via the Red Sea to invade Arabia from the west. The march was successfully made across the peninsula to the headquarters of the movement, which was destroyed (Riyadh, the present capital, is thus of more recent origin), and the Wahhabi power was vanquished for a generation.

During periods of revival Wahhabis are intolerant of other sects of Islam. To themselves they are the only man in the regiment in step, as it were; the rest are heretics every one. The theological and philosophical speculations which made Arabian civilization famous in the Middle Ages are heresies to be purged, if necessary by force, from the faith as delivered; the wearing of silk garment or gold ornament is a sin, and the delinquent is beaten; smoking is not tolerated, either, for who is to say whether the Prophet would not have forbidden it; but worse than this, the illumination of shrines of dead saints or the presentation of offerings to them is an abomination, so that some of the most beautiful architectural edifices of Islam are a reproach to the faith.

The Wahhabis consider their creed the pure and undefiled religion delivered through the Arabian Prophet. The Prophet to them is, as he taught, just a man, and the temptation to exalt him must be resisted. The attributes which Moslem sects have invested him with, but which he did not himself claim, are repudiated.

With the true Wahhabi laxity is sinful, and attendance at the mosque is obligatory. The wages of unbelief has, in times of crisis, been death, and chastisement for offences odious to their code is a commonplace; wherefore, in the later stages of my crossing of the south Arabian desert in 1931, I, as a self-confessed Christian, and my desert companions of Shafi'i tenets kept a careful watch to avoid collisions with any of these pious folk.

It is this movement which Arabia's outstanding figure, Abdul 'Aziz ibn Sa'ud, a religious man but by no means a fanatic himself had championed—as his forefathers did before him—when he regained possession of the state his father had lost. The hand of fate was against him in early life. Born at Riyadh, he had, at the age of nine, to accompany his father into exile after the latter's defeat by his northern rival, Ibn Rashid, whose star at that time was in the ascendant. As is often the case in Arabia, the way back to power lay through blood. His father, having from his exile in Kuwait made a final abortive attempt against his rival by open warfare, handed on the hereditary feud to the young boy.

Ibn Sa'ud, only nineteen at the time, set out in the winter of 1900 from his asylum at Kuwait, with forty men, on his reckless desert mission to win back his patrimony. Arriving overnight a short distance from Riyadh, he halted,

KING IBN SA'UD (ABDUL AZIZ IBN SA'UD).

(By courtesy of the Royal Legation of Sa'udi Arabia, London)

picked out six men to be his companions for the hazardous enterprise; the rest he enjoined to wait till the morning, when, if there was no news of him, they must fly for their lives back to Kuwait. Under cover of night he and his tiny party scaled the walls and made stealthily for the house next door to that of the governor, the representative of his father's usurper. They knocked upon the door, which was opened, forcibly made their entry, keeping the inmates under close arrest so as not to raise the alarm, then passed on to the governor's house and took the same precaution there, and so kept vigil during the dark hours against the governor's return in the morning, for it was his habit to sleep in the fort across the way. At dawn the fort gates were opened, and, oblivious of the presence of an enemy, the governor and his bodyguard came walking slowly towards the house. Ibn Sa'ud with his tiny party lying secretly in wait behind the door chose an opportune moment, rushed forth and took his enemies by surprise. There was a stiff fight, for the attackers were outnumbered four to one and, being in the open, were exposed to fire from the fort. The governor fell in the first onset; his death threw his companions into confusion, and the attackers quickly became masters of the situation, the guards surrendering in the belief that reinforcements must be at hand. Then, entering the fort of his fathers, the intrepid youth proclaimed himself governor of Riyadh, to the surprise and joy of the population.

A revival of Wahhabism was due, and a decade or two later the southern Nejd was aflame with zeal to purge the Arabian peninsula of its heresies, and the means to this end were the Ikhwan, the puritan army of Ibn Sa'ud. During the Great War Ibn Sa'ud, in receipt of a subsidy from the British government, remained benevolently neutral, though an embarrassing situation arose from the fact that he and our more actively engaged Arabian ally, the sharif of Mecca, were implacable enemies. Ibn Sa'ud's wartime attempt against Ibn Rashid, traditionally friendly with the sharif, though at the time client of the Turks, came to nought. But after the war had ended the Wahhabi leader marched (1922–23) to a more successful attack and wrested Ibn Rashid's territory from him, so that northern Nejd became his, and a few years later—by which time both he and the sharif had ceased to enjoy their war subsidies from Britain, and the sharif had ceased to enjoy British protection—he marched against the Hijaz. The sharif, who had meanwhile assumed the title of King of the Arabs, had become discredited with his own people and with Moslems overseas, from his inability to quell or satisfy Hijazi tribesmen who were plundering pilgrims, rendering the pilgrimage unsafe.

Taif fell, and King Husain's army was routed. Mecca submitted after a short siege, and a little later Medina and Jidda, too, passed into Ibn Sa'ud's hands, so that the Hijaz province was now added to his central Arabian possessions, and shortly afterwards he assumed the title of King of the Hijaz. The passing of the Hijaz under Ibn Sa'ud's sway came with a minimum of upheaval, not because Wahhabism was loved, but because misrule was ended and because Ibn Sa'ud enjoyed great personal prestige and reputation for just, wise and strong rule. It was the triumph of the great personal leader; Arabia had again been true to her tradition that it is the man, not the system that counts.

The possession of the holy places has been a pillar of strength to Ibn Sa'ud, but a source of weakness to the fanatical movement by which he rose to power. Pilgrim revenues are a vital means of keeping the hungry desert quiet, while the responsibility to an outside Moslem world compels a degree of toleration which is the very negation of aggressive Wahhabism. For the Sa'udi house, revenue and dynastic considerations must curb the desert ardour. Meanwhile, for pilgrims who do not go out of their way to offend mellowed Wahhabi susceptibilities, there is greater security for life and property under Ibn Sa'ud than normally fell to the lot of their predecessors down the centuries.

The livelihood of Arabia's natives is pitched low, by any Western standard. Over a greater part of the country it is a bare subsistence economy, where man counts his wealth in his camels or his oxen, his asses or goats—his menservants and maidservants perhaps—rather than his money. Of money there is very little indeed. Only in certain favoured coastal regions where towns are to be found—its most populous parts—is a wage system and other resemblances to a Western commercial mechanism found, and the houses of wealthy personages may know of the simpler Western amenities.

The pilgrimage brings considerable, if artificial, local prosperity. Of late years, on account of the world depression, it has declined. Medina, once a city of seventy thousand, has now a mere fifteen thousand inhabitants, though that is but the measure of its own fall. For centuries Medina was the main portal of the pilgrim's way, and the Pilgrim Railway from Damascus, built in the decade before the war, had its terminus there; but wartime destruction of the railway and the competition of postwar motor transport has been to Medina's hurt, and today most pilgrims come first to Mecca by way of the seaport of Jidda. The twentieth-century Moslem prefers the motorcar to the camel that was the vehicle of the Prophet's pilgrimages and that of his own ancestors for thirteen centuries past, though from a spirit of piety or as the penalty of poverty a few eschew the foreign machine in favour of walking. Many of the Negro pilgrims have thus accomplished the long journey from central or even west Africa. They spend years on the pilgrimage, working their way from place to place across the Dark Continent, some of their brothers falling by the wayside, others being born en route.

Another source of such wealth as Arabia can boast is her Persian Gulf pearl fisheries, centred in Bahrain. Two millions sterling was realized for the harvest of 1926, though a quarter of that income would be welcome today. Each year during the summer months when the inland sea is calm (and red, red hot!) the natives of Arabia's eastern littoral, freemen and slaves, abandon their normal avocations and swarm down to the coasts to become divers for the season. Dhows and other small native craft, packed with motley crews, go out and anchor over favourite banks, usually in about ten to fifteen fathoms of water, and carry on their diving in the selfsame way that the Moorish visitor, Ibn Batuta, saw and described six centuries ago. Nowadays the scene has one addition. A British naval sloop comes and goes, playing the traditional part in these waters of policeman and friend.

Thirty times a day the diver takes his deep breath and is lowered into the sea, to remain below for about a minute and a half and then be hauled up to the surface for a blow. He dives naked except for his loin cloth and a bag slung round his neck to hold the oysters which he wrenches off the sea bed; a leather clip, like a clothes peg, closes his nostrils; his finger tips and toes are protected by leather sheaths. The rest of the simple equipment consists of two

A SMALL DHOW ON THE PEARLING BANKS OFF BAHRAIN.

(By courtesy of Mr K. P. Narayan)

OVER A WATER–HOLE IN THE THIRSTY DESERT.

ropes, one weighted by a stone on which he is lowered, the other a communication rope to signal to his companions in the boat above when he has had enough, for a jinn sometimes enters the poor wretch's head, in which case his nose and ears are prone to bleed! Throughout the season divers eat little and must dive fasting except for a cup of coffee and a few dates. It is an unhealthy occupation, and divers usually die young, so that the lady who, on humanitarian grounds, shuns wearing fur and feathers, should, to be consistent, have misgivings about her pearl necklace if it is strung of rose pearls from the Gulf banks—the most precious of all their kind—unless of course she takes up the attitude: 'Would the diver who wants to dive be grateful for the unemployment?' The diving industry is in native hands, and the absence of modern methods of diving is due to native apprehension lest the goose be killed that lays the golden eggs. Arabian pearls go via Bombay to Paris, the world's pearl mart, and thence the most precious find their way to London and New York. In common with all luxury industries, pearling has suffered by the world slump, but a more insidious future enemy may be the cultured pearl industry of Japan.

If the world's most precious pearls come from eastern Arabian waters, the world's best coffee comes from south-western Arabia, where it is native to the mountains of the Yemen. At the port of Mocha—whence its trade name—Portuguese mariners, soon after their discovery of the Cape of Good Hope, met with it and introduced it into Europe, so that it was a novelty in England in the same century that saw the introduction of tobacco and the potato, both from the New World, of course. The Arabian crop today is small, and Arabian coffee a luxury mainly bought up by London and New York. For although coffee is the national beverage of Arabia, only the very rich can afford Mocha, and the poorer Arabs buy their everyday coffee from the outside world to which they first taught its use.

Another epicurean product of Arabia, fancied more by China and Malaya than the West, is the soup made from the fins and tails of sharks. The Persian Gulf and Indian Ocean swarm with sharks—the pearl diver is too good a fatalist to be afraid of them—and some hundred thousand are caught every year off the coasts of Oman alone. Indeed, these fisheries are an industry secondary only to date culture, and Oman's famous date groves extend for more than a hundred miles along its sandy tropic shores to a depth of a mile or two, from where the fruit, ripening earlier than elsewhere, is quickly rushed away to meet America's voracious needs.

The spices of Arabia are a more romantic source of income. Frankincense and myrrh, both the resinous substances of wild trees that made south Arabia famous in ancient times, come today almost exclusively from one province, Dhufar, possibly the Ophir of antiquity, a territory of the central south under the Muscat flag. On social occasions the frankincense brazier is passed around the assembly with the ritualistic coffee; and when evil is abroad it has a magical value for exorcism, but most of the crop goes overseas to be used in the service of Buddhist temples of India and the Farther East.

One other industry of coastal Arabia must be mentioned —its boatbuilding. The picturesque Arab dhow with its forward-raking mainmast carrying a big single stretch of sail, a tiny mizzenmast incongruously raking the other way, the high Elizabethan look of the poop and the graceful droop of the waist, are features that clearly belong to the distant past. He who has a sentiment for our old sailing ship meets with enchantment as he voyages across the Indian Ocean at any time except when the southwest monsoon drives these quaint fore-and-afters off the open sea into their summer anchorages. Here is a craft that has come unchanging across the ages. Almost every Arab seaport has its own traditional build and rig, Kuwait and Sur perhaps the most famous. Dhows up to two hundred tons burden carry dates and frankincense and shark's meat to India and Africa, and bring back rice, the staple food of the well-to-do, sugar, piece goods and other simple requirements of a poor oriental people.

The hardy Arab mariners, possessed of imperfect instruments and a nodding acquaintance with the rudiments of navigation, yet have a knowledge of the elements which even our more scientific sailors may envy. In the annual voyage to East Africa they run down before the northeast monsoon without too nice a sense of longitude and, on reaching the desired latitude, turn west to make a landfall. It is a common experience of British ships in these parts to be hailed at sea by one of these craft that has made a bad voyage with the request for water and its bearings. But the camaraderie of the sea is sometimes thought to be a trifle one sided when the Arab dhow, economizing in head or other lights up to the fifty-ninth minute, suddenly flashes her presence dead ahead out of a black night.

A thousand years ago such dhows were all that these oceans knew. From the Persian Gulf they sailed eastwards to Malacca and Java for the tin required by Abbasid metalworkers, an intrepid adventurer among them sometimes voyaging on into the China Seas. With India upon their way, an ancient trade with it stood at a high pitch of development, and Arab colonies sprang up in Bombay and

Sind, which survive to this day. Westwards, too, the Arabs sailed for gold to the islands of Wagwag, i.e. Madagascar—their name also for Japan—and sowed the seed which ripened into Arabian colonization and the annexation of Zanzibar little more than a century ago. From these voyages came the tall yarns ascribed to Arab sea captains, not hampered by too strong an addiction to the religious truth, which found their way into the literature of the times, though curiously enough the doings of Sindbad the Sailor and all the rest of his romantic kind in *The Arabian Nights*—to us as entrancing as Greek or Nordic folk tales—are a form of literature about which the serious-minded literate Arab is often a little scornful.

Dhows hauled up along the Arab beaches have a monstrous, whalelike appearance as they lean over at alarming angles on their bulging bilges. In process of building they are a joy to behold. The ribs take on a beautiful symmetry at the hands of craftsmen who appear to have no elaborate drawings to guide them and work by eye and rule of thumb. In Kuwait the barren woman comes by stealth at night to jump over a new-laid keel, an old fertility cult, while the watchman shoos her off lest she take virtue out of the ship.

Early Persian contacts and long seafaring intercourse with Iraq and India give the small seaports of eastern Arabia a cosmopolitan air and a comparatively advanced and tolerant outlook. The successful merchant-shipowner delights in bringing back to his date garden exotic plants he has met with on his travels. In the Hadhramaut, which province shares with the Yemen the pride of an ancient civilization and with New York a fancy for incipient skyscrapers, the tradition is with Java. The native goes off when young to the East Indies and returns, in later life,

DESERT CAMEL POLICE (TRANS–JORDAN).

(By courtesy of Major J. C. Glubb)

TERRACE COUNTRY OF THE YEMEN FOR COFFEE CULTIVATION.

(By courtesy of the Royal Geographical Society. Photo: Mr K. C. Twitchell)

with his fortune made; he has not ceased to be an Arab, though he has ceased to have an Arabian outlook.

But these are the coastal fringes. Arabia's great heart remains untouched and her mood forbidding. The nomadic tribes find the camel well-nigh sufficient for their simple wants. They subsist almost exclusively on its milk and occasionally its flesh; their houses are tents of hair made from its wool, their clothing in some measure from the same source too. In prewar days there was a camel-raising industry in the northwest for export via Damascus to Egypt. At that time the camel was the ideal means of transport in those neighbouring countries that lacked roads and much water, but the introduction of the American motorcar has brought great changes, and what was once a valuable export trade has decayed. So, too, a horse-raising industry flourished in the northeast, horses being exported to India where they were popular for polo, but the disappearance of the rule which imposed a height restriction and which in the old days made 'the Arab' ideal, has put the small and beautiful animal out of the game, and so the horse trade has greatly declined.

Cultural divisions of the Arabian society, if most marked between coast and desert, run also laterally across the various states. It is the old division between the settled Arab—cultivator, merchant, townsman—on the one hand, and our friends the Beduin on the other; the former wedded to ways of law and order, the latter to a wayward life which involves plundering each other or settled Arab, as occasion demands or opportunity offers. These two elements of the population are persuaded by long experience that their interests clash. They are mutually antipathetic. Each believes in armed force as a way of cowing the other. If you want peace with your neighbour the Arab proverb tells you the Arab way: 'In one hand bread, in the other a sword.'

Islam, the religion that had its cradle among the Arabs of Arabia, reflects their democratic spirit in its insistence on the equality of believers. For the non-Arab slave no equal social status is conceded, so that in this Arabia goes back on her democracy and indeed is today one of the very few countries left in the world to practise and justify slavery. Arabian male slavery is of two kinds, industrial and domestic. The former supplies the needs of date gardens and pearl fisheries. The latter, the more usual form, where the slave is the retainer, the bodyguard, the house servant, is not a harsh and pitiless exploitation of labour like the old industrial slavery of our West Indian colonies —the usual connotation of slavery in Western minds. Slaves are often treated as members of the family, fed and clothed every bit as well as others. I have, in fact, known of a slave who was liberated and then voluntarily returned to the bondage of his old master in preference to the insecurity that came with freedom. But slavery is intolerable for all that. The slave is a property. Slave dealers are free to traffic in their human wares, those who specialize in slaves being always in touch with intending buyers and sellers, and they conduct would-be purchasers to the houses where the slaves may be inspected. The majority of slaves, however, certainly the more fortunate among them, remain in the same family for generation after generation.

The answer to the question Why do the Arabs want slaves? is in part sociological, in part economic. Slavery is a traditional part of the social structure. It is congenial. The peninsular Arabs are in the mass far too proud to work as servants, far too independent in spirit to obey a master, so that the well-to-do have either to do their work themselves or to resort to slavery. This is why, among a poor people having little more than a subsistence culture, all attempts at the suppression of slavery have hitherto failed.

In the very early wars of Islam the practice was to treat prisoners as slaves and allot them to Arab warriors as part of the plunder of war. The end of these wars brought a fruitful source of slave supply to its close. Slave raiding into Africa was thereby given a greater stimulus, and for the last few centuries Africa has been the chief source of supply. Among slaves that one sees in Arabia today Negroes easily predominate, though Abyssinians and Baluchis are to be found.

My own experience after living for many years in parts of Arabia where slavery forms an integral part of the social structure is that few slave transhipments are coming in from overseas today. In the old days British naval activities did a great deal to make external slave dealing hazardous; today internal slavery perpetuates itself by slaves begetting slaves. They are usually married at puberty, and so fresh slaves are brought into the world ad infinitum, and these, by religious law as locally interpreted, are the property of the master and when he dies are inherited like any other form of property.

The British government, with some difficulty and much unpopularity, made slave agreements in times past with most of the coastal states of Arabia, under which slaves escaping to a British consulate are manumitted, while on the high seas British naval ships exercise the right to search native craft for slave runners. But within Arabia itself slavery flourishes with the full support of public opinion, and any extraneous authority interfering becomes odious in the eyes of the people. It is a vested interest of immemorial respectability.

Most enlightened Arabian rulers, though they doubtless privately consider that it would be a very good thing if slavery were no more, dare not affront influential subjects who favour slavery and possess slaves. These rulers, no less than Western ones, must not go out of their way to alienate the governed if they are to survive. And, short of coercive measures which no one is likely to take, only a change of public opinion—a new general attitude of mind—will ensure permanent abolition. Today King Ibn Sa'ud is tackling this very difficult problem sympathetically and wisely, but up to recent times the measure in which Arab rulers co-operated with a foreign power on an issue of this kind was construed as the measure of their dependence upon that foreign power. No really independent Arab ruler could attempt to overthrow the age-hallowed institution of slavery when he knew that such measures were equated in the minds of his people with a foreign and Christian policy, a policy obviously alien to, and subversive of, their own state of society. Changes in the social system have to be gradual if an upheaval is to be avoided. Certain pilgrims of affluence are being encouraged to buy a slave or slaves and set them free, and well-to-do Hijazis are said to be doing the same as an act of worship or to celebrate some happy occasion—the birth of a child, the recovery of a near relative from sickness and the like.

In the unabatement of slavery Arabia has been false to her Prophet. Muhammad, as we have seen, was no upholder of slavery—is held to have had no slaves himself. He exhorted his followers to manumit slaves and apportioned a part of the revenues of the state to the same ends. His goal may well have been total emancipation. In his

BEDUIN OF SOUTH ARABIAN DESERT BORDERLANDS.

TOWNSMEN: A FAMILY GROUP OF ARAB (PERSIAN GULF) PEARL MERCHANTS.

farewell sermon on Mount Arafat he did not forget them: 'And your slaves! See that you feed them with such food as you eat yourselves and clothe them with the stuff you wear; and if they commit a fault for which you are not inclined to forgive them, part with them for they are the servants of God and are not to be harshly treated.'

CHAPTER X

Rise of the West: Eastern Repercussions

WE MUST take leave of the Arabs of Arabia to resume our outline of the greater Arab world without, where we left it, as the sunset glories of the Arab caliphates finally faded under the shadow of Ottoman conquest. Arab civilization was already far gone in decay. Great Moslem architecture, it is true, continued in Egypt and in Persia—a country that had long ceased to be under Arab rule; the arts still flourished; indeed, Persian art was to grow in the seventeenth century to its zenith, surpassing the splendour of its Arab period. But science had declined among the Arabs some hundreds of years before (about the thirteenth century) with the hardening of dogmatic intolerance, when religious zeal revived and brought with it disapproval of philosophers because their works might lead to unbelief.

From the Ottoman conquest on through the subsequent four centuries to our own times was a period of further Arab eclipse and decay. The Arabs sank back into obscurity—from which the recent Great War has helped to rescue them—continuing to be content with their subordinate part in a supernational state of Islamic form—the Ottoman Empire.

This same period saw the rise of Western Europe to a position of world ascendancy. The West was destined to exercise far-reaching influence on Arab destinies, Western political philosophy was to weaken the Turkish shackles, Western arms to sever them. But the process was long delayed. The earlier forms of civilization, especially Islamic civilization, had, as we saw, at first been moulded by religion rather than nationality. It was religion that had differentiated social cultures and shaped political allegiances. Islam had evoked a loyalty transcending race or nation. With the remarkable rise of Western civilization, a civilization that in its later forms was inspired not so much by religion as by political ideals, oriental life and thought became more and more modified, and, since the Arab countries during this period formed part of the Ottoman dominions, their conversion is part of the Ottoman story.

The East, grown poor and backward, was first impressed by the material prosperity of the new West, a prosperity which seemed to lie at the roots of Western prestige and power. The growth of this prosperity, therefore, especially where it had Ottoman and Arab contacts, is of much more than passing interest. As Islam lost control of the western Mediterranean the early maritime expansion of Venetians and Genoese led to their later establishment by the crusades on the shores of the Levant; the Mongols, tolerant of Christianity, sweeping westwards, were next to lure Marco Polo and other merchant adventurers into unknown Asia and lift a corner of the veil that obscured remotest China. So came the growing knowledge of the wealth of the Indies that provoked

Western curiosity and further adventuring, and hence, at the very time the Ottomans were rising to imperial dominion in the Near East, Western mariners were circumnavigating Africa, rediscovering Arabia's seaboards, forgotten since Byzantine times, and opening up the treasures of India and the even greater opportunities of the Americas.

But Western influence, if founded in the material prosperity which sprung from this pioneering, was not confined to it. The flowering of Renaissance learning which continued increasingly to flourish along the subsequent centuries exalted the West and impressed its growing superiority on the declining East. Western enlightenment as well as Western prosperity gave a benediction to Western forms of political organization, and these in time came to find favour and acceptance. Thus nationalism, a Western concept of state organization and one running counter to Islamic internationalism, made headway in the Ottoman Empire and played a main part in Ottoman dissolution and Arab revival; democratic institutions of Western origin, too, that ran counter to traditional absolutism, also found champions in academic circles.

The struggle which had resolved itself in crusading times around three civilizations—Western, Near East, Middle East, or in other words, broadly speaking, Latin Christendom, Eastern Christendom and Islam—we left at the point where the West had withdrawn, unsuccessful, from the contest, and Middle East had triumphed over Near East as the Ottoman Turks established themselves in the Balkans. The subsequent centuries have brought Middle Eastern decay and Western world ascendancy.

The religious spirit was still active in the pioneer days of trade. The great explorers, Vasco da Gama, Christopher Columbus and De Albuquerque, all bore the Cross on their breasts and thought of themselves as inheritors of a sacred tradition. The first naval campaigns in the Indian Ocean in the sixteenth century were infused with this spirit, and the Portuguese records of their operations in the Red Sea thirty years after the discovery of the Cape of Good Hope show them bent upon the seizure of Mecca 'for the Glory of God and His most Catholic Majesty.' A setback before Jidda sent them scurrying back to Aden, which served as their base for voyages of exploration into the Red Sea whence they penetrated to the Isthmus of Suez itself.

To these Portuguese belong the honours of pioneers. In the great Western movement for world trade they were the first Europeans to make contacts, in Islamic times, with the Arabs of the peninsula. These early days saw their penetration into the Persian Gulf, too, where Hormuz, a flourishing medieval port on the Persian side, was their lure, and for its mastery they strove during a century and a half. De Albuquerque, their famous admiral, descended upon the opposite shores of eastern Arabia, built forts and threw garrisons into them as the splendid remains of the period at Muscat, the battered fort masonry and old muzzle-loading guns that litter the foreshore for two hundred miles to north and south, still bear eloquent testimony. But the West as yet had little to teach the Arabs. Portuguese activities were not even imperial; their purpose was trade, where possible by peaceful means, where not possible under armed occupation. Their enterprise must not on that account be belittled. He who is acquainted with these fearsome parts and can visualize their difficulties must be awed with admiration for their great qualities as seamen and adventurers. Their small sailing ships were scarcely bigger than the biggest of the opposing native ones, and by these many times outnumbered; they navigated waters about which they at first had no nautical knowledge; they engaged an enemy thousands of miles from their bases, so that in reality they had no bases; and to get supplies of food and water in times of war must land and fight an incalculable foe; they were unequipped for one of the hottest and most trying climates in the world, where indeed the Persian poet would have us believe 'the panting sinner receives a foretaste of his future destiny.' At times they were driven to drastic measures, and a tradition lingers in Muscat of an occasion when they cut off the noses of every male inhabitant they could lay their hands on. Among a warlike people overmuch given to revenge, and themselves alive to the danger of coming back again—which they must do—it is clear they were strong men possessed of indomitable courage.

By the seventeenth century British and Dutch traders had appeared upon the scene to share with Portuguese and Arabs what trade was going, the Turkish masters of Iraq taking as yet no active interest in Persian Gulf commerce. British mariners came and went; one of the most notable, the discoverer of Baffin Bay, left his bones to whiten there. As the official report of the day has it, 'Master Baffin went on shore with his geometrical instruments for the taking the height and distance of the castle wall for the better levelling of his piece to make his shot; but as he was about the same he received a small shot from the castle into his belly, wherewith he gave three leaps by report and died immediately.'[23]*

As the East India Company pushed forth its agents the Portuguese soon fell to third place and then dropped out of the race; while the Dutch, penetrating to Iraq itself with bigger ships and more astute factors, led the going. Such trading activities, part of a wider merchant enterprise the world over, resulted in the West laying the foundations of greater wealth and a higher standard of living for itself, but trade rivalry involved political action and brought the Ottoman Empire into the cockpit of Western diplomacy. Trade agreements made in Constantinople, unexceptionable as they may have been in their provision for uniform customs duties and other equitable arrangements, were of course not wholly effective in the remoter provinces; here the foreign trader who most prospered was he who bribed the local authorities most handsomely. Thus, however regrettable political pressure harnessed to economic interests may appear to a pious armchair student of foreign affairs today, it was often directed against corruption or abuse, and in any case the Western nation that sat back in those pioneering days saw privileges and prosperity pass to others.

In the Indian Ocean the French next came to share the Dutch trade, but in the eighteenth century both were eclipsed by the British in the race for the great market of India. The East India Company, soon to become the government of India, now began to dominate Arabian waters; it set about charting the coasts, putting down piracy (in later times slavery and gunrunning, too) and planting Indian trading communities, with political agents to protect them, on the Persian Gulf shores, where both make a living to this day. British mechanical genius, then preeminent in the world with inventions of railways, steamships and telegraphs, prepared the way for further exploitation. On the high seas the British steamer came to take a bigger share of the carrying trade at the expense of the native dhow, and on the internal waterways of

Iraq smaller British-owned vessels, through the personal interest of King William and Parliament, obtained a concession to ply for trade as they have continued to do down to this day. It was enterprise such as this, going on the world over, that laid the foundations of our foreign-derived income, which is reflected in our present-day prosperity, naval power and diplomatic prestige.

From the middle of the last century the Ottomans, and with them the Arabs, were brought into still closer political contact with Britain through new canal and telegraph enterprises. A telegraph line was constructed by British engineers, under Turkish auspices, linking up the Persian Gulf with the Mediterranean, and the power of British consular agents grew in a night. Whereas before they must come, cap in hand, to the local authorities to beg trade favours for their nationals, there was now direct and instant touch with India, London and Constantinople, and they found themselves armed with readier and firmer answers to local obstacle-makers concerning the 'rights' of traders, river navigators and even archaeologists. A new kind of local friction arose from a new kind of local balance of power. The native official did not like the foreign representative any better on this account, but he was awed by the amazing efficiency of the political organization behind him; it was educative.

Of much wider political importance was the opening of the Suez Canal in 1869, the work of French engineers, by which Egypt and Turkey came to have a new significance for Britain and India. Britain's need to protect the new trade route to her greatest market, India—the most valuable market in the world—led her almost at once to establish a protectorate along a strip of southwest Arabian coast immediately behind Aden, a fringe of Yemen territory where Turkey was nominally suzerain. For Turkey, too, the Arabian coasts came to have an added importance, and she tightened her control where she had a footing—the Hijaz and the Yemen—and extended control where she had not, thus claiming suzerainty over Kuwait and throwing troops into the mid-Persian Gulf littoral at Hasa and Qatar astride Bahrain. In deference to British susceptibilities she did not press her cherished pretensions to Bahrain; indeed, Turkey found herself everywhere thwarted in the Persian Gulf by the older and well-parapetted British-Indian entrenchments. Her tiny garrisons did, however, give her prestige with the two desert principalities of South Nejd (Ibn Sa'ud) and North Nejd (Ibn Rashid), and during the next half-century, down to the Great War, each of these from time to time turned to her in moments of internal weakness or from fear of the other, promising subjection as the price of support. But for Turkey these adventures did not pay, and her soldiers had been driven from the Hasa province of the Persian Gulf by Ibn Sa'ud a year before the Great War descended upon her.

Among these new Western agencies it was railways, however, that were destined to play greatest havoc with Turkey's future. So backward were the Arab countries under the Turks that up to the end of the century they still possessed no railroad. This was not the fault of foreign railway magnates, for these in very early days had formed plans of a railroad across Europe to India. A similar scheme was revived in London in the middle of the nineteenth century but again came to nought. In 1854 Lynch and Chesney, British pioneers of the Iraq river steamer enterprise launched a more modest and practicable plan for a short railway from the Mediterranean to the

Euphrates, thence to link up with the river boats to the Persian Gulf. Two years later capital of a million sterling for the Syrian Trans-Desert Railway was oversubscribed in the city of London. The Ottoman government were quite favourably disposed and went to the length of underwriting six per cent dividends and holding up the rival concession for cutting the Suez Canal for which the French had plans ready. The issue was decided by extraneous affairs. The Indian Mutiny broke out, Britain required certain concessions from the French in Egypt in connection with the movement of British troops. The British railway project was dropped, and the French canal project proceeded with. Had this railway been built the recent history of the Middle East might well have been different. British influence in Constantinople would probably have remained powerful despite Russia and German influence been denied the chance of growing. Turkey would then probably have escaped being drawn into the Great War, in which case the Arab countries, Palestine, Syria and Iraq, would have remained under Ottoman dominion, possibly to this day. But the railway was not built, and in the eighties British influence in Turkey began to decline under Mr Gladstone. The way was opened to Germany, and she was soon at work building all Turkey's railways. In 1885 the Balkan Railway was completed to Constantinople; during the last twelve years of the century German engineers brought into existence the railway system of Asia Minor; and early in the present century the Pilgrim Railway down the western side of Arabia to Medina. (See map, page 277.)

It was not local internal railways, however—these in political eyes were harmless enough—but projects for a strategic railway that came to have major interest for the great Western Powers. Round about the opening of the present century these various projects, first the Russian plan for a railway from Asia Minor to the Persian Gulf, then the German scheme for a railway from Constantinople to the Persian Gulf, had alarming significance for Britain. Both of these powers were known to cherish Eastern ambitions, and Britain as the one great Middle East imperial Power conceived herself challenged. Russia lay contiguous to Persia and Afghanistan in the north, so that the land threat to India via the northwest frontier, together with this foreshadowed sea threat by way of the Persian Gulf made a formidable combination. Since the Crimean War Russia had, however, been engaged in other tussles with Turkey, and the rumours of the Turkish railway concession to the Russians proved, in the event, to lack substance. The apprehension that it gave rise to, however, led the government of India to seek a closer relationship with Kuwait, the Arab port at the head of the Persian Gulf—the natural terminus for a strategic railway—where Turkish suzerainty had not been recognized, and under an agreement then made the ruler undertook to give no such concession to any foreign state.

Meanwhile Turkey had granted the more alarming railway concession to Germany, and the fat was in the fire. The future possibility of enemy submarine activities in the Indian Ocean in time of war was a less real menace than the threat to the Persian oil fields, which, as time went on, were developing and eventually formed a main source of Britain's oil supply. The interplay of international politics in the Arab countries which these activities involved was not lost upon the Arabs. They saw signs and tokens that presaged a great war, a war with which their own national destinies were to be bound up.

These great contending forces of the West were nations. Their mighty activities were inspired and sustained in the name of nationalism. Western nationalism began to have a curious fascination for the Arabs. What was at the bottom of the political organization which seemed to have all the solidarity of the tribe? It was a small, compact unit, a homogeneous group speaking one common tongue. Despite their common religion the Western nations were seen to be each acutely conscious of its own interests, anxious to maintain independent existence, zealous for its own preeminence. This was not at all like the Arabs' own Middle East tradition where Turks, Arabs, Kurds, etc., were loosely grouped within an Islamic framework—a heterogeneous collection of peoples speaking many tongues. True their own Ottoman Empire was no longer held together by religion but by the sword, though a general attitude of mind that encouraged Moslem unity was a legacy of its tradition. The caliphate, however, in its ideological form, had perished in the wars wherein Moslems fought Moslems for dynastic power, when the empire split into fragments and two or three caliphs could rule in different parts of the world at the same time. A phase of temporal rule had come. He was the ruler who could impose his will. 'The sovereign has a right to govern,' declared the fourteenth-century Moslem jurist, Ibn Jama'ah of Damascus, 'until another and stronger shall oust him from power, and rule in his stead. The latter will rule by the same title and will have to be acknowledged on the same grounds.'[20]* Tradition did not require that the blood of the rulers should be that of the people. It was a state of things where it was politically acceptable to render unto Cæsar the things that are Cæsar's. The realism of the age recognized that authority fundamentally and of right rests on force.

The late Western conception of the rights of nations to independent existence as being based on the homogeneous cultural group speaking one tongue was thus outside the Middle East tradition. In the East the traditional penalties of challenging him who held the sceptre did not encourage the growth of political self-consciousness among minority elements, much less of separatist movements. The imperial Islamic tradition was wider than nationalism, compelling men of diverse race and tongue into a common hegemony; thus the early triumph of Middle East civilization under the Turks had placed Arabs, Armenians, Assyrians, Kurds, Bulgars, Greeks and the rest under the caliphs of Constantinople, and none at first wished or dared to contest their authority.

In the West, on the other hand, individual nations developed their political institutions out of their inner consciousness, shaped by their history, their literature, their temper, their economic advantage. Such groups, geographically and ethnically compact, developed and gained strength. Their population increased, and to support themselves they must expand and in later times find ever fresh outlets for their manufactures and commerce. The Western nations ranged out and mastered the world—the Americas, India, Australasia, Africa—and even the Ottoman Empire itself was not free from their penetrating enterprises. By the late eighteenth century the Turks were having to look to their laurels and in the early nineteenth[1] were organizing their army on the Prussian model; they were being driven, in order to survive, to adopt the methods of a modern world that was enveloping them. And so

[1]Professor Temperley in his work *England and the Near East—the Crimea* has some new references to the caliphate in the nineteenth century.[27]*

with other aspects of the empire's political life. 'The reformers,' says Professor Gibb, 'were never given a fair chance . . . the highest Authorities (i.e. Sultans and religious leaders) were unwilling to do anything which might alienate from them the support of the mass of Moslem opinion. Did they desire to abolish slavery—the Sacred Law of Islam recognizes it. Did they desire to give equality of status to all citizens—the Law insists on the political subordination of non-Moslems. Did they desire to reform the administration of justice—the Law will not tolerate any code other than itself. Did they desire to create parliamentary institutions—the Law knows nothing of such and admits no right of legislation. And so on; on every point the reformers were met with a negative in the name of the Divine Ordinances of Islam.'[31]*

As time went on, however, both the army and the administration had to be brought more into line with Western practice. But the rigid self-discipline which was at the bottom of the Western technique was largely wanting in the East. What was natural and appropriate in the West was alien in the East. Still the wealth, the power, the prestige, the achievements of the West continued to apply the spur. Western results argued in favour of the West. Western political principles, it seemed, must be right; hence nationalism became a contagion. Greece, Roumania, Bulgaria, Albania and other countries in Europe one by one had been able to throw off their Ottoman fetters.

Nationalism spread into Asia. As the empire had crumbled in Europe under its influence, so in Asia it could only lead to disintegration. The first Asiatic groups to be affected were the Christian minorities of Armenia and elsewhere who were conscious of Near East rather than Middle East traditions. In her treatment of these minorities

Turkey had little to fear from her European neighbours, and her resistance to their aspirations, or their seditious activities, took the form of massacres. The conventional view that the Turkish massacres were primarily religious seems to have been too lightly accepted in the past. It is more probable that at root they were political (despite the close identity between religion and politics in the Islamic tradition). This at least is suggested by Turkey's own conciliatory policy in the early days. Indeed for the first two and a half centuries of Ottoman rule, before nationalism raised its head and made the Turks feel insecure, they had shown considerable tolerance and allowed minorities to enjoy a commendable measure of autonomy under a loose medieval form of government. They never forced Islam on their newly acquired subjects, though in traditional Moslem style they regarded Christians as an inferior caste. Most of their Balkan possessions—Bosnia, Bulgaria, Albania (Hungary excepted)—embraced of their own free will the faith of the dominant race, and if later they expelled the Turks and reverted to Christianity they did so under Western influence and with Western military support. It was the later Turkey, driven by force of circumstances to resist weakness within herself, that met separatist tendencies with abominable massacres.

As we have seen, in the earliest times Christian 'religious minorities' enjoyed 'protection' within the Islamic state so long as they were submissive and paid a small supertax. But the Middle East tradition had a different way with 'political minorities', a hard way for treason against the state. Under political absolutism minorities claiming to be different and opposed were not as respectable as they are in Western democratic states. Public opinion expected strong action and applauded resolute men. The minority, flaunting its racial and religious differences, was regarded as asking for extirpation. The recent Iraqi massacre of Assyrians—to the Iraqis the Assyrians were a militant and extremely provocative minority—is in some respects in the same political tradition. If England and Ireland had formed parts of a Middle East civilization instead of Western civilization the world would have had reason to expect some similar reactions. This is in no sense said as an argument for or against the spread of Western nationalism, which may well be as inevitable as the spread of taste or culture or disease. But its Western democratic forms that are taken for granted by untravelled Westerners do not form part of the common consciousness in the Middle East, nor do they appeal to the governing class where affection for strong and just and benevolent personal dictatorship is more in the historical tradition. If the Western democrat seeks with keen devotion the universal acceptance of his political deities, he should, if he abjures the sword, learn to be patient.

The spread of Western nationalism to the Arab countries under the Turks properly belongs to the present century, when the small literate class became genuinely converted but not the agricultural masses. The latter in many provinces, notably those of Iraq, had reverted to a social culture not much in advance of the deserts and were not nationally minded. The former—the townsfolk retaining something of their historic medieval traditions, and educated in Turkish-speaking schools—had on the other hand more in common with the Turks of the ruling class, their Sunni coreligionists, than with their own kith and kin who followed the plough and the Persian sectaries.

Iraq, to take as an example the Turkish-administered

Arab country I learned to know well, had this cultural division between the urban dwellers and tribally minded fellahin.

To the Arab townsman the Turk was no foreign tyrant. The Ottoman Empire was not narrowly Turkish in spirit; it was a loosely administered hegemony of diverse provinces, and if the local governor and the local general and the like were appointed from Constantinople, they were by no means always of Turkish blood. Arabs—generally from Syria—Kurds and even Cretans came, indifferently with Turks, to administer the provinces of Iraq.

The Turks, till recent times tribesmen themselves, were by no means inexpert handlers of the Arab tribesman either. They understood, if they no longer sympathized with, the wayward point of view that resented any close government control; their own careless medieval methods were indeed well suited to the taste of the tribes. These enjoyed much freedom from authority, and in the early days authority was exercised through their own local aristocracy, such as the Kurdish aghas in the north or the Sa'adun amirs in the south.

It was when the Turks began to 'improve' their administrative machine on Western lines and with Western applause that the old personal touch was lost and they grew less popular. They had come to think with the West that an efficient administrative machine was an effective substitute for personal rule. The fez was to replace the turban, the literate townsman to be promoted at the expense of the local aristocrat. But the conditions necessary for a Western regime were wanting. The bulk of the population were tribesmen and not impressed by literacy nor attracted by bureaucrats. If they had a sense of the well-being of their tribe or their area they lacked a sense of national public weal. Threat of closer control only hardened their opposition, and under the influence of their Shi'a divines they found religious justification for disputing the claims of Sunni caliphs. The demand on them for increased taxes only intensified their opposition to paying taxes at all. If they wanted water for their rice fields why shouldn't they cut canals? And what if this did flood highways? Food was an older and greater consideration for them than wheeled traffic, for which, indeed, they had no need at all.

The agents of Ottoman authority were the Arab townsmen, fit only, so the tribesmen thought, to scribble at their taxes. This local official class had greatly deteriorated since the old days. It, too, was deficient in the sense of public service, and chiefly preoccupied with the need of making a precarious living. It, too, identified the public good with the good of its own class. Flooding public highways was not to be tolerated. And did not evasion of taxes prove that the tribesmen were enemies of the state?

In the year 1869 came Midhat Pasha, a famous Turkish *wali,* to Baghdad, determined to break the tribes once for all. To this end he introduced an ingenious land reform which conferred a form of proprietary right on the individual members of the tribe, a hereditary lease, on easy terms, calculated to wean tribesmen from local allegiances. Though partly effective, and enduring to this day, its success was hindered by Midhat's less judicious measures to conscript the tribes. Hence those who might have been coaxed into a closer allegiance by the seductive appeal of property in land must keep their distance to avoid being whipped off to force a neighbour's submission to government's revenue demands or lured away to fight the Russians, whoever they might be!

The methods by which the Turks made their higher appointments were no more promising of success than were the ethical standards of local subordinate employees. Corruption ran from top to bottom. The very exalted, such as governors, bought their appointments in Constantinople, usually on a short-term lease, and came to the Arab provinces to make the investment profitable. Taxation was locally auctioned to tax farmers, who also must make good. The local subordinate Arab official received inadequate and irregular pay and restored to taking bribes. The police and local garrison, their uniform shabby, their pay often in arrears, must be nimble with their muskets—these often of various pattern—to bully and extort a living. Customs officials, who in theory took an eight per cent tax, were quite ready to reduce the burden to the importer in accordance with the size of the consideration passed under the table. In short there was wanting that public spirit in the service of the state which springs from a sense of personal security and from loyalty to clean and proud traditions, features which made bureaucratic government safe in the West. Thus Western panaceas compounded in a Turco-Arab dispensary brought little health to the extremities of the sick man of Europe. This is not to suggest that Turkish rule gave grounds for strong local dissatisfaction. It was too light to be irksome. If government is a necessary evil, a feeble evil is better than a virile one; in the measure of its weakness and inefficiency it was tolerable to the tribesmen; the taxpayer had the means of lightening his burden by his own ingenuity; the petty Arab official was not unhappy under a system which was the only one he understood. Ottoman authority varied not only from decade to decade with the personality of the wali, but within the country from town to town and from tribe to tribe. There was control in the towns, a light hand on the surrounding tribes, a faint supervision often vanishing altogether among remote marsh Arabs. Thus my own immediate postwar district of the Middle Gharraf (the ancient Lagash), midway between Tigris and Euphrates, had ceased to be administered by the Turks ten years before the war because of their inability to collect revenues, and three of my Turkish predecessors, who were too intent on revenue collection, had been murdered. Taxation was not uniform in Arab provinces of the Iraq, but then it never had been, and nobody expected it to be. The area under control must pay virtually a dozen times the amount that could be wheedled out of the inaccessible tribes who indeed often refused to pay anything. Arrears mounted up, and then would come a time when the sum owing must either weakly be abandoned on grounds of political expediency or an attempt be made at collection by means of a punitive column. Under the Turks the deciding factor was a simple arithmetical sum, on which side of the profit and loss account was a balance to be expected. The effect on public morality was scarcely salutary.

The administration of the law was various. The tribes were left to their ancient canons or their Shi'a sanctions; the Ottoman law of the towns, based largely on the Napoleonic code, was administered by judge or qadhi. Justice could usually be bought and sold. Yet however much illicit influence and bribery were brought to bear, the tendency was nearly always towards getting the prisoner off. There was humanity in it. Custom allowed the relatives of the prisoner to bring him his meals, which the underpaid jailer was pleased to share, a practice that encouraged friendly relations and was suited to the free and easy ways of the people; while quarantine officials, where these existed, were never so vexatiously efficient as to stand in the way of the truly understanding.

But in the present century a generation of Arabs was growing up dissatisfied with the Turkish connection. Under the influence of Western thought, achievement, example, the Arab intelligentsia was becoming growingly aware of the poverty and backwardness of their native lands under the Turks and saw before their eyes the growing prosperity of Egypt, under Western guidance. The official elements among them had tried loyally to cooperate in the reform policy of the Committee of Union and Progress which promised so much and from which they at first had hopes of greater autonomy, but when the young Turks, in the strength derived from association with Germany, seemed to steer an opposite course, the Arabs of Iraq fell more and more away. They had their own proud Umaiyyad and Abbasid traditions to inspire them.

But these politically minded Arabs were but a tiny fraction of the people. The mass of the fellahin were illiterate and apathetic to nationalist sentiment. They had drifted back to a rude tribal culture, wanted no government at all bigger than their tribal unit. Most of them would have wished above all to be left alone, free from any bureaucratic control including that of the official class of their own urban kinsmen. To the mass of the Shi'a tribesmen of Iraq, as indeed to any other Arab tribesmen, the constitutional reforms of Turkey, or any other constitutional reforms for that matter, gave them nothing that they needed or wanted.

Westernization, therefore, in effect weakened Turkey

in her Arab dominions. Turkey Westernized ceased to be acceptable to the Arab masses. Turkey, reeling under successive blows of the Balkan and Italian wars, ceased to hold its prestige with the Arab urban communities. These began to talk of Arab nationalism, to dream of freedom from the Turkish yoke.

Part Four

REVIVAL

CHAPTER XI

The Arabs and the World War

IN THE YEAR 1914 the Arabs of Syria, Palestine and Iraq and of the western provinces of the Arabian peninsula, the Hijaz, and, in a lesser degree, the Yemen, were under Turkish dominion. To all these lands Constantinople sent garrisons, to most of them viceroys and governors too. In the Ottoman army Arab soldiers and officers served side by side with Turks, Kurds and other representatives of the empire. The Arab officer class, educated in Turkish schools, served in military and civil capacities on the same terms as the Turks. There was no derogating distinction, as with Indians under the British *raj* in contemporary India, nothing to prevent the Arab from rising to the highest rank in the Ottoman services; though up to the war the Turks had resisted the Syrian demand that Arabic should be admitted as an official language along with Turkish. Arabs married Turkish wives—Sharif, later King, Husain of Mecca himself had a Turkish wife—Arabs were sent with Turks to German military staff colleges. Like army officers in any other army they took an oath of allegiance to their ruling sovereign—the Turkish sultan, and thus when war broke out, they found themselves fighting in Gallipoli, Mesopotamia and Palestine on the side of the Turks against the Allies.

But for many of them their heart was not in it. Their outlook had been affected by Western liberalism. They would have preferred to think of themselves as Arab patriots rather than Ottoman subjects. Their kith and kin at home in Syria and Iraq were of the same mind, and though these formed a small fraction of the Arab inhabitants they were the intellectual and vocal element. Here was a powder magazine within the Turkish territories ready to be fired by the war in which these politically minded Arabs saw their chance of flinging off the Turkish yoke. Secret Arab societies formed with such an object existed in the cities, as well as literary and scientific societies, which, while not secret, brought men together whose political aspirations doubtless trended the same way—the Arab Committee, the Arts Club and the Committee of the Covenant. With war joined, these Arabs could only expect to achieve their ends if Turkey were defeated.

The Turks were no tyrannous masters, however, to be got rid of at any price. Apart from their own easygoing ineffectiveness, the Turks in the Arab countries were crippled both in a financial and political sense. Their wars had led them to mortgage certain items of revenue such as fisheries, liquor, salt, stamps, the sale of tobacco. In Palestine they had conceded a form of foreign protectorate of the holy places from their earliest occupation. Capitulations, providing for the legal rights of Christian powers to try their own nationals in their own courts, and other extraterritorial rights which were in origin a lazy arrangement of the Turks to simplify their rela-

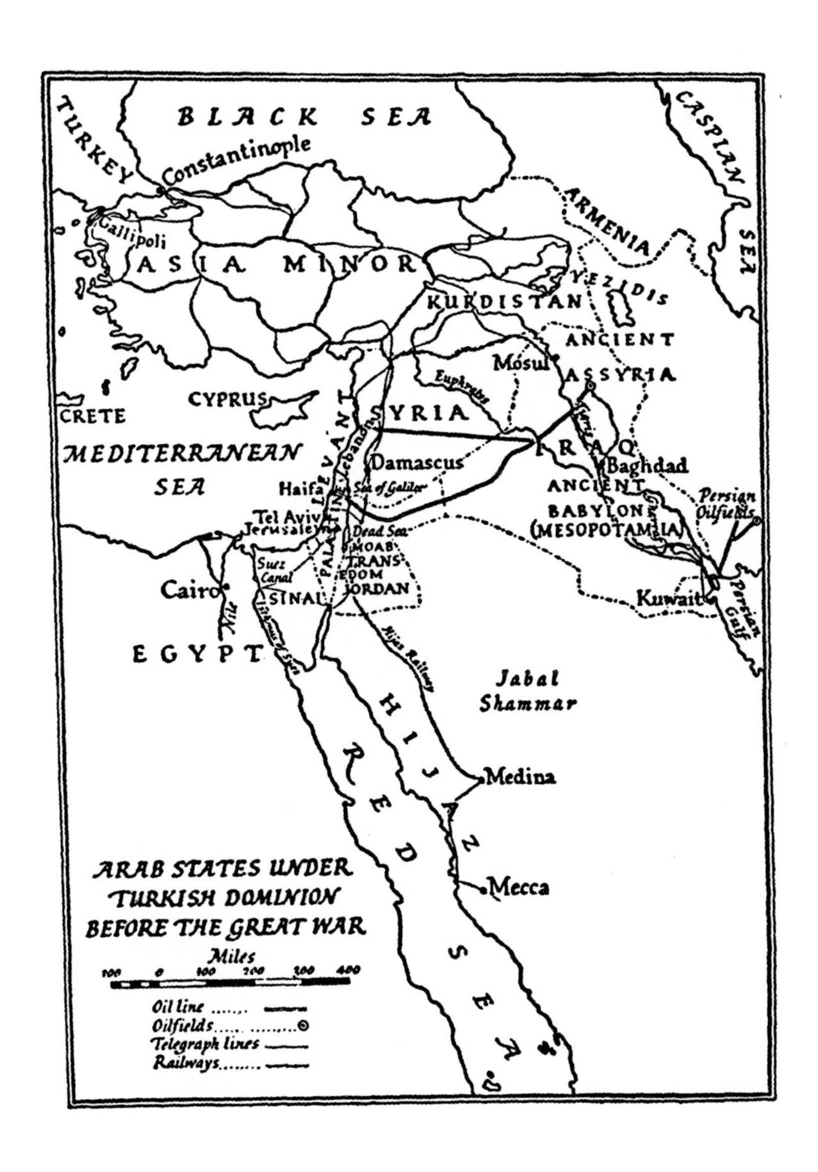
BLACK SEA
CASPIAN SEA
TURKEY
Constantinople
Gallipoli
ASIA MINOR
ARMENIA
YEZIDIS
KURDISTAN
ANCIENT
ASSYRIA
Mosul
Euphrates
CYPRUS
CRETE
SYRIA
MEDITERRANEAN SEA
Damascus
IRAQ
Baghdad
Haifa
Sea of Galilee
ANCIENT
BABYLON
(MESOPOTAMIA)
Persian Oilfields
Tel Aviv
Jerusalem
Dead Sea
MOAB
TRANS
EDOM
JORDAN
Suez Canal
SINAI
PALESTINE
LEVANT
Lebanon
Cairo
Nile
Kuwait
Persian Gulf
EGYPT
Hijaz Railway
Jabal Shammar
HIJAZ
RED SEA
Medina
Mecca
ARAB STATES UNDER TURKISH DOMINION BEFORE THE GREAT WAR
Miles
100 0 100 200 300 400
Oil line
Oilfields
Telegraph lines
Railways

tions with Genoese and Venetian traders and the like, grew to be another source of political weakness as the Western Powers arose to inherit the rights and exploit them to the full. And now for a century Turkey grew still weaker from the undermining effects of Western nationalistic doctrinairism.

Jewry, too, had already conceived an ardent desire to possess Palestine. The Jew minorities of the world, scattered throughout fifty nations of the earth, without a country, a government or a flag to call their own, had, like the Arabs, become nationalists and started their movement of Zionism. Indeed, at the first Zionist Congress Dr Herzl had prophesied the World War and said, 'It may be that Turkey will refuse or be unable to understand us. This will not discourage us. We shall seek other means to accomplish our ends.'

The French enjoyed a special position in the Turkish territories. They were the acknowledged protectors of Catholic Christian communities, so that Syria with its predominantly Catholic seaboard of the Lebanon had a special interest for France. From crusading times on through Napoleon's adventures there a French footing in the eastern Mediterranean was an axiom of their policy. French influence had always been stronger in Syria than that of any other European power. French was the most popular foreign language taught in Syrian schools; French hospitals and French schools had long flourished.

But Germany, already strongest of all powers in Constantinople circles, was attaining growing prestige in the Arab countries, her great engineering skill displaying itself in Turkey's railways, her great project, which threatened the British position in the Persian Gulf, reinforcing the mighty name she had as the first military power in Europe. Moreover, Germany had given diplomatic support to Turkey in all her recent wars, had showed a steady indifference to Turkey's treatment of her subject populations, had followed that close friendship with the Turks which foreshadowed alliance in time of war.

British interests in the Arab countries were most considerable in the Persian Gulf and at one or two strategic points on the Arabian coasts. Aden, the rocky furnace commanding the entrance to the Red Sea, was a British protectorate; Bahrain, looking across the Gulf to our Persian oil fields, was 'protected territory'; and Muscat, facing India, a cherished ally, though in the eyes of Arab pirates, gunrunners, and slave dealers a sort of maritime Scotland Yard, and perhaps no more popular on that account.

In Turkey any kindly sentiment towards Britain, dating from Crimean associations, had waned before a later Gladstonian attitude, which, during the Balkan Wars, ranged our sympathies on the side of Turkey's Christian antagonists. When Turkey did try to put her house in order Europe, as a whole, had not been conspicuously helpful. Austria and Bulgaria repudiated her suzerainty of Bosnia-Herzegovina; Italy invaded Turkish north Africa and took Tripoli; and though Britain withheld her hand in Egypt and France maintained a benign neutrality, Germany was the only power who openly cherished her.[26]*

When the Great War came the matter of moment in the British-Arabo-Turkish relationship was the fact that the sultan of Turkey was the nominal head of orthodox Islam and master of the holy cities of Mecca and Medina, while Britain was the greatest Moslem power. In India alone, British Indian Moslem subjects outnumbered all the Turks and Arabs the world over. To the Sunnis among these—a large majority—the sultan of Turkey, as caliph, could declare *jihad,* or holy war,[1] upon the infidel, and even among Shi'as there was a considerable sentiment in favour of Turkey as the one great Islamic power. Much of the best fighting material in India was recruited into the Indian army from the Moslem northwest. This explains why British officials, raised in the Indian school and faced with the possibilities of Indian upheaval, were traditionally pro-Turk, or, at least, why they looked askance when prewar governments at home inclined to sympathize with any and every adversary of Turkey.

Just before the outbreak of the war the British *sirdar* in Egypt was Lord Kitchener. He had come from India, where he had served as commander-in-chief under Curzon and was therefore alive to caliphate influence among Indian Moslems. He had foreseen that if Turkey were ranged against Britain, as she must be as the ally of Germany, there would be unrest and probably Moslem upheaval in India. He therefore saw political advantage in the Arab movement towards independence. In any case Arab co-operation would be clearly useful as a means of discouraging jihad in India and of thwarting German ambitions in the Middle East. The holy places of Islam, where Indians came on annual pilgrimages, had a special significance in the former connection, and hence Kitchener and their keeper, the Sharif Husain, were in touch before

[1]The original meaning of the word seems to have been 'striving', i.e., 'striving after good.' It can mean fighting in defence of freedom of thought and on behalf of the oppressed. As a military weapon for political ends it is not today regarded by enlightened Arabs as an Islamic institution, though as such a weapon it has been traditionally met with, even in the recent war.

Turkey had openly joined her fortunes with those of Germany.[2]

In the immediately preceding years Turkey, emboldened by her alliance with the first military power in Europe, had stiffened in her attitude towards the Arabs. Arabian princes had in places been called upon to acknowledge Turkish suzerainty afresh, Turkish troops had been sent to the Yemen, and the sharif of Mecca had for the first time been told he must introduce conscription into the Hijaz. Between the sharif and the Turks there was little love lost. He had long desired an opportunity to shake off their mastery. His sons were educated princes who, having spent some of their youth in Constantinople, had met everyone who mattered among the Arabs in Turkey, Syria and Egypt; they were in sympathy with the Arab nationalist movement and personae gratae with its leaders. Thus Sharif Husain became the spokesman of the Arab nationalist movement—the spokesman of a movement that now primarily concerned not Arabia itself but the Arab countries outside. The 'heart of Arabia' under Ibn Sa'ud had already won its freedom from Turkish influence by its own efforts. The new Arab revolt was thus not the revolt of Arabia so much as the revolt of the Arabs; it drew much of its political inspiration from the Turcofied Arab countries without, and if sackfuls of 'golden horsemen of St George' brought needy Hijazi tribesmen to its banner, the great bulk of peninsular

[2]An interview between Lord Kitchener and the Amir Abdullah, the sharif's second son and at that time a Turkish deputy, took place in Cairo in February, 1914. I am informed by Professor Harold Temperley and Dr G. P. Gooch, editors of *British Documents on the Origins of the War,* that an account of this interview by Lord Kitchener himself and other relevant material will appear in Vol. X, Part II, shortly to be published.[28*]

Arabia remained indifferent to its activities, while Arabia's greatest figure, Ibn Sa'ud, was at the time hostile to its Hashimite leaders on old and personal grounds. Had the Arab Revolt been a spontaneous Arabian movement Sharif Husain would scarcely have been the acceptable leader, even with the lure of gold and arms, poured forth like water to tribesmen fulsomely appreciative of them.

Sharif Husain was told he could count on British support only if and when Turkey joined the Central Powers in the field, for Britain, up to the last moment, was using her efforts to keep Turkey out of the war by promising recognition of Turkey's territorial integrity, and this, of course, included her Arab possessions. When the Turks had come in Husain did not at first move. He had many things to consider. Arabs of known nationalist sympathies were fighting on the Turkish side and would continue to do so until they could be taken prisoner and change their allegiance; others were living behind the Turkish lines and openly declared Arab revolt would bring suspicion upon them if not worse. Also it was by no means clear that the Allies would win the war and so be able to fulfil Arab aspirations, and the Arabs never quite lost belief in the invincible might of the German army. Sharif Husain in Mecca was able to save his face with the Turks by making a pretence of complying with their conscription measure and by affording protection to some of the crew of the shipwrecked German raider Emden. The summer of 1915 came and saw the Turks to the south make an abortive attack on Aden from the Yemen.

In the north a challenge was now thrown down to the Arabs. The Turks ruthlessly set about attempting to exterminate Arab nationalism in Syria, its fountainhead. Suspected Arab patriots were taken out and hanged as traitors, and a regular reign of terror was instituted. This inspired Arab loathing for the Turks everywhere. Fear spread and dismay and a thirst to be revenged; and the Arab refugees from Syria came to Mecca to implore Sharif Husain to throw in his lot with the Allies and raise revolt in the name of Arab independence.

Arab intervention at this stage had less value to the Allies than it would have had a year before, and the sharif's terms concerning the future of Syria, Iraq and Palestine were not acceptable. He demanded that these Arab territories should be recognized as an Arab kingdom. Britain, already in negotiation with France and other Allies who had prewar interests in Turkish territories, replied, setting forth qualifications both in the scope of the area concerned and in the degree of administrative freedom she deemed prudent. Negotiations continued, and by the early part of 1916 the sharif, on behalf of the Arab nationalist movement, felt he had reached a sufficient measure of agreement.[3] But he was not as yet prepared for intervention and suggested a wait of six months or so. The Arab Revolt was, however, precipitated a few months later, when Turkish troops started arriving by the Pilgrim Railway to reinforce the garrison of Medina. To dally might have invited the same tragic fate as had befallen Arab patriots in Syria. The sharif's two sons, the amirs Faisal and Abdullah, were already impatient of delay, and they now cut the railway north of Medina to start the Arab Revolt, the people of Mecca having already taken an oath of allegiance. Thus the sharif joined the Allies without obtaining guarantees about French claims in Syria; in ignorance, necessarily, of later Zionist commitments in Palestine.

[3]For Macmahon's letter of October 24, 1915, see Philby, *Arabia*, p. 242.

The military value of the Arab Revolt led so gallantly by his son, the Amir Faisal and T. E. Lawrence, won the unstinted praise of our famous general, that most noble of men, the late Lord Allenby. And however much the postwar activities of the revolt movement made for unrest and agitation, to our acute discomfort in Mesopotamia, the immediate political influence of the revolt, with which we are here more concerned, is not in doubt. When Arabs fought Turks for Arab independence the patriotic issue must have had considerable effect on Arabs behind the Turkish lines in Syria, through which British troops must later advance, while the repudiation of the Turkish caliphate by the sharif of Mecca, descendant of the Prophet, living head of the Prophet's tribe, and keeper of the holy places, had, at the time, an effect on Indian opinion which could not be overestimated.

Britain conducted two separate military campaigns against the Turks in the Arab countries, a western one in Palestine and Syria operated from Egypt, an eastern one in Iraq operated from India. The Arab revolters were a guerilla force who came to co-operate on the desert flank in the western campaign of Allenby's which drove the Turks out of Syria and Palestine.[4] They took

[4]As regards military strength and the cost of the Arab Revolt, which was borne by the British exchequer, I owe the following figures, necessarily approximate, to the kindness of Captain Liddell Hart. In the early part of the Hijaz campaign the Arabs had a nominal fifty thousand men who might have been tapped, and their three 'armies' had a nominal total of about sixteen thousand. In the advance to Wejh, Faisal's army numbered just over ten thousand, but this was a very fluctuating quantity, and most of the British officers who took part are convinced that the totals given them were actually exaggerated. In the later stages of the campaign in the north the Arab tribal forces were similarly an uncertain and fluctuating quantity, simply gathering for some particular expedition in numbers that sometimes reached a few thousand, but were more often only a few hundred. The only consistent part of the Arab strength was the Arab regular force which was raised after the revolt broke out. The bulk of this

no part in the eastern campaign of the Mesopotamian Expeditionary Force which drove the Turks out of Iraq. Although less publicity is reserved for this latter Arab theatre of war, a campaign in which the Indian army took a large and loyal part, its scope was actually bigger than the South African war. The successful prosecution of these two campaigns freed the Arab countries from the Turkish yoke, and when the war ended British armies occupied the enemy territories, and provisional military administrations directed local affairs.

The problem of the future government of these Arab territories had now to be faced. There were many interests to be considered. It was not possible to hand the territories over to the Arabs, even if that had been considered desirable. There had been strong foreign interests under the Turks as we have seen, and these in 1916 had formed the subject of secret agreement between the pow-

was shifted up to Aqaba in August, 1917, and it then comprised eighteen hundred men. This was somewhat increased by 1918, when it consisted of a brigade of infantry, a battalion of camel corps and about eight guns. By the middle of 1918 the total Arab regular forces, counting those under Faisal and also the further forces raised by Ali and Abdullah in the Hijaz, amounted to about ten thousand men. But only a small number of these was available at any time for offensive operations at a distance from their base. Thus, when the decisive campaign was launched in September, 1918, the striking forces moved up north to Azraq for this totalled a little under six hundred picked men. It was reinforced by about two thousand picked tribesmen.

The total cost to the imperial exchequer of the Arab Revolt is thought to have been in the neighbourhood of £4,000,000 in gold, of which rather more than half came back in purchases of food and clothing. Of this Lawrence himself was given a fund of £200,000 by Allenby after the latter's arrival in 1917, which was increased to £500,000 by the time Damascus was reached; there was a balance of £10,000 remaining at the end. It is, of course, impossible to estimate the cost of weapons and personnel lent to the Arab forces, but in any case it represented only an inconsiderable fraction of that of the theatre of war of the Egyptian Expeditionary Force as a whole. The actual subsidy to the Arabs is thought to have been about £1,000,000.

ers principally concerned. By this agreement (Sykes-Picot) Britain, France and Russia had mutually agreed upon spheres of influence.

Zionist aspirations complicated the issue as regards Palestine. During the course of the war the Foreign Offices of the Allied Powers had been approached by Zionist organizations concerning the future of Palestine, to which they advanced claims. On the Palestine front itself, a British-Hebrew battalion, known euphemistically as the Jordan Highlanders, had fought loyally, and Jews played their parts on other fronts; while a considerable military contribution was made by a distinguished Jewish scientist in the form of an invention of a cheap high explosive. This scientist, Dr Weizmann, a keen Zionist, too, pleaded his nation's cause to a grateful British prime minister. The British War Cabinet became persuaded of the deserving nature of Zionism, and Lord Balfour, the then British foreign secretary, expressed this official view in November, 1917, in a letter to Lord Rothschild, a letter which has come to be known and hated in Arab circles as the Balfour Declaration. It read:

> I have much pleasure in conveying to you, on behalf of His Majesty's Government, the following Declaration of sympathy with Jewish aspirations, which has been submitted to and approved by the Cabinet.
>
> His Majesty's Government view with favour the establishment in Palestine of a National Home for the Jewish people, and will use their best endeavours to facilitate the achievement of this object, it being clearly understood that nothing shall be done which may prejudice the civil and religious rights of existing non-Jewish communities in Palestine, or of the rights and political status enjoyed by Jews in any other country.
>
> I shall be glad if you will bring this Declaration to the knowledge of the Zionist Federation. A. J. Balfour

The United States, French and Italian governments endorsed this action, and the League of Nations approved, four years later, of the establishment of a national home for the Jews in Palestine on these conditions.

America had joined the Allies halfway through the war, and her powerful and decisive contributions entitled her spokesman, President Wilson, to a strong voice in the matter of peace terms. America favoured the maximum liberty of the small nations, favoured universal self-government and a policy of multinationalism. As she was a vast country, rich to repletion from her own ever-expanding home markets brought about under liberal immigration laws, she was less understanding of the traditional jealousies of her allies—small, close-knit industrial nations—for overseas spheres of influence, in much the same way, perhaps, as Britons today, with a great empire and feeling no need for fresh territory, are impatient of the claims of Italy or Germany for space in Africa. The rights of small nations to independent existence, the promotion of nationalism, based on self-determination, found its most powerful champions in America, and this doubtless had its influence on Allied counsels. At the conclusion of the war, November, 1918, an Anglo-French Declaration was issued which ran:

> The end aimed at by France and Great Britain is the complete and final enfranchisement of the people so long oppressed by the Turks, and the establishment of National Governments and Administrations drawing their authority from the initiative and free choice of the native populations. . . . Far from wishing to impose upon the populations any particular institutions the Allies have no other desire than to assure by their support and active assistance the normal functioning of the Governments and Administrations which the populations have freely given themselves.

The 'support and active assistance' Britain and France envisaged was administrative advice and the garrisoning of the regions covered by the Sykes-Picot Agreement, but the Arab leaders considered this agreement—it had come to light in Russia following the revolution—as incompatible in spirit with war promises to the Arabs, while the Balfour Declaration was even more irreconcilable with the new declaration of Allied aims. The position, all very confused, was regularized by a new political principle, a contribution of President Wilson, known as the mandatory system. By this device the Powers were to have their spheres of influence, but so devoid of advantage as to ensure the ultimate rights of native populations. The mandate was designed to prevent the sphere of influence becoming an old-time veiled protectorate. A League of Nations was envisaged, under whose authority the mandate was juridically conferred on some great power, to guide and assist the young and backward state until such time as it could stand on its own feet. It would then become free and sovereign and able to join the League as a member, and the mandatory connection would automatically end.

These principles differentiated the mandatory system from the old colonial system or even the protectorate.

1. The mandatory Power must administer the territory as trustee solely in the interest of its ward and share on equal terms with other members of the League whatever economic or commercial opportunities there were.

2. It must be a temporary arrangement whose ultimate aim was emancipation and independence of the territory.

3. The mandatory was to be answerable not to its own conscience, but to the public opinion of the world before the bar of the League of Nations.

The historic interests of France and Britain in the Middle East, the major share borne by British armies in the two campaigns which freed the Arab territories from the Turks, namely about fifty thousand battle casualties in Palestine and Syria and eighty thousand in Mesopotamia (Iraq)[5] marked these two Powers as the natural mandatories. But the political idealism of the times gave rise, both in Peace Conference circles and in Syria itself, to the notion that the Arabs could choose their own mandatory. A new kind of history was to begin. French interests from crusade times onwards could be set aside as though France didn't matter and 'history is all bunk.' The Arab nationalist leaders declined to recognize a French mandate for Syria or, indeed, have any dealings with the French, pointing out that their war negotiations had been with Britain, and Britain must satisfy Arab national aspirations. The Arab revolters now revolted against the French (the British army of occupation having evacuated Syria in favour of France in accordance with agreement). Anglo-French relations became strained as postwar events then taking place in Turkey showed, for France supposed that Lawrence and the British officers attached to the Arab Revolt movement were at the bottom of Arab opposition to them.

The French landed an army in Syria and expelled the Amir Faisal, who thereupon fled to London. In the same year, partly under the inspiration of members of the Arab Revolt, an Arab rebellion took place in Iraq directed against the local British administration. While the French resisted Arab demands in Syria, the British followed a con-

[5]British figures, including disease casualties, for Mesopotamia alone, were: killed 14,814, prisoners of war and missing 13,494, wounded 51,386, dead of disease 12,807=92,501.

ciliatory policy in Iraq. The Amir Faisal was allowed to offer himself for the throne of Iraq and was, with British support, accepted by the inhabitants, and the administration was Arabized.

Legally the country was still enemy-occupied territory, for the Turks did not ratify a peace treaty recognizing Iraq's independence till 1923, i.e. five years after the war ended. Its real independence, moreover, could only be assured by recognition of its other neighbours, and at first neither Persia in the east nor Ibn Sa'ud in the south was disposed to recognize the new Arab regime. The mandatory used its good offices to bring about this end, though its task was rendered more onerous and thankless by the internal situation, for, if the mandate was to live up to the moral standards behind its design, not only must the mandatory guide, but the mandated must accept guidance. But Arab official elements in Iraq, like those in Syria, did not consider mandatory guidance necessary; they preferred to be untrammelled. They held that they were quite competent to manage their own affairs and were morally entitled to release from an enforced status of tutelage. Meanwhile Britain, as mandatory, had laid the foundations of a clean, progressive and well-ordered administration under two brilliant servants of the government of India, Sir Percy Cox and Sir Arnold Wilson. Subsequently, when Iraq's neighbours recognized the new experiment of Arab king, Arab parliament and a constitutional government, Britain found it expedient to recommend to the League the abrogation of the mandate and the election of Iraq to membership of the League as a sovereign state (October, 1932).

France, after attempting at first to follow a different course in Syria by tightening control under a large army

THE AMIR (LATER KING) FAISAL.

(By courtesy of Mr Lowell Thomas)

of occupation, has lately announced her intention of abrogating her mandate, too, in favour of treaty relations on lines somewhat similar to those followed by Britain in Iraq.

Peninsular Arabia was also finally freed from the Turks by the Great War, the Yemen and the Hijaz both obtaining their independence. The Sharif Husain, the Arabian chief who played the leading part in Arab participation, and who, shortly after the war, proclaimed himself king of the Hijaz, did not long maintain his position, for the Wahhabi invasion under Ibn Sa'ud drove him from his throne to die in exile, not, however, before he had lived to see his line established dynastically on two new Arabian thrones, his son Faisal as king of Iraq, his son Abdullah as amir of Trans-Jordan.

King Faisal ibn Husain was doubtless one of the two outstanding Arab figures of the war and postwar period, as King Abdul Aziz ibn Sa'ud was the other; the one, of Constantinople upbringing and sophisticated mien, nominal leader of the Arab Revolt and spearpoint of wartime Arab nationalism, who came, as a result of Allied victory, to be raised to a throne; the other, the supreme product of the deserts, the puritan warrior-statesman of Nejd, to-day the master of the holy cities and most influential among Arab rulers, a Cromwell who carved out his own kingdom and founded a royal line. Europeans who have come under the influence of his personality and admire his wonderful exploits are given to bemoan the day when the Allies, in supporting Faisal, 'backed the wrong horse.' But in the early war days it was Faisal's sire who had the prestige which must attach at all times to the possession of the holy places, nor did Ibn Sa'ud's influence—with Ibn Rashid in the way—reach far enough northwards to admit of his rendering effective military assistance on General Allenby's flank. Yet coming events had cast their shadows, and though Ibn Sa'ud did not take a more active part in the Great War, his benevolent neutrality brought him a handsome subsidy from the British government[6] as a palliative to the resentment he felt for the recognition and support given to the Sharif Husain, his hated enemy, and as a means of pacifying the tribes in Allied interests. Despite the fact that it was Ibn Sa'ud who was the first to raise the standard of revolt and expel Turkish influence from Arab soil—this before the Great War—the Arab nationalist movement during the war, as we have noted, was, in effect, a movement of the politically minded Turcofied Arabs outside Arabia. Thus the conception of the two great Arab figures of the period as the embodiment of the two Arab cultures led to a view that the 'fancy' of the Arab backers in the nationalist stables, at the time, would be for Faisal's colours.

[6]£60,000 per annum.

CHAPTER XII

Palestine

And I will give unto thee, and to thy seed after thee, the land of thy sojourning, all the land of Canaan, for an everlasting possession. JEHOVAH'S PROMISE TO ABRAHAM.

We have come not as Conquerors but as Deliverers.
GENERAL ALLENBY.

THE military campaigns of the Allies, waged in the lands of the Arabs, have nearly everywhere brought these Arabs political emancipation. Of the five Arab provinces that had for centuries lain under Turkish dominion—the Iraq, the Hijaz, the Yemen, Syria and Palestine—three have achieved independence; the fourth appears about to achieve it; only Palestine remains. Viewed in a wide perspective, therefore, the Arabs have done better out of the Great War that ravaged their countries than many of its regular participants. The Palestine Arabs are the exception, and their country, too, they say, must be an Arab state.

The word 'Palestine' (= Philistine) connotes to a stranger a country of considerable significance. In point of fact it is a province rather than a country, being in size no bigger than Wales; its population is but that of a European city, having only recently passed the million mark; its entire revenues would scarcely pay for a modern battle cruiser. Yet for its mastery a local struggle goes on as bitter in spirit as any that it knew in crusading times; though the disputants are no longer the rival peoples of Christendom and Islam, but Jew and Arab, and the issue is no longer religion but nationalism.

At present Palestine is administered by neither Jew nor Arab, but by the Christian power that conquered it from the Turks—a curious echo of the crusades, if a false one, being an adventitious result of an unwanted war. But however small the area involved and scant its population today (1,300,000), yet the postwar course of events in Palestine has been no smooth one. At intervals of every few years, recurring all too regularly, violent collisions between its Arab and Jew inhabitants have disturbed the peace of the land. The cause of such outbreaks, whether attributed to some immediate local disaffection, over land or religion, for instance, has been at bottom nationalistic. The Arabs avow that they want an Arab state; the Zionists declare they want a Jewish majority. At the root of racial antagonism is the impelling desire of each for political ascendancy. Local agitation is further encouraged by the very nature of the mandatory system, namely that the mandatory connection is only temporary.

The League of Nations is under commitments to the Zionists and to the Arabs. The mandate expresses itself in the same terms as the Balfour Declaration, namely that the aim is to bring about 'the establishment of a National Home for the Jewish people. . . . it being clearly understood that nothing shall be done which may prejudice the civil and religious rights of existing non-Jewish communities.'

The mandatory's difficulties in implementing this policy

A PALESTINE MOSLEM ARAB.

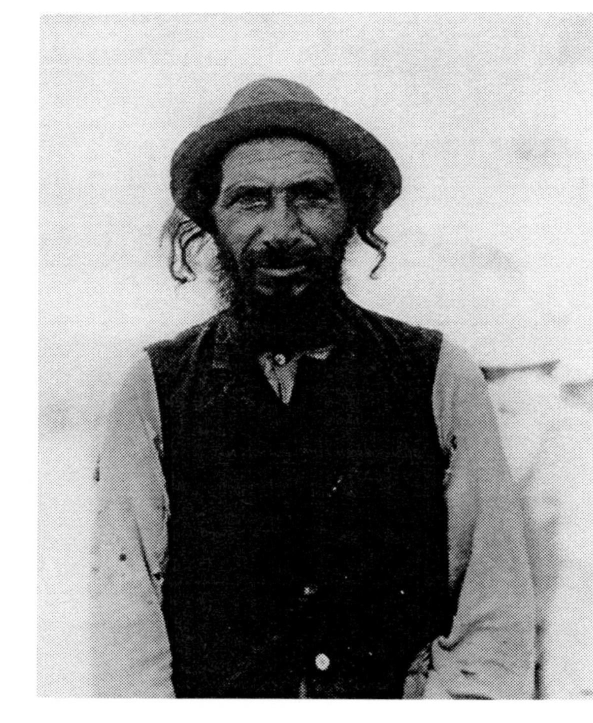

A PALESTINE JEW.

(By courtesy of Mr Lowell Thomas)

need only be stated to be understood. Palestine's population is predominantly Arab and has been so for the last twelve centuries. At the time of the British conquest Arabs formed ninety per cent of the population. Today no less than seventy per cent are Arabs, nine tenths of them Moslem Arabs, and their political leaders oppose the League's policy and declare that the outside world has no right to dispose of their country in opposition to its own wishes and contrary to the League's early declared principle of the rights of small nations to self-determination. The Zionists, similarly, insist on the rights of their own gifted people to a place in the sun, point to the unique position in the world today of a nation sixteen millions strong, scattered in hopeless minorities among the other nations of the earth, without a country to call its own. They urge that it is with Palestine that the ancient glories of their nation are associated, claim that all down the centuries, both before and after the Arab conquest in the seventh century, Jews have continuously lived there and that world Jewry has never ceased to regard Palestine as its spiritual home.

The Zionist Jews consider, moreover, that they have moral claims upon an enlightened world because of the great contributions in music, art and science, in philosophy and religion made by the Jews to Western civilization, while non-Jewish sympathizers have urged that a Jewish national home in Palestine is but compensation for the persecution Jews suffered at the hands of Western Europe in the Middle Ages. Persecution is still their lot in Germany and parts of eastern Europe. They are tired of being unwanted guests in the houses of others and demand a home of their own, this home to be their own historic one where David and Solomon ruled three thousand years ago, the background of their ancient and superb literature, our Scriptures. The problem has been aggravated by their increasing numbers and by that spirit of renewed antipathy which is manifesting itself in Germany and elsewhere today. The Jews in the time of our Lord are thought to have numbered three millions. Under the persecutions of the Middle Ages their numbers fell so that at the beginning of the seventeenth century world Jewry numbered but a million or so. Early nineteenth century estimates place them at two or three millions; by the middle of that century they had doubled their numbers, and today there are some sixteen or seventeen million Jews. Their voice is therefore a growing one, however much it may be a voice in the wilderness.

When the war ended and found Palestine occupied by a British army and ruled by a British administration, advanced Zionists were urging that Palestine must be as Jewish as England was English, and enthusiasts among them in the outside world are said to have left some part of their new buildings unfinished as a sign that they were pilgrims in a strange land. At the Peace Conference the Zionist Organization put forward three demands: the recognition of Jewish claims to Palestine, opportunities to settle three to four million Jews there and the request that Britain should be the mandatory Power. A favourable reception was accorded Dr Weizmann, the Zionist representative and the distinguished chemist, who by his scientific discoveries had done great service for the Allies; the immigration demand was, however, left to the discretion of the mandatory.

The Arabs also had their claims to Allied consideration. The value of the Arab Revolt in India and Syria has already been noticed. The Sharif Husain in his negotiations which brought about the Arab Revolt had asked, at the outset, for the autonomy of all the Arab lands, which of course included Palestine, and although this was not explicitly agreed to, the Arab revolters considered that they entered the war without foreseeing a policy in Palestine which, in their view, was more damaging to Arab interests than the old Ottoman rule had been. The Balfour Declaration, therefore, came as a bombshell and was utterly distasteful to them, and the name Balfour among politically minded Arabs today is a name of execration. On the other hand the Amir (later King) Faisal, who represented the Arab cause at the Peace Conference, is said to have been on friendly terms with the Zionist leaders and to have sent a letter to Dr Weizmann expressing cordial sympathy with the idea of the establishment of the Jewish National Home in Palestine, though it is clear that he could not have foreseen all the present political developments.

From the day the mandate came into existence, onwards, the proportions of Jewish immigration have been a matter of the deepest concern for both Arabs and Jews, for on it rests the ultimate numerical superiority of one or other within the state. In the exercise of the mandate, therefore, this has been the most delicate of its problems. A stony strip of territory along the eastern Mediterranean coast, bordered eastwards by the Jordan Valley and stretching northwards to end well short of the Sea of Galilee, Palestine clearly has limited potentialities for supporting population. The Zionists, anxious for Jewish immigration on a large scale, place its capacity high. The Arabs, anxious to stop the inflow of Jews, place it correspondingly low. Some estimators, who have no obvious political bias, have supposed that Palestine is capable of supporting a population of not much more than double its present number, estimates varying with the degree of industrialization permitted. But as a pastoral and agricultural country, with about two thirds of its soil already under cultivation, any considerable increase in the population inevitably means changing the face of the land. Immigration of workmen from countries having a higher standard of living leads to new wants, for different food, clothing and housing, imposes on Palestine the necessity for changing her ways, of no longer contenting herself with her own milk and honey; in short, she is being compelled, by outside influences, to become progressive according to one school of thought, to become alienized according to another.

The Jews claim that with greater industrialization the population could be vastly increased, the amenities of life added to and the country made prosperous. Already a big electrification scheme from the waters of the Jordan is progressing under the Rutenberg Concession. But the highest hopes are reserved for development of her chemical wealth. Estimates that she is capable of supplying the world with all the potash it will need for a thousand years may be exaggerated, but of the existence of large and valuable deposits there is no doubt, and with proper exploitation it is said that Palestine potash could be produced at half the recent German monopoly price and at a fraction of American war prices. That curious phenomenon, the Dead Sea, with its concentration of chemical salts ten times that of sea water, has always attracted the chemical minds of the world, so that as long ago as 1867 some sixteen hundred memoranda had already been published. Harbour development is another feature of Palestine's recent progress, and Haifa, with its oil refineries at the end of the transdesert pipe line from the new Mosul fields, is already the third seaport in the eastern Mediterranean.

If the Arab political leaders see in developments, coupled with foreign capitalistic interests, an undermining of their own hoped-for leadership, or for some other reason prefer the old order of things to the new, if they desire to stop Jewish immigration and Jewish concessions as prejudicial to the interests of their native land as they conceive them, the onus for measuring their complaints and applying a remedy where one is thought necessary rests with the mandatory Power.

The political difficulties inherent in the Palestine mandate are clear. The liquidation of Zionist claims in full involves the repudiation of Arab claims and vice versa. The problem is one that calls for fine adjustment, one that entails, in practice, a partial repudiation of the full-blooded claims of both sides, and therefore can be satisfactory to neither. In the administrative sphere it is possible to hold the scales evenly between the two, but the moment an incident happens vital and irreconcilable political principles emerge to complicate the situation. Protagonists on either side avow that some sacred principle is involved that does not admit of compromise. The problem is on the face of it insoluble peaceably, unless the terms 'national home' on the one hand and 'Arab rights' on the other are given a more limited meaning than partisans on the Zionist and Arab sides will at present allow. The situation is not made easier by the fact that the mandatory is only a trustee, an agent rather than a proprietor, in law, and that the Arab-Jew problem is not merely a local problem but has world ramifications. Moslems throughout the world, especially Arab kinsmen in Iraq, Syria and Egypt, sympathize with the Palestinian

Arabs, and their newspapers condemn Zionist aspirations while doubtless in narrow religious Moslem circles Palestine is thought of as Islam Irredenta. On the other hand the Zionists also represent a world movement with the backing of wide financial and political interests and the ear of many influential chancelleries.

For both Zionist and Arab politicians Jewish immigration is of fundamental importance as affecting vitally the ultimate constitution of Palestine's population. The mandatory, in its role of establishing a national home, has allowed Jewish immigration; in its role of safeguarding Arab civil rights it has set limits to it. The principle it has normally followed has been based fundamentally on Palestine's absorptive capacity at the time. There have been two half-yearly quotas. These, when announced, have produced violent and opposite reactions in the Arab and Jewish press. To the Arabs the figures have been as a red rag to a bull; by the Jews they have, till the last few years, been bitterly criticized as niggardly and inadequate.

According to the last census figures the total number of immigrants allowed in during the thirteen years 1919–1931 was 101,400; that is to say, one immigrant to every ten natives; expressed in another way, ten immigrants to the square mile; or in still another, an average of 7,800 per annum.

The countries of origin were as follows:

Russia and Poland	67,000
Roumania	4,400
Lithuania	3,500
United States	1,400
Germany	1,000
British Empire	400
Miscellaneous (Bulgaria, Czechoslovakia, the Yemen, etc.)	23,000

That sixty-seven per cent of the immigrants should have come from Russia and Poland constituted a grievance, according to the Arabs, namely that the less desirable, not the best, Jews were being brought into Palestine. They held that the old native Palestinian was, for the most part, a simple, God-fearing, conservative-minded son of the soil, whereas the incoming Jew was the proletarian from eastern Europe, of advanced left-wing political and moral opinions, obnoxious to the Palestinians and subversive of their way of life. Against this it was said that the personnel of the incomers, which was left to the Zionist organizations, was the subject of their special care and that none was allowed in unless possessing capital or under promise of work.

But the capital backing of Jewish immigrants, often made possible by American generosity, was another subject of Arab grievance, for this influx of capital, they held, was upsetting the economic equilibrium of Palestine's agriculture. This agriculture, the country's basic industry, was founded not in raising crops to sell overseas; it was primarily a subsistence economy. The cultivator was a small holder who worked not for a profit or a wage, but for subsistence—for food for himself and his family. Immigration, it was argued, with capital backing and modern machinery from outside, tended to upset this equilibrium by creating a demand for land; land values soared, and the urge of individual Arab landowners—often absentee landowners—to enjoy sudden wealth, led in places to a change of owner from native to immigrant. This produced unrest, because it tended to make for a landless class of native suddenly deprived of his habitual means of livelihood.

Hence on the one hand it is held that every fresh inflow

of immigrants with its fresh demand for land means a fresh tendency to dislocation; on the other, that the new technique and more up-to-date methods of the incoming agriculturist must increase productivity and result in a higher standard of living for the country as a whole. This is a feature which may lend itself to exaggeration, because only one tenth of Palestine's agriculture is in Jewish hands, and Zionists strenuously deny that Jewish immigration has brought about a landless class of Arab.

It is industry, trade and commerce that have attracted Jewish enterprise. According to the 1931 census already one third of Palestine's commerce was in Jewish hands. This is the basis of another fear of the Arab politician, namely that even where immigrants today are agriculturists, their sons, the Jews of the second generation, will be agriculturists no longer. Natural propensities and superior education will draw them into nonproductive but more remunerative callings—they will be lawyers, shopkeepers, landowners or, at all events, members of the rent-drawing classes, while the native Arabs of the country will be their hewers of wood and drawers of water. The Zionists answer that this fear is groundless and that the bulk of the immigrants have been absorbed in productive forms of industry which the Jews themselves have established in the country.

In manner of living, dress and occupation the Arab community falls into three main classes, the Beduin, the fellahin and the city dweller. The Beduin are the poorest and the most primitive element—shepherds, who culturally correspond most nearly with their kinsman, the desert nomad. They are scarcely producers and do not participate in politics except indirectly, in times of political upheaval, to indulge the inherited instinct of improving the shining

RISHON-LE-ZION: JEWS AND ARABS WORKING TOGETHER HARVESTING GRAPES.

(By courtesy of Mr Norman Bentwich)

hour by robbing and looting, which they regard as a legitimate phase of war. There may be sixty thousand of them, but they are said to be dwindling.

The fellahin are the agriculturists—the peasants and farmers who form the backbone of the population and are Palestine's producers. The average holding of a family is about twenty acres, which is sufficient for a peasant life in the Old World but means a low standard of living where the land is stony and poor and the methods of farming old fashioned.[1] Tenancy conditions are severe, and the fruits of labour small, generally twenty per cent to thirty per cent of the crop, or, if the cultivator supplies the seed, fifty per cent. A view of the Zionists is that the lot of the wretched fellahin of the hills, living a precarious existence and often in the grip of the local usurer, will be greatly improved by their activities.

The Arab town dwellers consist of the professional propertied and trading classes, with a small but growing labouring class. Here, as elsewhere in the world, it is the lettered urban circles that produce the politically minded and vocal elements. They voice the Arab opposition to a Jewish national home in Palestine and clamour for Arab freedom and independence from a foreign yoke.

Palestine's population figures according to its census for the ten years 1922–31 were as follows:

	Population in 1922	*Population in 1931*	*Percentage increase approx.*
Arabs (Moslems)	591,000	760,000	28.5
Arabs (Christian)	82,000	101,000	23.0
Jews	84,000	175,000	100.0

[1]The Sir John Hope Simpson Report (October, 1930) states that the minimum requirement to support an Arab agricultural family, under present methods, is about thirty acres.

The birth and death rates in 1931 were:

	Deaths per 1000	*Births per 1000*
Arabs	26	48
Jews	9.4 cf. England 10.5	32

Taking these figures together, the percentage of Jewish increase was four times greater than the Arab increase. On the other hand the absolute figures show that the Arabs increased more than the Jews had done, viz:

Arab increase	169,000
Jew increase	91,000

Thus the expansion of Palestine's population for the period up to 1931—an astounding one of 36.8 per cent in ten years—came about primarily not from immigration, but from fertility of the existing population; Arab fertility exceeded Jewish fertility to an extent which largely offset Jewish immigration, and the population, at this rate of fertility plus immigration, must double itself in the short space of twenty years unless checks occur according to Malthusian principles, that is to say, checks imposed by subsistence limits.

With the prospect of saturation in view—assuming that Palestine cannot support a population more than double its present one—the Zionist grievance was that, under the rate of immigration allowed for the decade 1922–1931, there was no chance of catching up with the Arab lead, so that the National Home, as they understood it, was not being brought about by the mandatory.

During the past few years a greatly accelerated rate of immigration has taken place. This would appear to have been stimulated by external world affairs. As has been seen, the normal policy of the mandatory has been to base the quota on the purely economic consideration of Palestine's ability to absorb. But the persecution of Jews in Germany and a far-reaching economic and political discrimination against Jews through eastern Europe generally seem to have introduced a new feature. Abnormal periods of prosperity, or at least unusual labour demands in Palestine, have coincided with a large exodus of Jews from central and eastern Europe at a time when the United States, Canada, Australia and other countries of great spaces where, normally, they could have turned to, have closed their doors during a world slump. The pressure to emigrate from Poland, Austria, Roumania and central and eastern Europe generally seems to have encouraged Palestine, as their appropriate asylum under the National Home, to open wider its doors, while the inflow of fresh capital created scope for them, in the mandatory's judgment.[2]

Hence, as against the ten years 1922–1931, when only 71,000 Jewish immigrants were allowed in (an average of 7,100 a year touching its low point in 1929 with 4,000), the past four years have seen the annual quota zoom up by 400 per cent and last year to 800 per cent, so that almost as many immigrants came in last year as were allowed in the ten years ending 1931, viz:

1932	9,553
1933	30,327
1934	42,359
1935	61,854
1936	14,646 (up to June)

[2]Immigrants are distinguished by those having capital backing and those being allowed in under the labour schedule. During the peak year, 1935, the labour schedule accounted for 11,000 approximately.

Of these, 35,000 came from Germany alone—Jews who have left under the Hitler regime—of which number 8,000 came in the peak year 1935.

It is this increased rate of Jewish immigration during the past few years that is at the bottom of the present Arab unrest (1936). The new figures, if maintained, will bring about a Jewish majority, and it is the prospect of a Jewish majority which has so alarmed the Arabs. Population capacity, at this rate, will soon be reached, and Zionists are said to be looking beyond Palestine, across the Jordan to the emptier spaces of the ancient lands of Edom and Moab, familiar nowadays as Trans-Jordan, the Arab buffer state against the desert, under the rule of the Amir Abdullah. The Arabs are hostile to this, holding that Trans-Jordan's exclusion from the National Home is explicitly provided for by promises made to them. Today there are no Jews there, and in times past so fierce has been the local antagonism that a Jew crossing the Jordan without government's permission or protection did so at the peril of his life. Not all Arabs are politicians, of course, and not all Jews are Zionists, but the conflict of extremists in Palestine has, unfortunately, been to stir up racial antipathies.

Both Arab and Zionist movements have their political organizations whose aims, naturally, are mutually conflicting. There are right-wing, left-wing and centre parties in each movement, the greatest hope of co-operation lying where respective right and left wings touch. But the wing of a movement is, in the nature of things, not representative, and men of most moderate opinion on one side with sympathies for the most moderate opinion on the other are swept aside by mass emotion as political crises periodically recur.

The Arab Higher Committee today, the official mouthpiece of Arab nationalism, is formed of representatives of a number of Arab bodies. The Arab Congress, a representative body formed in 1921, immediately voiced its protest against the Balfour Declaration and denounced Jewish immigration on principle. When in 1922–23 the mandatory made certain proposals for a legislative council, then for an advisory council of nominated Arabs and Jews, and finally, when these fell through, for an Arab agency parallel to the Jewish Agency, these proposals, as made, did not satisfy the Arabs who were averse to co-operation because it seemed to them to be an act of recognition of the Balfour Declaration and to invalidate the principle of the Arab state.

A representative but ostensibly nonpolitical Arab body of considerable influence today is the Moslem Supreme Council under the presidency of the grand mufti of Jerusalem. This purely Moslem body administers *waqfs,* or sacred endowments, and so enjoys great influence as the source of patronage. Some of the advanced Arab nationalists desire to see the lessening of the great influence wielded by religious leaders, as such, but religion is still a potent factor with the Arab masses, and such leaders have as much power as the political leaders, if indeed the offices are not in many cases identical.

In 1934 there were three main parties, the Palestine Arab party, the National Defence party and the party of Independence.

The Palestine Arab party is the majority party and supported by the representatives of the fellahin and labour groups. It is opposed to co-operation with the mandatory.

The National Defence party is the moderate party and attracts the wealthier and bureaucratically minded class of the people, including some of the intellectuals. It is regarded as a party aiming at co-operation with the government.

The party of Independence is the extremist group, an offshoot in 1932 of the Palestine Arab party. It is Pan-Arab rather than Pan-Islamic and has for its aim the unification of Palestine, Syria and Iraq into one Arabian independent nation as existed in the two centuries following the Prophet.

In spite of religious differences between Palestine Moslems and Palestine Christians—and the massacre of Nestorian Assyrians in Iraq immediately following Iraq's achievement of independence a year or two ago bodes not too well for minorities who get above themselves in the young Arab state at this stage—politics transcend religion in the nationalist movement in Palestine. If the masses, Moslem and Christian, that are being brought together under the common banner, as yet scarcely understand politics in the Western sense of the word, their leaders do and avow enthusiastic discipleship of the political philosophy of John Morley, namely that self-government is to be preferred to good government, and also avow a fondness for the dictum of his successor at the India Office, Edwin Montagu, himself a Jew, as applied to India, namely that the masses should be stirred out of their apathetic content. The demand of Arab nationalism is for self-determination.

The Jewish parties in Palestine are parts of larger parties in the Zionist movement throughout the world. In some cases divisions have occurred in Palestine itself, for the ideals formed outside have undergone modification when coming into contact with the realities of the internal situation. If the underlying ideal is a common one, namely the establishment of the Jewish National Home, there are several parties among the Jews with different programmes reflecting distinctions of class and of interests. The left-wing party, called the Labour party, is Socialist with a few Communists. It is composed largely of immigrants from eastern Europe who, having been oppressed, come with advanced political views. The Federation of Jewish Labour in 1932 numbered 34,000 members, and these with their wives and children constituted about one third of the Jew population of Palestine (at the end of 1935 it was 67,800). They have a daily newspaper, hospitals and schools. Their first plank is to insist on a large and steady immigration of Jews into Palestine as a means of attaining the National Home; their second plank is the nationalization of land; their hope is that Palestine ultimately becomes a co-operative commonwealth, though it is to their interests at present to stand for co-operation with the mandatory.

The Jewish right-wing party, founded in 1923, is called the Revisionist party. Its critics describe it as Fascist, if that is not a paradox in view of the anti-Semitism of European Fascism. An anti-Socialist movement, it would replace the class struggle by the ultimate ideal of the state; it finds support among youth who hold strong views and believe in strong action to bring about an out-and-out Jewish state. Its object is to create a self-governed Jewish commonwealth in Palestine with a population predominantly Jew on both sides of the Jordan. And to attain this predominance it demands the sequestration of all uncultivated lands and a rate of immigration at the recent tempo, holding that the end could be achieved in twenty-five years by a yearly quota of forty thousand or, if Trans-Jordan be included, fifty thousand to sixty thousand. The Revisionists reject self-governing institutions in Palestine so long as the Jews are in a minority, reject negotiations with the Arabs so long as they do not recognize the Balfour Declaration and favour, for the time, the continuance of British legislative and administrative control. They form a small party outside the Zionist organization.

The middle party or liberal party of Palestine Jews are the General Zionists, who demand the immigration of the middle-class Jew rather than the wholesale admission of workers. It is mostly anti-Socialist and anti-Revisionist and is broadly attached to the principles of private enterprise and personal freedom and, generally speaking, is a central party with a social and economic programme similar to that of traditional centre parties in Europe. It attracts the merchant, the orange grower, the educationist and the like, and co-operates with the mandatory Power.

An orthodox religious organization among the Palestine Jews, the nearest thing perhaps to the grand mufti's council among the Moslems, is the Orthodox or Mizrachi party. It is traditionalist in spirit as opposed to modernist, is inspired by ideals of religious and pious upbuilding of the state founded in the law and traditions and opposes the irreligious and unorthodox in the Zionist movement. Its activities have most to do with religion and education, while politically it inclines to the right wing of Zionism.

Lastly there exists a Jewish society whose influence, more especially outside Palestine, is greater than the meagre membership suggests. It is known as Brith-Shalom, or Covenant of Peace. It criticizes the Zionist leaders for looking to the West for support instead of coming into closer contact with the Arabs among whom the Jews will have to live, and it advocates buying from Arabs instead of boycotting them. The Brith-Shalom enjoys neither the confidence of the Arabs nor the Zionists. The Arabs welcome its moderation but suspect it for that very reason and see in it a greater danger to their ideal of the Arab state. Brith-Shalom's main idea seems to be that Palestine should be neither an Arab nor a Jewish state, but a biracial state in which Jews and Arabs should enjoy equal civil, religious and political rights without distinction between majority and minority. It is a group of intellectuals who construe the term 'national home for the Jews' less as a Jewish sovereign state than as a spiritual home. Both the Labour and the Revisionist parties oppose it as standing for 'just another minority group of Jews, this time in Palestine.'

Perhaps this underestimates what has already been done for the Jews by the mandatory, for the status of the Jews in Palestine is equal to that of the native Arab; though the native Jew was in 1918 in a minority of one to nine, to-day the Jews are to the Arabs as three is to seven and for the most part are of foreign birth; the Hebrew language has been elevated to an equal official status with that of Arabic; the postage stamps and coins are in three languages: Arabic, Hebrew and English; a Jewish university has sprung up in Jerusalem, and everywhere there has been a revival of the ancient Hebrew, so that from being almost a dead language it has now become the common tongue of Jewish immigrants coming from all over the world. All Jewish children growing up in Palestine learn Hebrew as their mother tongue, and whereas in the old days the private schools were Anglo-Jewish, German-Jewish, French-Jewish, today the Zionist schools are Hebrew-Jewish.

The twin terms of the mandate that (*a*) Palestine must be a national home for the Jews, and (*b*) the civil and religious rights of the Arabs must on no account be permitted to suffer, may be a counsel of perfection and are without doubt unimpeachable in intent, but for the high commissioner called upon to translate them into action they are often the horns of a dilemma. Periodical rebellion and the resultant impasse is, in origin, perhaps less the fault of the Arabs or of the Jews than of those in authority during the war, who, by idealistically framed declarations or verbal promises, have led both Jews and Arabs to expect too much, so that each one is demanding and expecting more than is compatible with the demand and expectation of the other. It is another unfortunate war legacy. The momentous issues involved at that time led authorities in closest touch with Jews and Arabs severally to make promises, in moments of enthusiasm or gratitude, which are incapable of fulfilment side by side.

The issues are deeper than the agrarian discontent or the religious incident which in the past has been the immediately preceding cause of communal strife; though the pursuit by one side or other of some unenlightened self-interest has been the means of bringing latent anger to white heat and leading to riots and rebellion.

The occasion of the flare-up in 1929 was a religious incident connected with the Wailing Wall of Jerusalem. The visitor to Jerusalem who has witnessed the interesting ritual of the Jews praying at the Wall will remember that the sacred structure forms part of the temple of Herod—the lower six courses of original stonework still actually remain—and is the traditional site of Solomon's temple. Here the Jews have been accustomed from time immemorial to bewail the departed glories of Judah. Tradition goes back to the prophet Jeremiah that the Jews who remained in the Holy Land during the Babylonian captivity were in the habit of worshipping on these ruins; the Pilgrim of Bordeaux who visited Jerusalem in A.D. 33 mentions that all Jews came once a year to this place, weeping and lamenting; Jewish writers of the tenth and eleventh centuries mention repairs, while in 1840 a Turkish decree forbade the Jews from paving the passage in front of the wall, it being only permissible for them to visit it 'as of old', so that under the Turks there was no hindrance to the old Jewish usage.

The troubles of 1929 were brought about by the Arabs erecting in this place of special sanctity for the Jews—a place from which God's presence has never departed—a new structure at one end, and at the other end converting a house into a *zawiyah,* fitting up a lavatory close by, and making a new doorway that opened up a thoroughfare from the sacred pavement under the Wall into the mosque of the Dome of the Rock, so that the Jewish worshippers were interrupted by a stream of men and animals over the pavement. The Jews did not put forward a claim to ownership but asserted that the Arabs were behaving malevolently, and bickerings led to riots.

The Arabs alleged provocation. They held that this was not the crux of the matter. The Jews, they said, were doing what they had no right to do and had never done before, namely they were making use of benches, a screen for separating men and women, an ark with the Scrolls of the Law and ritual lamps, which together constituted an open synagogue, and this on Moslem property, for the Wall forms part of the western wall of the plinth on which the Dome of the Rock (otherwise known as the Mosque of Omar) is erected. This, too, is a place of special sanctity to the Moslem world, for, according to a medieval Arab writer, it was 'here that God called David and Solomon to repentance, here that he put all that worked in the earth or flew in the air under subjection to David, here was discovered to Solomon the Rock which was the first corner of the whole earth to be created, here unto Mary (peace be upon her) winter fruits came in summer, and summer fruits in winter, here did Jesus speak when in the cradle, here where angels ascend and descend every night, here Gog and Magog shall conquer the whole earth except the sanctuary, and here shall take place the gathering of all men on the Day of Resurrection.'[22]* But perhaps the greatest stress on the sacredness of the Wall and pavement lies in the belief that it was here that Muhammad the Prophet tied up his aerial steed on the occasion of his miraculous visit through the seven heavens to the throne of the Almighty, as the Qur'anic version, in tiles around the mosque dome, recalls, and the name of this steed Boraq is the name by which the local Arabs know the Wailing Wall to this day.

The magnitude of the disturbances and the delicate nature of the religious implications led the League of Nations to send out a commission of inquiry. It consisted of three non-British members, under the chairmanship of a former Swedish minister of foreign affairs, and its findings were legally enacted and are now enforced under mandatory authority. These were that the Wall and pavement belong to the Moslems, but Jews have the right of usage for their services, except that they must not introduce screens and other appurtenances which constitute a synagogue. Moslems are forbidden the right of structural alterations impairing Jewish access, and the new doorway into the mosque must be closed on Jewish holy days and a prohibition placed on the driving of animals along the pavement during certain hours daily, when Jews are performing their devotions; the maintenance of the Wall and pavement being the joint concern of Moslems and mandatory.

Disturbances broke out a few years later in Jaffa following a bitter press campaign around the Arabs' grievances and fears, chief among which was the question of illicit immigration, the Arabs declaring that during the preceding twelve months over fifteen thousand Jewish immigrants had come in illicitly over and above the quota. Emphasis was placed on the land question too. The Jewish population in 1932–33 was at about the two hundred thousand mark, representing approximately a fifth of the entire population. Nearly a quarter of the Jews lived in agricultural settlements (today it is relatively much less) forming the highest proportion of Jewish rural population in the world. They were largely self-contained and autonomous communities. The Arab grievance was this: that lands acquired by the Jewish National Fund, whether from government or from a Palestinian landowner (often absentee), became henceforth forbidden territory to the native Arab cultivator. The Jewish National Fund acquired land, evicted the native Arab peasant and installed the Jewish immigrant. Zionist leases quite openly contained a clause forbidding the employment of non-Jewish labour. Inquiries after the troubles, by a judicial officer of the government, following Sir John Hope Simpson's report, established six hundred cases of Arabs who had been rendered landless by Jewish purchase of land, whether privately or under the National Fund, and these have since been offered land by the government in compensation. The Arabs complain of a systematic boycott of Arab labour by the Jews. The Zionists affirm that more Arab labour is employed in Jewish orange gardens than Jew.

Such questions appear to be subsidiary. The rising of the Arabs this year (1936) in the form of national political strike, as we have seen, arose from the fundamental grievance—the sudden great increase in the quota of Jews being allowed in. The Arabs are indifferent to the causes which have impelled acceleration, they being concerned only by its effect for themselves, as they see it. The Arabs do not want the Jews and they do not want the mandate. Recent history in the Arab countries, as well as Palestine, does not suggest that they are amenable to political subordination. Political domination under the sword of the strong, such as they themselves originally imposed upon the world, is in their recurrent moods more honourable to them, however distasteful for others, than a voluntary surrender of rights they consider sacred. The give and take of Western democratic politics is as yet alien to Middle East tradition.

The recent remarkable growth in Palestine's population is an index to its prosperity. It is a country which, under the mandate, has, comparatively speaking, been without an unemployment problem. It has balanced its budget, year after year, without recourse to foreign loans. Where almost every other country has experienced economic setbacks, Palestine has been largely free from them. This is due principally to the copious inflow of gold that has accompanied Jewish immigration and, in part, to an efficient and enlightened form of administration.

Politically Palestine has undergone a great change. From being a small, Turkish-administered province it has acquired the status of a country and is ruled under an elaborate crown colony form of British administration. The direction of affairs rests in a high commissioner, an executive council composed of four senior members of his staff and an advisory council, made up of these and five other chiefs of departments. Though Palestinian Arabs and Jews do not as yet hold these senior posts they provide nearly all the subordinate personnel, while in their respective social, economic and religious affairs they enjoy great freedom, in keeping with the spirit of the mandate.

As yet there is no representative government in Palestine. Indeed to make government truly representative on the basis of numbers, at this stage, would entail a predominantly Arab and actively anti-Jew majority; and the mandatory has therefore resisted Arab demands in this direction. The mandatory is in the position of not being able to allow Arab nationalist aspirations to debar the fulfilment of basic promises made to the Zionists. On the other hand it cannot allow Jewish immigration on the scale demanded by Zionists in utter opposition to the wishes of the native population, who claim an Arab Palestine as their birthright, a right, they say, as ancient as the Englishman's right to England. The mandatory role is to hold the scales evenly between Jew and Arab, to mitigate their differences as far as possible by inclining to the extremist of neither and to use its power and influence to bring the two communities in Palestine nearer to each other in the hope of making future co-operation between them possible.

Sympathizers will be found for persecuted Jews of central and eastern Europe faced, in these days of world unrest and depression, with closed doors by almost every country in the world and looking to Palestine as their principal hope.

Sympathizers will be found for the Arabs of Palestine who, under the recent tempo of immigration of Jews, are witnessing the population of their native country passing against their wishes and without their consent to an alien majority.

Palestine is Holy Land to Jewry, to Islam and to Christendom, and as such it has claims to consideration which transcend both those of Arab nationalism and Jewish nationalism, though the special interests of each cannot be overlooked. Its meagre size is such that it represents but a fractional part of the Arab territory freed from the yoke of the Turks by British armies; its scant capacity for population is such that it could only support a small fraction of the Jews of the world. That this little shrine of three world religions should be sacrificed to any one exclusive nationalism, apart from the unlikelihood of a one-sided settlement surviving unscathed another world war, is probably distasteful to the most liberal and enlightened thought of today.

EPILOGUE

Epilogue

We have traced briefly the life story of the Arabs: their deliverance from a pagan barbarism in the seventh century by one of the great figures of history—the Prophet Muhammad, 'threefold founder of a nation, of an empire, and of a religion'; their marvellous world expansion in the century that followed; their splendid medieval civilization for three centuries more; then disintegration and decline amid the buffetings of foreign invaders from East and West, crusaders, Mongols and Tartars, and so to submergence within the Ottoman Empire during the past four centuries; emergence, finally, and signs of new life in a post-war world swept by a wave of nationalistic revival.

Today the Arab world in common with the rest of the world is stirred to its foundations. Under the pressure of modernism Middle East civilization is in the melting pot; many of its distinctive features are disappearing or becoming modified out of recognition. Politically the caliphate system of government has gone, an anachronism in the twentieth century even for the Arabs themselves, and in its place limited, constitutional, nationalistic forms of government of Western form and evolution hold the field.

Universal education, once the glory of Arab civilization, but abandoned in the later centuries of decay, is enthroned again, and with the universal cinema and the universal press is producing a new shape of mind in the young, while industrialization under the invasion of Western capital is changing the livelihood of their elders. This is true not of the Arabs of Arabia, of course, but of the Arabs without, the historical Arabs who have been liberated from the Ottoman yoke and awakened to the sense of a new destiny, whose territories, forming the ancient land bridge between East and West, have today as airway and oilway acquired a fresh world significance.

Politically the many Arab states pursue their separate existences, but behind the mosaic façade are the ties of common blood, common tongue and a predominantly common historical and religious outlook. Educated Arabs naturally cherish the hope of ultimate political federation, conscious as they are not merely of a tradition of empire, but of empire that once dominated a civilized world.

To a foreign observer, however sympathetically disposed, the obstacles in the way of immediate realization of this aspiration seem considerable, arising as they do not from outside political influences alone, but from inherent cultural and economic conditions. We have seen a clear-cut division between Arabs. The peninsular Arabs, among whom intertribal and interstate wars have been perennial through the centuries and down to our own times, are jealous to preserve their own light, indigenous tribal forms of government, still more their individual personal liberties. In Palestine unqualified political sovereignty, whether Arab or other, seems remote in view

AN ARAB SCHOOL IN A PALESTINE VILLAGE.

(By courtesy of Mr Lowell Thomas)

of the essential internationalism of that problem, and the present communal discord between Arab and Jew is likely to need the safeguard of a guide and friend as far into the future as it is possible to foresee. There are observers, of course, who suppose that during the next twenty years the mandatory system will everywhere disappear by common consent of interested parties, as has recently taken place in Iraq and is about to take place in Syria, but Palestine may well be the exception. The present antipathy between Arabs and Jews should, however, be softened with the closing of the doors of immigration which must ultimately and at no very distant time come about from the operation of a law of saturation, and future generations of Palestine Arabs will then come to regard Palestine Jews not as alien colonists as they can and do today, but as fellow natives. In Iraq the recent coup d'état in which an elected, constitutional government was overthrown by the army, a popular and distinguished minister was assassinated and his two most important colleagues, one of them the prime minister, were driven into exile, suggests that ruthless and overmastering individualism is still a paramount quality in Arab leadership—not a propitious quality for the wider teamwork required by real federation.

Between Syria and Iraq we have seen a historic rivalry even before the Arabs came. The Syrian Arab considers himself and was considered by the Turks to be more advanced and more capable than the Iraqi Arab, which, if true, may be expected to lead to Syrian dominance in any relationship between the two. Iraq, on the other hand, is the one part of the Arab territories with an assured economic future; it has great wealth in oil, great cotton potentialities, may well become another Egypt. Iraq, therefore, is not likely to be persuaded by its poor relations to abdicate its place of natural priority in the family councils.

It would seem that the chief political prerequisite of Arab federation is the building up of an educated and strong public opinion. Here the Syrian Arabs seem most likely to lead the way. With them, Arab nationalism is founded in the homogeneous cultural group speaking the common tongue, irrespective of religious allegiance; it is, in other words, the geographical-linguistic grouping of Western form. Thus Syrian Moslems and Syrian Christians find a superloyalty in the ideal of Arab nationality. While revolting against Western domination, they are converts to Western political philosophy.

The political problem of great importance in the dealings between East and West, one that has loomed large in the past and may do so again in the political evolution of the Middle East, is the problem of minorities. It was a problem that faced the Ottoman Empire and was bequeathed by it to the Arab states on their dismemberment.

What the West conceives of as morally unjustifiable massacre of Christian minorities in Ottoman times the East holds to have been a perfectly legitimate suppression of revolt. There is a divergence of traditional viewpoint as to the legitimacy of agitation against authority and of the ways and means of dealing with it. Public opinion in circles with absolutist traditions differs from our own, as the feelings evoked among us over the attitude towards minority movements in Fascist Germany and Communist Russia show. In the Middle East repression springs primarily from political motives, not religious bigotry; indeed, as we have seen when Jews were outlaws in Christendom it was the Moslem countries that gave them refuge. Nor is the traditional Middle East absolutism illiberal so long as subjects are obedient to authority and law abiding, but clearly where political power is an entrenchment and not democratically derived minority movements aimed at weakening it live unhealthy lives.

The Turks were by no means illiberal, for they allowed minorities a large measure of autonomy. Kurds, Assyrians, Yezidis, living in groups in the mountains, were encouraged to maintain their own laws, language and customs and were dealt with through their own native leaders—aghas, begs, patriarchs and the rest. Indeed the easygoing way of the Turks proved to be a weakness when nationalism came to raise its head in Asia and liberalism had gone as far as it might. Intimidation and terrorism were then resorted to as a prevention of political disintegration. The young Arab state of Iraq, on the threshold of independence a brief decade ago, was not for repeating the Turkish experiment. The state within the state had no attractions for Iraq. It wanted the solidarity of a Western state, a thoroughgoing absorption of all minorities, without recognition of administrative distinctions for each such as the Turks had conceded, but providing constitutional safeguards for equality before the law and complete religious toleration, such, for instance, as Jews enjoy in Britain or France; and this was approved by the League under mandatory advice. Assyrian resistance was met in the traditional Middle East manner, in other words, a manner which was locally considered justifiable.

Those who laboured for the spirit as well as the letter of constitutional, democratic and parliamentary government of Western form for Iraq may have had their convictions shaken, but 'distinctive traditions of civilization cannot be surrendered or borrowed precipitately without a shock to the system,'[26]* and political institutions in an

English sense require a long apprenticeship and an educated public opinion, and in the Middle East time is needed. Indeed, our system of combining a democratic form of government with an aristocratic organization of society is, in a sense, the converse of the Eastern system. There we have a social democracy side by side with a governing class imbued with ideas of political autocracy. Certain left-wing political movements in the West appear to have aims not dissimilar.

However important the political reforms that are coming about, a more revolutionary change, because it intimately affects the everyday life of the common people, is the industrialization of these Arab countries. It is a change that springs not merely from the world's appetite for oil and phosphates or its profits in selling machinery, but from a genuine demand on the part of the progressive, especially the youthful elements of the local populations. These are looking to the royalties from their oil fields, to the development of irrigation projects and power plants to bring them a higher standard of life, and they are well aware of the need of security to serve such ends.

The oil pipe line, completed but a year or two ago, which brings oil from the new Mosul fields across the Syrian desert to the Mediterranean, is a triumph of a new order of things in desert security. Enterprises have sprung up along the shores of the Dead Sea oblivious of the proximity of the desert raider, which again would not have been possible under the Turks thirty years ago. What is the explanation? It is not that the desert man on the 'fringes of the sown' is no longer the man he was, has suddenly lost his lust for plunder, but that his raiding has ceased to pay him, has ceased to be a menace for others. However unpalatable the thought, it is the deadly modern weapons that organized governments now possess that intimidate him—the bomber cruising through the skies at incredible speed, the steel bulletproof coach with its machine gun scorching along the frontiers—that have driven the desert man back into his sandy wastes. It took a Roman legion to do ineffectively what a few airplanes and armoured cars do today in making the frontiers secure. It is weapon superiority, or rather the inventions of the internal-combustion engine and wireless telegraphy enabling a lightning use of weapon superiority, that have made possible the development of these borderlands, where the native warlike man would not otherwise have permitted intrusion. It is the fear of force which has compelled peace and progress. And thus Iraq, with wealth enough from her oil royalties to maintain airplanes and tanks, has, by this fact, the prestige to compel obedience in her lawless tribal areas, a peace which without them would be wanting. Science in the East as in the West is making governments more powerful, the governed more at their mercy, and thereby increasing the moral responsibility of those in authority.

But if security, necessary for progress, is indirectly affecting the habits and outlook of the borderlands the effects of industrialization among the sedentary populations are even more far reaching. In the construction of the desert pipe line alone some fourteen thousand natives were drawn into new forms of activity, leaving their ploughs, their sheep, their primitive crafts, many of them doubtless never to return to them. Novel dress, novel food and clothing perhaps, novel working conditions certainly, must have left their mark. If the pipe line is one day followed by a railway—the preliminary surveys for which have been made, its cost computed in millions, and the time required to build several years—the ramifications will be still wider and deeper. The effect of industrialization is to Europeanize the Arab. Whether for good or ill great sociological readjustment is in progress. The shepherd must discard his loose skirt when he comes to drive a lorry, for the gears demand it. It may seem a small thing, but clothing and habits in the common people as well as changes in the traditional methods of government are signs of the extent of the change taking place in Middle East civilization.

Nor is the religious outlook unaffected. In the East as in the West it is a time of intellectual questioning. A wider and more secular education and the impact of modern ideas, especially progressive ideas which challenge the whole basis of the fatalistic attitude, are naturally tending to a modern outlook. The familiar European notion that modernism and Islam are a contradiction in terms, that modernism is the death knell of Islam, is one, however, which the educated orthodox Arab vigorously contests. He points with conviction to the great age of Arab civilization, which indeed immediately followed the birth of Islam, when the Arabs assimilated Greek philosophy and Persian culture without ceasing to practise their faith. He holds that the depressed condition of today is not the result of an unprogressive religion but of an unenlightened interpretation of it in these later centuries of decay; that its original spirit was free, liberal, progressive, and only when the doors of research and independent thought were closed, when the laws well suited to medieval times as evolved by the findings of the early doctors came to be established as a final and irrevocable interpretation of religion, that stagnation and narrow-mindedness brought their trail of woes.

EPILOGUE

Among Arabs of the enlightened world modernism takes a variety of forms. To one school the rationalizing influence of modernism is welcomed as getting rid of superstitions and outworn interpretations of religious belief which discredited Islam in the eyes of a scientific world. Although Arabs of this school are often rationalists who no longer believe in revealed religion and share the general outlook of the ruling class in Turkey they cherish Islam on historical and sentimental grounds as the faith of their fathers and see in the adherence thereto of the masses a valuable counterpoise to Bolshevism and other alien revolutionary movements. This attitude is found among the Arab governing classes of Syria and Iraq who are alive to the value of Islam as an instrument of political solidarity, especially among communities not reached by the secular and intellectual claims of nationalism.

Modernism in Islam has its genuinely religious side too. In intellectual circles a phase of agnosticism has been followed by one of religious revival. There are movements afoot among young Arabs who believe that there can be no health in the political state unless it is rooted in the religious life, no health in the world until its peoples are drawn into a closer brotherhood of mutual understanding, toleration and good will. Last year at a congress of world faiths held in London a paper written by a most distinguished Moslem scholar, the rector of Al Azhar University of Cairo, on the subject of 'World Fellowship through Religion', attracted wide interest. It showed how much closer in spirit the religions of the world are today than ever before, deplored that exponents of them should misuse their energies in attacking one another when their ends and aims are the same and pleaded for an allied front to combat the real enemy—the evils of the world, and for a common ideal—the achievement of good fellowship among the peoples of the earth.

The bitter legacy inherited by East and West from the centuries of medieval warfare—lies, misrepresentation and hatred one of the other—is happily dwindling. Old intolerances, old bitternesses are disappearing before the spread of another spirit now cherished by good men of all religions, the spirit of peace on earth, good will towards men.

The Arabs, in their many ways, are feeling the influence of modernism, their receptiveness varying with their cultural condition; hence educated circles in Syria and Iraq occupy a position midway between backward Moslem communities of the Arabian peninsula and advanced Moslem communities of India and Egypt. But it is Egypt whose influence must tell in the long run, for its Arabic press occupies a commanding position throughout the Arab countries, its thinkers and publicists are becoming known to an ever-widening circle of literate Arabs, its theological, social and political controversies are echoed in the press and the diwans of Baghdad, Damascus and Jerusalem. Egypt, the first of the Arabic-speaking countries to accept Westernization and adopt the European philosophical outlook, is preaching modernism to the Arab world.

Thus has the wheel of fate turned full circle. A thousand years ago the Arab was teaching modernism to Europe. His civilization was then pre-eminent, his influence of imperial extent. Great warrior though he was, his sword could clearly not alone have wrought his splendid achievements. Besides strength of purpose, there must have been creative genius and qualities of the spirit. Yesterday and today pride, honour, love of freedom—these are the strong elements of nobility in his character.

EPILOGUE

If much of the cultural side of Arab civilization had its roots in the earlier civilizations of the Arab conquests some of its great human qualities derived as surely from the hard school of Arabia herself. Among them generosity and heroism stand nobly forth. There is no people in the world more naturally generous than the Arabs. They give with both hands, they give with all their heart. It is no niggardly, calculating generosity impelled by the hope of something better in exchange. It springs spontaneously from a nature that is made that way. Not once but twenty times during my journeyings in south Arabia I have been moved to admiration by little acts of humanity among my Beduin companions. After long thirsty hours in the saddle I have trotted ahead—one or two of them accompanying me—to be first at a longed-for water hole. There they have watched approvingly as I have eagerly slaked my thirst, yet would none of them allow a drop of water to moisten his lips till the rest of his companions—an hour's march behind perhaps—came up that they might all drink together. A crust I have given to one I have noticed that he saved to share with a companion; and rarely has it been possible to pass a tent, however humble, but the owner has come running out with a greeting on his lips to insist on our sharing his bowl of milk, his few dates or whatever else he had, though his supply were inadequate perhaps for his own wants. You are a stranger, he has never seen you before, he will never see you again, yet he unstintingly gives you that of which he has dire need himself.

Impulsive, unmeasured generosity has its counterpart in another quality of the spirit. The usage of sanctuary when the desert Arab, without any claims upon him, will protect with his life the outcast or the weak who has sought his protection has already been noticed. Driven by hunger to raid, he observes in a true sporting spirit the rules of the game, unless a blood feud absolves him. To shed blood is lawful enough if his adversary is unyielding, but let him heed in time and he will be allowed to retain a camel, be given rations and so return to his tribe, free to prepare a counter raid.

Proud of his dominion within his horizons, the Arab will allow none to trespass without his permission or that of his kindred. On many occasions the writer, engaged in camel journeys through the unknown south Arabian borderlands, has been obliged to draw rein by a hail of bullets, some of them passing uncomfortably close—carrying the haughty, wordless challenge: 'Halt! Who goes there?' But if the Arab brooks no uninvited invasion of his domains and is roused by it to immediate militancy, he is no unchivalrous exploiter in cold blood. True the short list of European travellers is not free from victims; those who met with violent ends include Palmer, a professor of Arabic at Cambridge, Seetzen, a Swedish botanist of European reputation, and Huber, a French-Alsatian naturalist and archaeologist—the last two professing Moslems. Yet never in the history of Arabian exploration has a European been held up to ransom. To be shot in the raid, that is legitimate; the unwanted intruder, too, who comes ignorantly without safe-conduct, or the suspected spy, must take the consequences of his ill-mannered ignorance or his bad luck, but methods such as those of the gangster in America or the bandit in China are foreign to the sporting legitimacies of the warlike Beduin.

In my fifty-eight days crossing of Rub' al Khali, Arabia's great southern sandy waste, I, the first European to penetrate its depths, moving with the utmost secrecy possible, used as my saddle bags by day and my pillows by night gunny bags stuffed with many thousand-dollar pieces; my companions, fully aware of it, were hungry, penniless Beduin whom I had never seen before and who could not be called to account by any authority for my life—the life of a self-confessed Christian. Their honourable conduct and their personal loyalty are memories I shall always gratefully cherish. The Arabian custom of going forth to battle with a woman's name as a war cry, the time-honoured practise of being led into action by a girl mounted on camel back—the latter no longer possible since the introduction of firearms—speak alike of the gallant in their attitude of mind. Chivalry was ever the quality exalted in their heroes, and chivalry, be it not forgotten, found its way into general European practice during the Arab period first by way of Spanish, then of French contacts. Had the Arabs, then, no other claims upon us—and their claims, as history shows, are both many and significant—their contributions to chivalry alone would entitle them to a proud name among the nations.

Appendix

RACIAL ORIGINS OF THE ARABS

APPENDIX

Racial Origins of the Arabs

WHO and whence are the Arabs? Traditions they cherish tell of the Flood, of Noah, of a survivor of that catastrophe and the father of the human race, of his three sons, Shem, Ham and Japheth, the respective progenitors of the peoples in their three divisions of the world, namely Arabia, Africa and the rest—this a very simple and satisfying reconstruction of the history of mankind as seen by the desert man twenty-five hundred years ago, and all very clearly an inheritance from the Arabs' linguistic cousins and ancient neighbours, the Jews.

The son Shem—from whose name, of course, our words 'Semite' and 'Semitic' derive—had two sons, they go on to tell us, Qahtan and Adnan. Qahtan (our Biblical Jokhtan?) was the begetter of the Arabs of the south, Adnan of those of the north; and elaborate genealogies piously devised in the desert and analogous in some ways to Old Testament genealogies that enjoyed credibility in the days of Bishop Ussher, purport to show the Arabs as all descending from a common ancestor. All are Semites, i.e. sons of Shem.

But how does modern science regard the Semites and an Arabian origin for them? In popular parlance the Jew is the Semite par excellence of course. Now anthropologists believe the Jews' original home, as that of the Semitic types of ancient Assyria and Babylonia, to have been not Arabia at all, but the uplands to the north of Arabia, probably of Asia Minor. The Abyssinians have a Semitic tongue, too, but their physiognomy suggests evolution in their native Africa or some corresponding low latitude. Language is no longer accepted as a criterion of race, and the term 'Semitic' like the term 'Latin' or 'Aryan' is used not in a racial sense, but in a cultural or linguistic one. A Latin race or an Aryan race as understood yesterday, or even today by the man in the street, is no more spoken of. The French, for instance, are Latins only in the cultural sense—they speak a Latin tongue. Racially they are something else. In the north the tall, blue-eyed, fair-haired, long-headed Normans, such as largely make up the scrums of the national rugby fifteens visiting these shores, are of Nordic type; the small, spare, dark, long-headed southerner is said to be a Mediterranean man. In Germany, too, with its common Aryan tongue, the Nordic type in the north is of different racial origin from the typical thick-set, roundheaded Alpine man principally in the south. And so with our Arabs, Abyssinians and Jews; linguistically they are Semitic; racially the dark, long-headed, woolly-headed Abyssinian is a Hamite, the hawk-nosed, roundheaded Jew is an Armenoid (a racial group, incidentally, to which the Assyrians of Semitic tongue and the ancient Hittites and modern Armenians, both Aryan-speaking peoples, belong). Yet it must be supposed that the Semitic family of speech has evolved within the bounds of the peninsula and that the peoples among which this tongue has become nature have some distant relationship of one kind or another—just as the Aryan tongue has broadly dominated certain peoples who appear to have had a similar origin.

What then is the racial make-up of the Arabs? The answer may or may not be found in their cultural and geographical inheritance, their tongue and their traditions; it is more surely inherent in their bodily inheritance—their anatomy, the shapes of their heads, the nature of their hair, their pigmentation and the like.

The original inhabitants of Arabia, then, according to Sir Arthur Keith, one of the world's greatest living anthropologists,[1] who has made a study of Arab skeletal remains, ancient and modern, were not the familiar Arabs of our own time, but a very much darker people. A protonegroid belt of mankind stretched across the ancient world from Africa to Malaya. This belt, by environmental and other evolutionary processes, became in parts transformed, giving rise to the Hamitic peoples of Africa, to the Dravidian peoples of India and to an intermediate dark people inhabiting the Arabian peninsula. In the course of time two big migrations of fair-skinned peoples came from the north, one of them, the Mongoloids, to break through and transform the dark belt of man beyond India; the other, the Caucasoids, to drive a wedge between India and Africa.

The Caucasoid wave took place in prehistoric (probably late Pleistocene) times when Arabia was a well-watered and inviting land. The more virile invaders overcame the dark-skinned peoples, absorbing most of them, driving others southwards where my own exploration is believed to have discovered vestiges of them in a natural sanctuary beyond the great sandy ocean of Rub' al Khali.

[1]See Appendix to *Arabia Felix*, by Keith and Krogman.[36]*

The cultural condition of the newcomers is unknown. It is unlikely that they were more than wild hordes of adventurous hunters. But conditions must then have been favourable to their attraction; certain it is that at the time of our last Ice Age, perhaps twenty thousand years ago, when Europe and Northern America lay under a cap of ice and were uninhabitable by man, Arabia must have been enjoying a Pluvial Period, been well fitted for habitation. Considerable dried-up river systems I came upon in the southern borderlands, and the fauna I collected in the Qara Mountains—fauna that have African rather than Arabian affinities—bear witness to a common climate with a wet tropical Africa at some remote time and to a land bridge that made the Red Sea an inland lake and which later submerged to form the shallow straits of Bab al Mandab. As the ice of the Northern Hemisphere receded and the rain belt moved north behind it Arabia was bereft of its rains, its climate changed; it became drier with the passing of the ages until today it is one of the hottest and most rainless parts of the earth's surface.

What then are we to understand by 'the pure Semitism' of the Arabs? Primarily we must accept its cultural implications. On the threshold of history we find the Arabs and the Jews, cheek by jowl, on the northern desert fringe. If they were successive waves of a prehistoric culture-spread from the north there were already physical differences, for the ancient Arab appears to have been a long-headed man, the Jew predominantly a roundhead.

The long and gradual desiccation of Arabia brought about a shrinkage and a segregation of its peoples—a common climate, common conditions of life and suchlike common evolutionary influences led to the establishment of well-defined desert types. In other words, Shem was an environment rather than a grandfather; and in this sense Semitic man was the pastoralist of southwest Asia when we first hear of him from the lettered peoples of the Nile and the Euphrates.

The inhabitants of Arabia within historic times have experienced invasions of foreign peoples so rarely, and the effect of these, nearly all of them on her periphery, must have been so slight, while her conditions of life are so broadly and uniformly severe, that her culture is exceptionally homogeneous; indeed, may be without parallel in any other land of comparable size. So, too, Arabia's ancient tongues, as we have seen, belong all of them to one Semitic family. No wonder then our authorities, historians and philologists alike, have been content to accept without question the racial purity of an Arabo-Semitic people.

Yet, anthropologically considered, the Arab peoples are representative of several distinguishable racial types. Physiological data, including head and skull measurements, ancient and modern, show recognizable differences within the peninsula and recognizable affinities of groups with races outside the peninsula that establish diverse origin.

The Arab tradition of Adnan and Qahtan would appear almost certainly to preserve a memory of two racially distinct ancestors. The traditional Arab view of their brother kinship we may the more easily dismiss when we are told by the same tradition that only a generation separated them from Shem and Japheth, the one the ancestor of the Arab and the other the reader's own ancestor, who are also two blood brothers according to these Arab lights.

Three races clearly have contributed to Arabia's blood: the dark, gollywog, Hamitic man of the south, the roundheaded Armenoid, the narrow-skulled Mediterranean.[2] Popular imagination in the West, with stage and cinema to minister to it, requires that the Arabs shall belong to the middle type resembling the handsomer kind of Jew, that is to say, a refined hawk nose with hair black and wavy; closer attention may show a flat back to the head and the ear placed conspicuously far back. This is the Armenoid, whose evolutionary home is probably Asia Minor. Prehistoric waves westwards may help to account for some of these features in the Alpine man of central Europe, but whether or not, southern waves planted these Jew-Arab types on the shores of the Levant and projected them into the peninsula. A late Armenoid invasion from the north, distinguished for opening up the most ancient trade route known to man and for the introduction of copper, took place in about 3000 B.C. It was a forked wave that ran down both sides of the Syrian desert to invade the river civilization of Egypt and Sumer and to leave its mark on the physiognomy of Syria and northern Mesopotamia (Jews and Arabs) as we see to this day. Himyaritic kings of fourth century southwest Arabia, judged by their coins, were of this Armenoid race, and today many of the tribes of Oman, who claim to have emigrated from the Yemen at about that time, display the same features and have the characteristic roundhead.

On the other hand most north Arabian tribes are not roundheaded, hawk-nosed Armenoids at all. They are Mediterraneans of characteristic long narrow skull. And such ancient skeletal remains as have been dug up suggest

[2]The reader, interested, will find a splendid series of photographs and measurements in Henry Field's *The Arabs of Central Iraq.*[83]*

There is also some admixture of Negro blood outside the nomadic tribes that has come about from union with slaves. This is very common in the Hijaz and the Oman.

ARAB RACIAL TYPES:

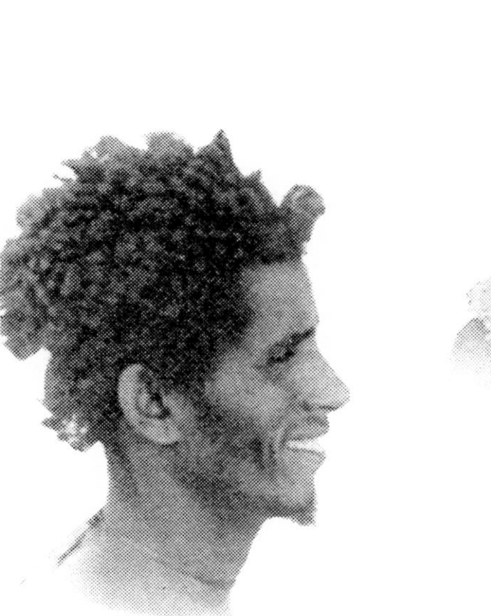

(a) A Hadhramauti Donkey–Boy

(Hamitic Characters)

(By courtesy of Mr Carleton S. Coon, Division of Anthropology, and the Peabody Museum, Harvard University)

(b) A Trans–Jordan Policeman

(Mediterranean characters)

(By courtesy of Major J. C. Glubb)

(c) An Iraqi Tribesman

(Armenoid Characters)

(By courtesy of Mr Henry Field, Curator of Physical Anthropology, The Field Museum, Chicago)

that this was a common—perhaps the most common—Arabian type in the early centuries of our era.

Still different, doubtless, were the earlier inhabitants of southwest Arabia, the dark, indigenous Hamitic type of marked affinities with the Abyssinian. Such blood probably dominated southwest Arabia down into the times of the ancient kingdoms. The Sabæans, the Minæans and the rest who disappeared before the rise of the Himyarites may well in part have belonged to this ancient stock. Their inscriptions are in a character of which the Ethiopic character is a direct development; the dialectical survivals of their tongues in south Arabia today are spoken exclusively by gollywog, Hamitic-looking tribes, and although these tongues are now greatly Arabicized they are still incomprehensible to the Arabs of the north.[3] (See pp. 22–24.)

The persistence in Arabia today of distinct racial groups suggests that earlier waves of peoples rigidly maintained a front against later intrusions, whether or not the basal stocks from which they sprang were kindred. It provides a reason for supposing that when the lettered peoples of antiquity used the term 'Arab' only in the restricted sense of 'nomad', and to differentiate themselves from Arabs, a usage found in Sabæan and Himyaritic inscriptions and common to the Jews, they were conscious of a distinction deeper than a cultural one; the term 'Arabia', in the sense of the land of them all, is, as we know, a later Greco-Latin appellation for a geographical conception of the Hellenistic world.

[3]For grammar and vocabularies of these tongues known as Mahri, Shahari, Harsusi, Botahari, see my *The Geography and Ethnography of South Arabia,* Cambridge University Library.[37]*

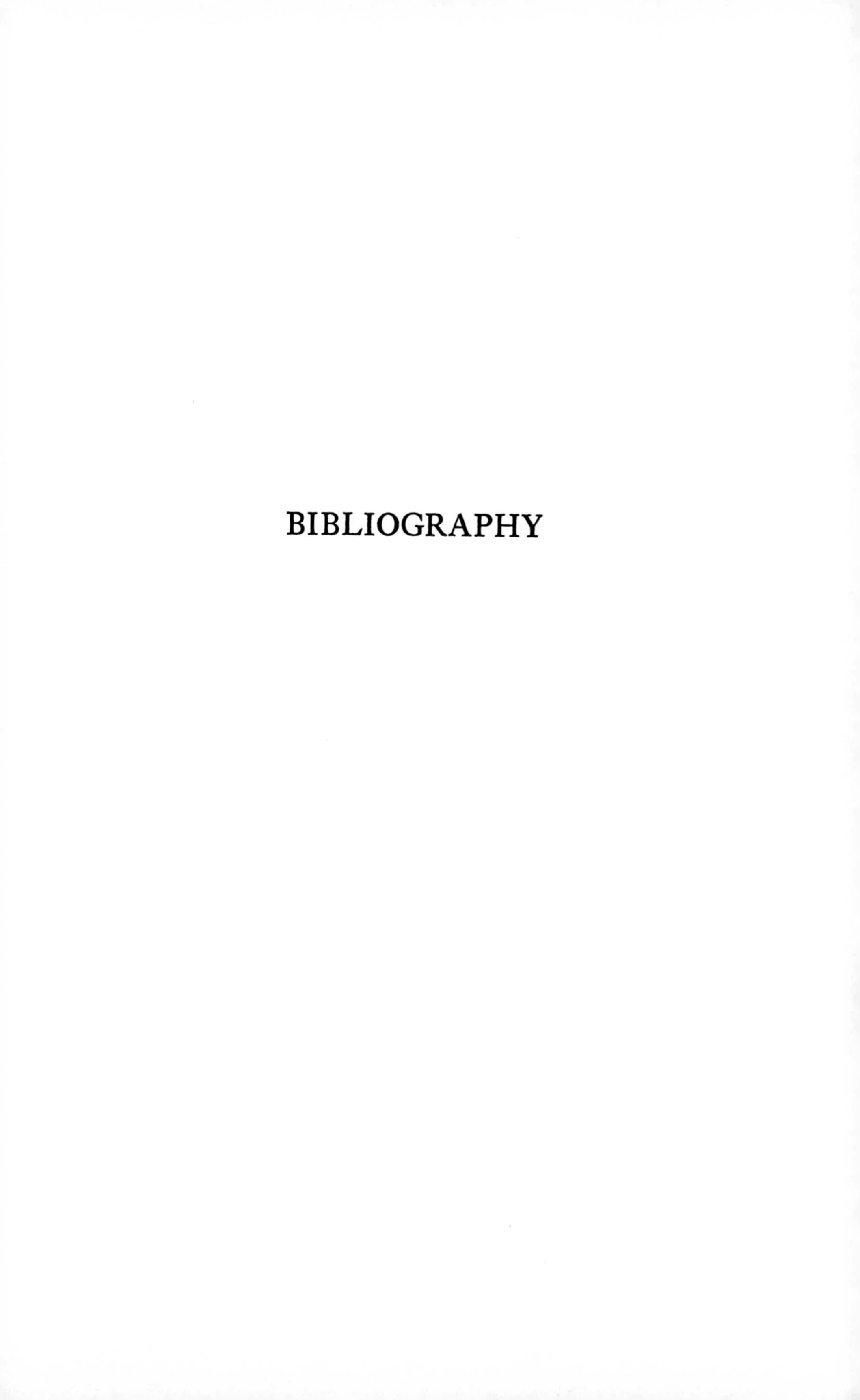

BIBLIOGRAPHY

BIBLIOGRAPHY

The works hereunder are those to which I am specially indebted. The student will find fuller references in the works quoted. Invaluable to him also is the *Encyclopædia of Islam* (Luzac) in process now of publication by instalments.

1 DE LACY O'LEARY: *Arabia before Muhammad.* Kegan Paul, 1927.

2 D. S. MARGOLIOUTH: *The Relations between Arabs and Israelites prior to the Rise of Islam.* (The Schweich Lectures.) Oxford University Press, 1931.

3 D. S. MARGOLIOUTH: *Mohammed.* G. P. Putnam's Sons, 1906.

4 MAULANA MUHAMMAD ALI: *Muhammad The Prophet.* Lahore, 1924.

5 CARLYLE: *Heroes and Hero Worship.* Chapman & Hall, 1897.

6–7 *The Cambridge Medieval History* (Vol. II). Cambridge University Press, 1932.

6 A. A. BEVAN: *Mohamet and Islam.*

7 C. H. BECKER: *Expansion of the Saracens.*

8 BUDGETT MEAKIN: *The Moors.* Sonnenschein, 1901.

9 REUBEN LEVI: *The Sociology of Islam* (2 vols.). Williams and Norgate, Vol. I, 1931; Vol. II, 1933.

10 MARMADUKE PICKTHALL: *The Cultural Side of Islam.* The Committee of 'Madras Lectures on Islam', 1927.

BIBLIOGRAPHY

11 GIBBON: *Decline and Fall of the Roman Empire* (Vol. V). Henry G. Bohn, 1854.

12–21 *The Legacy of Islam*. Edited by Sir Thomas Arnold and Alfred Guillaume. Oxford University Press, 1931.

12 A. H. CHRISTIE: *Islamic Minor Arts and Their Influence upon European Work.*

13 MARTIN S. BRIGGS: *Architecture.*

14 H. G. FARMER: *Music.*

15 CARRA DE VAUX: *Astronomy and Mathematics.*

16 J. H. KRAMERS: *Geography and Commerce.*

17 MAX MEYERHOF: *Science and Medicine.*

18 ALFRED GUILLAUME: *Philosophy and Theology.*

19 J. B. TREND: *Spain and Portugal.*

20 D. DE SANTILLANA: *Law and Society.*

21 ERNEST BARKER: *The Crusades.*

22 E. T. RICHMOND: *Moslem Architecture, 623–1516, Some Causes and Consequences.* Royal Asiatic Society, 1926.

23 D. G. HOGARTH: *The Penetration of Arabia.* Lawrence and Bullen, 1904.

24 D. G. HOGARTH: *A History of Arabia.* Oxford University Press, 1922.

25 ERNEST BARKER: *The Crusades.* Encyclopædia Britannica, 1922.

26 ARNOLD TOYNBEE: *The Western Question in Greece and Turkey.* Constable, 1922.

27 H. W. V. TEMPERLEY: *England and the Near East—the Crimea.* Longmans, 1936.

28 G. P. GOOCH AND H. W. V. TEMPERLEY: *British Documents on the Origin of the War,* Vol. X, Part II. H.M.S. Office, 1927–1937.

29 STEPHEN LONGRIGG: *Four Centuries of Modern Iraq.* Oxford University Press, 1925.

30 *The Palestine Census Report, 1931.*

31 H. A. R. GIBB: *Whither Islam?* Victor Gollancz, 1932.

32 R. A. NICHOLSON: *The Idea of Personality in Sufism.* Cambridge University Press, 1923.

33 HENRY FIELD: *The Arabs of Central Iraq.* Field Museum, Chicago, 1935.

BIBLIOGRAPHY

[34] JUDGE PIERRE CRABITES: *Things Muhammad Did for Women*. From the magazine *Asia*. U.S.A., 1927.

[35] BERTRAM THOMAS: *Alarms and Excursions in Arabia*. Allen and Unwin, 1931.

[36] BERTRAM THOMAS: *Arabia Felix*. Jonathan Cape, 1932.

[37] BERTRAM THOMAS: *The Geography and Ethnography of South Arabia*. Not yet published.

INDEX

INDEX

INDEX

INDEX

INDEX

INDEX

INDEX

INDEX

T

Lightning Source UK Ltd.
Milton Keynes UK
UKOW04f1905161215

264885UK00001B/113/P